PRINCIPLES OF INSURANCE

Dr. (Ku.) Shakti Prathaban
M.Com., LL.B, MBA (HRM), Ph.D.
Assistant Professor (Sr. Scale),
G.S. College of Commerce and Economics, Jabalpur (MP).

&

Dr. N.P. Dwivedi
PGD-DSW, DPA, DCPA, M.A., MBA (HRM), Ph.D.
Section/Court Officer
Central Administrative Tribunal, Jabalpur (MP).

Himalaya Publishing House

MUMBAI • NEW DELHI • NAGPUR • BENGALURU • HYDERABAD • CHENNAI • PUNE • LUCKNOW • AHMEDABAD • ERNAKULAM • BHUBANESWAR • INDORE • KOLKATA • GUWAHATI

FIRST EDITION : 2013

Reprint : 2025

Published by : Mrs. Meena Pandey for **Himalaya Publishing House Pvt. Ltd.**,
"Ramdoot", Dr. Bhalerao Marg, Girgaon, **Mumbai - 400 004.**
Phone: 022-23860170/23863863, Fax: 022-23877178
E-mail: himpub@vsnl.com; Website: www.himpub.com

Branch Offices :

New Delhi : "Pooja Apartments", 4-B, Murari Lal Street, Ansari Road, Darya Ganj, New Delhi - 110 002. Phone: 011-23270392, 23278631; Fax: 011-23256286

Nagpur : Kundanlal Chandak Industrial Estate, Ghat Road, Nagpur - 440 018. Phone: 0712-2738731, 3296733; Telefax: 0712-2721215

Bengaluru : No. 16/1 (Old 12/1), 1st Floor, Next to Hotel Highlands, Madhava Nagar, Race Course Road, Bengaluru - 560 001. Phone: 080-32919385; Telefax: 080-22286611

Hyderabad : No. 3-4-184, Lingampally, Besides Raghavendra Swamy Matham, Kachiguda, Hyderabad - 500 027. Phone: 040-27560041, 27550139; Mobile: 09390905282

Chennai : No. 8/2, 2nd Madley Street, Ground Floor, T. Nagar, Chennai - 600 017. Mobile: 09345345055

Pune : First Floor, "Laksha" Apartment, No. 527, Mehunpura, Shaniwarpeth (Near Prabhat Theatre), Pune - 411 030. Phone: 020-24496323/24496333; Mobile: 09370579333

Lucknow : House No 731, Shekhupura Colony, Near B.D. Convent School, Aliganj, Lucknow - 226 022. Mobile: 09307501549

Ahmedabad : 114, "SHAIL", 1st Floor, Opp. Madhu Sudan House, C.G. Road, Navrang Pura, Ahmedabad - 380 009. Phone: 079-26560126; Mobile: 09377088847

Ernakulam : 39/176 (New No: 60/251) 1st Floor, Karikkamuri Road, Ernakulam, Kochi - 682011, Phone: 0484-2378012, 2378016; Mobile: 09344199799

Bhubaneswar : 5 Station Square, Bhubaneswar - 751 001 (Odisha). Phone: 0674-2532129, Mobile: 09338746007

Indore : Kesardeep Avenue Extension, 73, Narayan Bagh, Flat No. 302, IIIrd Floor, Near Humpty Dumpty School, Indore - 452 007 (M.P.). Mobile: 09301386468

Kolkata : 108/4, Beliaghata Main Road, Near ID Hospital, Opp. SBI Bank, Kolkata - 700 010, Phone: 033-32449649, Mobile: 09883055590, 07439040301

Guwahati : House No. 15, Behind Pragjyotish College, Near Sharma Printing Press, P.O. Bharalumukh, Guwahati - 781009, (Assam). Mobile: 09883055590, 09883055536

DTP by : Sudhakar Shetty (HPH Pvt. Ltd., Mumbai)

Printed at : Geetanjali Press Pvt. Ltd., Nagpur on behalf of H.P.H.

PREFACE

There are innumerable threats of financial losses in one's family and business. At present, economic security has become paramount for human beings in all spheres of their lives. To eliminate or reduce the financial risk, it has become utmost important for all the human beings to get their movable/immovable property and their life insured. Insurance is not only beneficial for the individual concerned but it is an effective tool for economic development of the community and the nation at large.

Today, insurance has become an important device for risk management as it affects people in all walks of life. That is why insurance industry secures an important place among financial institutions operated in service sector throughout the world. Due to increasing complication of life, trade and commerce, individuals as well as business entities tend to move to insurance to manage various risks. Every human being in the world is exposed to unforeseen and unexpected hazards or dangers, which may make him and his family vulnerable. Insurance is a system that ensures an individual to protect against adverse consequences by compensate the individual his/her loss financially.

In this book, an attempt has been made to throw light on some important aspects of principles of insurance, as prescribed in the syllabi for the course. Accordingly, Chapter-I: includes concept of Insurance; Chapter-II: Insurance Agent; Chapter-III: Life Insurance; Chapter-IV: Elements of Contracts and Life Insurance Contact. Further, Chapter-V: Marine Insurance, Chapter VI: Fire Insurance, Chapter-VII: Misc. Insurance; and Chapter-VIII: Insurable Interest, Procedure of Claims settlement. Chapter-IX: Organization of General Insurance Corporation and its subsidiary companies. Thereafter Chapter-X: New emerging trends in Insurance Sector; Chapter-XI: Indian Life Insurance Corporation — Establishment, Objectives, Functions, Development and Evaluation. Finally, Chapter-XII: Study of main insurance policies in practice. Further, at the end of this book, short answer, long answer, multiple choices type questions, fill in the blanks, glossaries and bare acts which are required have been included for continuous and comprehensive evaluation of the contents.

The authors are deeply indebted to the management of M/s. Himalaya Publishing House Pvt. Ltd. for well designing and promptly publication of the book.

Apart from this, I would like call the bright students who are the best judge to recognize the book as to what extent this book caters to their needs for perceiving the concepts and subsequently, for preparation to the examination. Finally, I request to the readers/students to express their views as well as their suggestions for improvement of the contents of this book at my email id. npd1976@rediffmail.com.

Best wishes to all the students and teachers who wish to refer to this book.

Date: 29th Sept. 2012

Authors

Department of Higher Education, Govt. of M.P.
B.Com. (Graduate) Semester Wise Syllabus

As Recommended by Central Board of Studies and Approved by the Governor of M.P.

Class	B.Com. 3rd Year
Semester	Vth Semester
Title of Subject	Economics (optional)
Group	Group C: Insurance and Investment
Title of Paper	Principle of Insurance
Compulsory/Optional	Optional
Maximum Marks	85

PARTICULARS

Unit	Particulars
Unit-I	**Insurance:** Meaning, Need, Types, Function and Principle. Insurance Agent — Rights and Working of Insurance Agent.
Unit-II	**Life Insurance:** Introduction, Need, Importance, Elements of Contracts and Life Insurance Contact.
Unit-III	Marine Insurance, Fire Insurance, Miscellaneous Insurance, Various Types of Agreements. Insurable Interest, Procedure of Claims settlement.
Unit-IV	Organization of General Insurance Corporation and its Subsidiary Companies New Emerging Trends in Insurance Sector.
Unit-V	Indian Life Insurance Corporation — Establishment, Objectives, Functions, Development and Evaluation. Study of Main insurance Policies in Practice.

CONTENTS

CHAPTER 1

INSURANCE

Insurance: Introduction, Meaning, Definition, Need, Types, Function and Principle of Insurance.

1.1 OBJECTIVES OF LEARNING

- *Explain the meaning of insurance.*
- *Discuss the need of getting insured and its benefits to individuals and business firms.*
- *Describe the types of insurance and their meaning.*
- *Trace the evolution of Insurance, and*
- *Explain the functions and principles of Insurance.*

1.2 INTRODUCTION

Today, insurance has become an important device for risk management as it affects all walks of life. That is why insurance sector secures an important place among financial institutions operated in service sector throughout the world. Due to increasing complexity of life, trade and commerce, individuals as well as business entities tend to move towards acceptance of insurance to manage various risks. Every human-being in the world is exposed to unforeseen and unexpected hazards or dangers, which may make him and his family vulnerable. Insurance is a system that ensures that an individual is protected against adverse consequences by compensating the individuals loss financially. Thus, an appropriate knowledge of insurance, its need, functions and principles is necessary for all of us.

Insurance is a co-operative form of risk management mainly used to avoid against the risk of a contingent, uncertain loss. It may be defined as the reasonable transfer of the risk of a loss, from one body to another, in exchange for payment. An insurer is an Insurance company selling the insurance; the insured or policyholder, is the person or entity buying the insurance policy. An amount to be charged by the insurer for a certain sum of insurance coverage is called the premium. The insured receives a contract known as the insurance policy, which contains the terms, conditions and circumstances under which the insured will be financially compensated.

In the course of business deal, the insured (Policy holder) assumes a guaranteed and known reasonably small loss in the form of payment as premium to the insurer in exchange for the insurer's promise to compensate (indemnify) the insured in the case of a financial or personal loss.

In a general parlance, insurance of anything other than human life is called general insurance. Insuring property like house, factory or other belongings against fire and theft or vehicles against accidental damage or theft are examples of general insurance. Unforeseen injury due to accident or reimbursement of medical expenses on hospitalization for illness and surgery can also be insured. Liabilities to others arising out of the law can also be insured and is obligatory in some cases like third party motor vehicle insurance.

1.3 HISTORY OF INSURANCE

We can say that insurance emerged along with the emergence of human society. In ancient time, the method of transferring or distributing risk was practised by Chinese and Babylonian traders as long ago as in the 3rd and 2nd BC. The Babylonians developed a system which was well known as Code of Hammurabi, in about 1750 BC. In this system, if a merchant received a loan to fund his shipment, he would pay the lender an additional sum in exchange for the lender's guarantee to cancel the loan should the shipment be stolen or lost at sea.

The first example of insurance is related to marine activities. In many ancient societies, merchants and traders gave assurance of their ships or cargo as security for loans. In Babylon creditors charged higher interest rates from merchants and traders in exchange for a promise to write-off the loan if the ship was robbed by pirates or was captured and held for ransom.

In post medieval England, local groups of working people associated together to create 'friendly societies,' and they are now known as ancestors of the modern insurance companies. The members of these societies made regular contributions to a general fund, which was used to compensate for losses suffered by members. At that time the contributions were determined without reference to a member's age, and without specifying the insurance face value. In absence of a effective system to predict risks and possible liability, several friendly societies were incapable to pay claims, and ultimately they disbanded. Insurance had gradually been seen as an affair which can only be handled by an organized company engaged in the business of providing insurance.

In the present time, a large number of General and Life Insurance companies are providing insurance services in different countries in the world. Similarly, insurance in India is broadly categorized into two types: life and general. Life insurance can be further classified into term life insurance, whole life insurance, money back plan, endowment policy and pension plan. Health, home, accident, motor and travel insurances fall under the general insurance category. Various private as well as public sector companies provide life and general insurances in India.

1.4 MEANING OF INSURANCE

Insurance means *a promise of insurer to insured towards compensation for any potential future losses. It facilitates financial protection to insured against a loss arising out of happening of an uncertain event.* In other words, insurance is used as *an effective tool of risk management* as quantified risks of different volumes can be insured. An immense benefit of insurance is that *it spreads the risk of a few people over a large group of people exposed to risk of similar type.* Thus, the *insurance basically, works on the fundamental principle of risk-sharing.*

Several insurance schemes provide comprehensive coverage with reasonable premiums. Premiums are periodical payment and different insurers (Insurance Companies) offer a variety of premium options. The rates of premiums are calculated according to periodicity of its payment and total face value of insurance amount. There are different insurance companies that offer wide range of insurance options and an insurance purchaser can select as per own convenience and preference.

Fund is created through contributions made by persons willing to protect themselves from common risk. Insurance companies collect the premium and act as custodian of this fund. In case of any loss happening of an uncertain event to the insured is compensated out of this fund. Thus, insurance schemes use to transfer the loss (premium) of exposures to an insurance pool (common fund) and the redistribution (compensation) of losses among the members (actually suffered) of the pool.

1.5 DEFINITION

For systematic understanding of the concept, the definitions of *Insurance* can be categorized in following categories:

(a) General Definitions

(b) Functional Definitions and

(c) Legal Definitions.

(a) General Definitions:

Following definitions may be considered under general definition of insurance:

(i) *'Insurance is a co-operative form of distributing a certain risk over a group of persons who are exposed to it.'* ***— Ghosh and Agarwal***

(ii) Focusing on risk factor, insurance has been defined as *'The collective bargaining of risk is Insurance.'* ***— Sir William Bevridge***

(iii) *'Insurance is a device for the transfer to an insurer of certain risks of economic loss that would otherwise be borne by the insured.'* ***— Allen L. Mayerson***

(iv) *'Insurance is a provision which a prudent man makes against fortuitous contingencies, loss or misfortune. It is a form of spreading risk.'* ***— Thomas***

(v) *Insurance has been defined as 'A plan which large numbers of people associate themselves and transfer, to the shoulders of all, risk attach to individual.'*

— Magee, D.H.

(b) Functional Definitions

Considering the functional importance of insurance, some of important definitions of insurance are as follows:

(i) *'Insurance may be defined as a social device providing financial compensation for the effects of misfortune, the payments being made from the accumulated contribution of all parties participating in the scheme.'* ***— D.S. Hansell***

(ii) *'Insurance may be described as a social device whereby a large group of individuals, through a system of equitable contributions, may reduce or eliminate certain measurable risks of economic loss common to all members of the group.'*

— Encyclopedia Britannica

(iii) *'Insurance is a method in which large numbers of people exposed to a similar risk make contribution to a common fund out of which, the losses suffered by the unfortunate few due to accidental events are made good.'*

— Federal of Insurance Institute

(c) Legal Definitions

Having being contactual obligations for both of the insurer and insured, some important definitions of the Insurance are as follows:

(i) *'In its legal aspects, it is a contract, the insurer agreeing to make good any financial loss the insured may suffer within the scope of the contract and the insured agreeing to pay a consideration (Premium).'* ***— Regal and Miller***

(ii) *'Insurance is a contract in which an individual or entity receives financial protection or reimbursement against losses from an insurance company.'*

http://www.investopedia.com

(iii) *'Insurance is a contract in which a sum of money (premium) is paid by the assured to insurer as consideration of insurer's incurring the risk of paying a large sum upon a given contingency.'* ***— Justice Tindall***

(iv) *'Insurance is a contract by which one party, for a compensation called the premium, assumes particular risk of the other party and promises to pay to him or his nominee a certain or ascertainable sum of money on a specified contingency.'*

— E.W. Patterson

(v) *'Insurance is an agreement to pay, assurance against loss, bond against risk, compensation for injury, compensation for loss, contract against future loss, contract against unknown contingencies, guarantee against loss, indemnity against loss, pledge, promise, protection against loss, security against loss, stipulation to compensate for loss, warranty against loss.'* ***— http://legal-dictionary.thefreedictionary.com***

1.6 NEED OF INSURANCE

All assets have some economic worth attached to them. There is always a possibility that these assets may get destroyed/damaged or become useless due to risks like breakdown, fire, floods, earthquake etc. In other words, life is full of uncertainties and insurance is based on uncertainties and if there are no uncertainties about the incidence of a disaster, the thought of insurance will cease to exist. Thus, we are not able to predict the future dangers correctly and hence we seek for insurance of our lives as well as our tangible and intangible assets. Different assets are uncovered of different types of risks, like a human is exposed to risk of death, accident or illness, whereas a Motor Vehicle has a risk of theft or meeting an accident and a house is uncovered to risk of catching fire. Finally, Insurance is deemed necessary or needed vitally because of following reasons:

(i) As a tool of Social Security: Insurance acts as a significant tool providing a common sense of security to the society on a whole. In a general case, where the bread earner of a family is dead, the entire family has to face the financial hardship as family's income ceases. Consequently, economic condition of the family gets affected adversely unless there are any other alternate to rescue the family from this situation.

Life insurance is one alternate arrangement that offers some relief to the family from financial suffering. Otherwise, such family would have been pushed into the lower strata of the society, which would be an additional burden to the society as subsidies would have to be given to the family to enable it to stay alive and enjoy the primary rights at par with other people. In addition, it is, generally, seen that poor families have a large family size with family members who are illiterate. Ultimately it affects the society as a whole and makes an extra cost to the society.

Insurance compensates the insured/dependant family members, not only in case of death, but also in other situations such as unemployment, disability, sickness or any other circumstances out of his control. Thus, insurance shares the burden of the state and accordingly, helps the state to maintaining social security for his population.

(ii) Uncertainty: The fundamental need of insurance arises as risks and hazard are uncertain and unpredictable in nature. Getting insurance of an asset does not imply that the asset is protected against risks or its coverage to risk is reduced, but it actually implies that in case the asset suffers any loss in value due to such risk which is covered under the contract, the concerned insurance company bears the loss and compensates the insured by making payment to him.

(iii) Economic Development: The premium paid by policy-holders to the insurance companies is a part of their savings. Hence, insurance works as a useful instrument in encouraging savings and investments, mainly within the lower-income and middle-income groups of the society. These savings are finally used as investments contributing to economic growth of the nation.

(iv) Indemnifies the loss: Insurance reinstate people to their previous financial position in case of any loss (except death of insured) is occurred. It facilitates them to remain financially safe without any worry to recoup the capital after a loss. It also helps business firms to continue their normal business operations without disturbance even if the loss occurred.

(v) Generates employment at large: For carrying out its business operations, insurance industry offers regular and full time employment to a large number of unemployed people of the country. In addition to this, number of agents, professionals etc., are also engaged in rendering professional insurance services.

(vi) Makes available funds for investment: Economic development of a nation depends upon investments and saving makes available funds for such investments. An insurance company acts as an important device for mobilizing people towards savings, and funds collected from these savings are used in investment promoting economic growth. Besides, it provides stability in trade and commerce, by covering the risks that could hinder the economy and thus ultimately helps the economy to grow.

(vii) To educate people about loss prevention: Insurance companies play a vital role in educating people about loss prevention. In our country the General Insurance Corporation has formed a loss prevention association of India to promote and propagate about loss prevention.

(viii) Reduces fear: Insurance is very useful in reducing concern and fear before and after any loss takes place, as it is well-known to the insured that the insurance company will compensate the loss if any such mishap occurs.

(ix) General Purposes of Insurance: As far as Life insurance is concerned, it is widely popular and beneficial for not only to the policy holder but also to the nominee because of its following general purposes:

(a) ***Term insurance plans*** are best suited for people till the age of 35 years as it provides higher protection at low cost. Such plans are also useful for a person whose income is low and wants to protect ones family from financial hardship in case of his death.

(b) ***Endowment type plans*** provides the benefits of saving and protection.

(c) ***Unit Linked plans*** are helpful in Speedy growth of money and in risk coverage.

(d) ***Money back plus*** provides saving, protection and liquidity of the investment.

(e) ***Children plans*** are very useful for education or marriage of the child/children.

It is pertinent to mention here that above purposes (mentioned against (a) to (e)) are applied for life insurance only. However, the basic purpose of General Insurance is to protect the insured in case of financial loss suffered by the policy holders due to the causes covered in the policy.

1.7 TYPES OF INSURANCE

Insurance companies sell different types of insurance policies by assuming the economical worth attached to the insured and probability of risks according to their specific viewpoints. This provides a measure of standardization in the risks that are covered by a type of policy. It permits the insurers to predict their anticipated losses and accordingly decides the premiums for different types of policies. At present, variety of insurance policies including life, fire and casualty, marine, health, automobile, personal property, and other social & miscellaneous policies are popular among the people. In view of the above, insurance can be classified in the following categories:

(A) Classification on the basis of nature.

(B) Classification on the basis of business.

(C) Classification on the basis of risk.

(A) Classification on the basis of nature:

(1) Life Insurance: Life insurance provides a financial assistance to a deceased's family or other nominated beneficiary. Sometimes, insurance provides burial, funeral and other expenses also to an insured person's family. According to terms and conditions stipulated in Life insurance policies, insurance companies may, sometimes, allow the beneficiary to opt either for a lump sum cash payment or an annuity. Some of life insurance contracts accumulate cash values, which may be withdrawn by the insured if the policy is surrendered. Annuities and endowment policies are financial instruments to accumulate or liquidate wealth when it is required.

Generally, life insurance companies disburse lump sum cash payment to beneficiaries in case of death of insured person or on maturity of policy along with bonus applicable as per scheme and prevailing rate.

(2) Fire Insurance: Fire insurance covers tangible assets from risks of fire. Fire insurance compensates losses arising due to fire. The property or business of an individual is protected from such losses and helps to restore it in the same position in which it was before the loss. The fire insurance does not compensate only losses but it also provides compensation on certain consequential losses. Main type of policies available under fire insurance are:

(i) Comprehensive policy.

(ii) Valued policy.

(iii) Valuable policy.

(iv) Consequential loss policy.

(v) Floating policy.

(vi) Average policy.

(3) Marine Insurance: Marine insurance and marine cargo insurance provides protection against loss of marine perils. The perils may be of any kind such as collision with rock, ship attacked by pirates, catching fire etc. Marine insurance policies insure transporters and owners of cargo shipped on an ocean, a sea, or a navigable waterway. Marine risks include damage to cargo, destruction or disappearance of the ship, damage to the vessel and injuries to passengers. Besides, many marine insurance companies also include time element coverage in such policies, which extends the insurance to cover loss of profit and to recover other business expenses attributable due to delay in operations. Most common types of marine policies are:

(i) Voyage policies.

(ii) Time policies.

(iii) Valued policies.

(iv) Hull insurance.

(v) Cargo insurance.

(vi) Freight insurance.

(4) Social Insurance: Various types of insurance serving the purpose of society are available in market. Some of these are as under:

(i) Unemployment Insurance: Unemployment insurance provides benefits to insured persons who are unemployed and actively seeking for job. It is a bunch product, which covers general credit risk of insured during a loss of job. In India, ICICI Lombard & Bharti AXA General Insurance, etc., are providing Unemployment Insurance which is actually available as a Top-Up to a general insurance.

(ii) Sickness Insurance: Health insurance policies cover the reimbursement of medical expenses incurred on treatments. Different types of treatment and diseases are covered under health insurance and as per requirement the medical treatment can be availed by the beneficiaries, subject to the conditions that the same is covered under a policy.

(iii) Old age insurance: Old age insurance provides financial support to elders and the aged.

(iv) Disability insurance: These policies provide financial support to the policyholders in the event of incidents due to which they would be unable to work because of disabling illness or injury. It provides monthly financial support to policyholders in repaying such obligations on account of mortgage loans and credit cards.

(v) Total permanent disability insurance: When a person is permanently disabled and he can no longer work, the policy provides benefits which often paid as an addition to life insurance.

In addition to these, many more social insurances are also available.

(5) Miscellaneous Insurance: All other insurance which are not covered under, life, fire, marine and Social insurance may be defined as miscellaneous insurance. Some important form of miscellaneous insurances are as follows:

(i) Vehicle Insurance: Vehicle insurance protects the policyholders against financial loss in the event of an incident involving a vehicle they own. For instance, vehicle insurance would normally cover both the property risk in case of theft or damage to the vehicle and the liability risk in case of legal claims arising from an accident.

In India, vehicle insurance covers for the loss or damage caused to the vehicle or its parts due to natural and man-made calamities. Accident cover is provided for individual owners of the vehicle while driving and also for passengers and third party legal liability. Auto Insurance in India is an essential requirement for all new vehicles used whether for commercial or personal use. The claims of vehicle Insurance can be accidental, theft claims or third party claims. The vehicle insurance generally includes:

(a) Loss or damage by accident, fire, lightning, external explosion, burglary, housebreaking or theft, malicious act.

(b) Loss/damage to electrical/electronic accessories; on payment of appropriate additional premium as prescribed by the insurer.

(c) Liability for third party injury/death, third party property and liability to paid driver.

The vehicle insurance does not include:

(a) Depreciation, mechanical and electrical breakdown, failure or breakage.

(b) When vehicle is used outside the geographical area.

(c) War or nuclear perils and

(d) Drunken driving.

(ii) Crop Insurance: Crop insurance is for farmers to get protection from various types of risks associated with growing crops. Crop insurance covers risks related to crop loss or damage caused by weather, flood, drought, frost damage, insects or disease. Agriculture in India is highly subjected to risks like droughts and floods. Considering the risks associated with crops, the Government of India has introduced many agricultural schemes throughout the country.

(iii) Legal liabilities insurance: Legal liabilities insurance covers the probable costs of legal action of policyholders against an institution or an individual. There are mainly two types of legal expenses insurance *viz.*, (1) before the event insurance; and (2) after the event insurance.

(iv) Crime Insurance: It is a form of casualty insurance that covers the policyholder against risk of losses arising from the criminal acts of third parties. For example, a company can obtain crime insurance to cover losses arising from theft or fraud.

(v) Burglary insurance: It is provided to reimburse the insured party for any losses which he may incur due to burglary, robbery, or theft of his property or belongings as well as any damage thereto. In recent times, burglary insurance has become a highly specialized branch of the insurance industry.

(vi) Personal Accidental Insurance: Personal Accident is an insurance cover wherein, in the event of the person sustaining bodily injuries resulting solely and directly from an accident caused by external, violent & visible means, resulting in death or disablement. An accident may include events like:

(a) Rail/Road/Air Accident.

(b) Injury due to any collision fall.

(c) Injury due to bursting of gas cylinder.

(d) Snake-bite, frost bite/dog bite.

(e) Burn Injury, drowning, poisoning etc.

These are only illustrative and not an exhaustive list of accidents.

(B) Classification on the basis of business:

(1) Life Insurance: Life insurance provides financial security to the nominee on the death of the insured. There are different forms of life insurance. Some provide for payment only upon the death of the insured; others allow an insured to withdraw profits before death on maturity. Life insurance policy can be taken by a person on his own life for the benefit of a third person or persons. Individuals may even purchase life insurance on the life of another person. Presently, life insurance has enough scope because every person has need of insurance. It provides protection to the family at the premature death of insured or gives sufficient amount to the insured at old age when his earning capacities are reduced. In India, different types of insurance plans offered are listed below:

(i) Whole life plans.
(ii) Term assurance plans.
(iii) Endowment assurance plans.
(iv) Endowment policies with health insurance benefits.
(v) Unit linked plan.
(vi) Assurances for children.
(vii) Family income policy.
(viii) Life annuity joint life assurance.
(ix) Pension plans.
(x) Policy for maintenance of handicapped dependent.

(2) General Insurance: General insurance deals with all types of insurances excluding life. Generally, it includes property insurance, liability insurance and other forms of insurance. It is necessary to confirm here that the fire and marine insurance also comes under property insurance. Whereas liability insurance also comes under general insurance and includes motor, theft, fidelity and machine insurance to a certain extent. Fidelity insurance is the strictest form of liability insurance whereby the insurer compensates the loss to the insured only when insured is under the liability of payment to the third party. Some of important policies governed under general insurance are as follows:

(i) Personal accident policy.
(ii) Group insurance policy.
(iii) Automobile insurance policy.
(iv) Health insurance policy.
(v) Medi-claim policy.
(vi) Worker's compensation policy.
(vii) Liability insurance policy.
(viii) Aviation insurance policy.
(ix) Business insurance policy.
(x) Fire insurance policy.
(xi) Travel insurance policy, etc.

(C) Classification on the basis of risk:

1. Personal Insurance: Personal insurance mainly deals with reimbursement of medical expenses and provides financial support in case of accidental death. Personal insurance policies, cover only specified risks. Generally, claim is admitted on account of expenses incurred from injury, disability, sickness, and accidental death. Personal insurance may be purchased for oneself and for others.

2. Property Insurance: Property insurance provides protection against certain risks to property arising out fire, theft and weather damages. This includes specific forms of insurance such as fire insurance, marine insurance, flood insurance, earthquake insurance, home insurance and other different types of insurances related to property. The term property insurance consist of various subtypes of insurance, some of which are listed below:

(i) **Home insurance:** Provides risk coverage in case of damage or destruction of the policyholder's home. Depending upon geographical areas, the policy may exclude certain types of risks, such as flood or earthquake that require additional coverage. However, maintenance of home is the responsibility of the owner. In some countries, insurance companies offer umbrella packages which include both the liability and legal responsibility.

(ii) **Earthquake insurance:** It is a kind of property insurance that compensates the policyholder in the event of an earthquake that causes damage to the property. Normally home insurance policies do not cover earthquake damage. Risks of earthquakes vary from one geographical zone to another depending upon sensitivity attached with respective zone. Hence, rates depend on location the likelihood of an earthquake, as well as the construction quality of the home.

(iii) **Aviation insurance:** Provides risk coverage for aviation business as it protects not only to aircraft hulls and spares but also to associated liability risks, for instance, passenger and third-party liability.

(iv) **Boiler insurance:** Boiler insurance (also known as boiler and machinery insurance, or equipment breakdown insurance) protects against risks resulting from accidental damage to boilers including equipment or machinery connected to it.

(v) **Builder's risk insurance** provides protection against the risk of physical loss or damage to property during construction. Builder's risk insurance generally includes all associated risk from any cause including the negligence of the insured.

(3) Fidelity Guarantee Insurance: Fidelity bond covers policy holders for losses incurred as a result of fraudulent acts by specified individuals. It is a form of casualty insurance that generally insures a business for losses caused by the dishonest acts of its employees.

(4) Liability Insurance: Liability insurance covers a wide area including legal claims against the insured. Several types of insurance have an aspect of liability coverage. The protection offered by a liability insurance policy is dual in nature as it provides legal defense in the event of a claim made against the policyholder and payment on behalf of the policy holder with respect to a settlement or court decision. Liability insurance can be:

(i) Public liability insurance protects a business or organization against claims if its operations injure a member of the public or damage his property in some ways.

(ii) Environmental liability insurance provides protection to insured from physical injury, property damage and cleaning costs as a result of the dispersal, release or escape of pollutants.

(iii) Professional liability insurance, also known as professional indemnity insurance (PI), covers the risk of certain insured professionals such as medical practitioners and architectural firms against possible negligence claims made by their patients/clients. Professional liability insurance is sold on different names according to profession. For example, professional liability insurance pertaining to medical profession may be called medical malpractice insurance.

(5) Credit insurance: Credit insurance provides financial support to insured in repaying some or the full loan amount if any adverse circumstances arise to the borrower such as unemployment, disability, or death. Credit insurance provides creditability to borrower insured against a loan.

1.8 FUNCTIONS OF INSURANCE

The objective of insurance is to provide indemnity, or reimbursement, in the occurrence of an unforeseen loss or tragedy. The function of insurance is to spread the loss over a large number of insured who are willing to co-operate with each other in the event of loss. It is pertinent to mention here that risk cannot be prevented but loss occurring due to a certain risk can be spread amongst the agreed persons. Persons insured for insurance agree to share the loss because the probability of loss, (*i.e.*, the time, amount) to a person who might be any one of them are not known. In other words, anyone of them may bear loss to an uncertain risk, so, the rest of the insureds tend to share the loss for gaining mutual benefit of insurance. The loss is shared by insured by paying of premium to insurance company which is estimated on the prospect of potential loss.

It is an admitted fact that insurance contributes significantly to economic growth by improving the investment climate and promoting savings among the people. This contribution helps in balancing growth of banking and other financial systems. Life insurance makes a large contribution to development generally in developed countries, since life insurance is usually a smaller part of the total insurance market in developing countries.

Function of insurance according to its nature and characteristics can be classified as follows:

(1) Primary Functions
(2) Secondary Functions and
(3) General Functions.

(1) Primary Functions:

(i) To provide certainty: Insurance provides certainty of payment at the uncertainty of loss to the insured. Indeed, the uncertainty of loss can be reduced by better planning and administration. However, the insurance helps the person in such complex task. It will be costlier if someone bears his loss by himself. Different types of uncertainties are attached to a risk, *i.e.*, whether risk will occur or not, when will it occur or how much loss will be there? Insurance eliminates all these uncertainties and accepts liability of payment in case of loss. The insurance company charges premium for providing the said certainty.

(ii) To provide protection: Every human being, all the time, wants to be secured from all types of risk, loss and uncertainty in his life. It is imperative to mention here that insurance cannot prevent any mishap, accident or calamity but it can protect the sufferers/insured by paying compensation. The main function of insurance is to provide protection against the probable chances of loss to the insured. The time and amount of loss may not be determined and at the occurrence of risk, the person has to suffer loss in the absence of insurance. The insurance guarantees the compensation of loss and thus protects the assured from suffering.

(iii) Risk sharing: Risk is uncertain and therefore the consequential loss arising out from the risk is also uncertain. When risk arises, the loss is shared by all the persons who are exposed to the risk. In ancient time, usually the risks were shared by a group of people at time of damage or death; but now-a-days, on the basis of probability of risk, an anticipated share is obtained from every insured in the form of premium without which protection against loss is not guaranteed by the insurer.

(2) Secondary Functions:

(i) Prevention of loss: The insurance companies associate themselves with institutions which are engaged in preventing the losses of the society because reduction in loss causes lesser payment to the assured and as a result more saving is feasible which will help in reducing the rate of premium. Lesser premium attracts more business and more business cause lesser share to the assured. In other words, reduction in rates of premium stimulates more business and more protection to the masses. Therefore, the insurance provides financial supports to organizations such as health organization, fire brigade, educational institutions and other organizations those are working for prevention the losses of the masses from death or damage.

(ii) Provision of capital: The scarcity of capital of the society is reduced to a greater extent with the help of investment of insurance. Insurance provides financial assistance to the individuals, Institutions and to the Government for expansion of their different financial activities such as business, industry, trades and for infrastructural development. Therefore, industry, business and the individual all are benefited by the investment and loans provided by the insurance industry.

(iii) Improvement of efficiency: Insurance eliminates fear and misery related to unforeseen losses at death or due to damage of property. It improves not only his effectiveness, but the efficiencies of the masses are also improved.

(iv) It helps economic progress: Insurance protects the society from massive losses of damage, destruction as well as death and encourages the masses to work hard for their betterment. In addition to this, the insurance provides risk coverage to large scale industries especially where probability of risk is higher. Having secured their resources from risk, such industries utilize their resources optimally and contribute to the economic progress of the nation.

1.9 PRINCIPLES OF INSURANCE

Insurance is an agreement executed between insured and insurer towards financial protection to insured against a loss arising out of happening of an uncertain event. In the course of business deal, some general and legal principles are complied with for ensuring the authenticity of contract executed for insurance. Basically insurance acts on the principles of co-operation and theory of probability. In view of this, some important principles of insurance discussed in brief are as follows:

[I] BASIC PRINCIPLES

(1) Principle of co-operation:

Insurance is a co-operative form of risk management mainly used to avoid the risk of a contingent, uncertain loss. Hence it is a co-operative device. It may not be an insurance if someone bears his own losses, as in insurance, the loss is shared by a group of persons who are willing to co-operate. Similarly, in ancient times, the members of a group used to share the loss of a member of the group. They collected sufficient funds from the society and paid to the dependents of the deceased or the persons suffering property losses. Therefore, mutual co-operation prevailed from the very beginning in most of the countries.

Recently, this social co-operation took a systematic form of insurance mechanism wherein it was agreed between the individual and insurers to pay a certain sum in advance to be a member of the insured group. If an insured stopped the payment of premium he ceases to be a member of insured group and will be deprived from insurance coverage. Thus, without mutual co-operation insurance cannot be operated.

(2) Principle of probability:

There is a probability that losses already happened in the past may recur if other conditions remained unchanged. That is why the chances of loss are anticipated in advance to determining the amount of premium. The loss in the form of premium can be spread appropriately only on the basis of theory of probability. As the degree of loss is uncertain and it depends upon different factors, the related factors are analyzed before determining the sum of loss. The trend of events helps in ascertaining liabilities for insurance. Past trends of events are kept in account for anticipating the future trend of events if situation is same. It is purely a mathematical process to determine the risk of loss based on future trends which is applied in the business of insurance. Applying the principle of probability, the uncertainty of loss is converted into certainty. While determining premium, it is taken care that the insurers neither have to suffer loss nor gain too much. Therefore, the insurer has to charge reasonable amount which is sufficient to meet the losses.

Finally, no co-operation is possible without premium and the premium cannot be determined without applying the theory of probability and as a result without it no insurance is feasible. Therefore, these two principles are the two pillars on which whole system of insurance stands.

[II] ALLIED PRINCIPLES:

(1) Utmost Good Faith:

Both the insured (Policy holder) and the insurer (Insurance company) are bound by a good faith bond of honesty and fairness. In other words, there should not be any fraud, non-disclosure or misrepresentation of material facts. Therefore, it is an important duty of the every individual, seeking for insurance, to disclose all the facts truly and fully as insurance shifts risk from one party to another. A material fact is information that would influence the mind of a careful insurer while making the decision as to whether or not to accept a risk for insurance and on what terms. This duty to disclose the material fact is operated at the time of commencement, at renewal and at any point midterm. At any point of time breach of good faith renders the contract voidable at the discretion of the aggrieved party. Thus, the principle of utmost good faith includes:

(i) The insured and the insurer, both the parties, should all the time have a good faith towards each other;

(ii) The insured ought to provide the complete, correct and clear information of subject matter to the insurer for assessing the factual risk;

(iii) The insurer ought to provide the complete, correct and clear information regarding terms and condition of the contract.

The doctrine of utmost good faith is applicable to all contracts of insurance, *i.e.*, life, fire and marine insurance.

(2) Insurable Interest:

Insurable interest must be present in all the cases irrespective whether it is property insurance or insurance on a person as the insured has to suffer directly from the loss. The concept implies that the insured have a risk in the loss or damage to the life or property insured. If an insured wishes to enforce an insurance contract before the Court of law, he must have an insurable interest in the subject matter of the insurance, which means that he has benefits from its preservation and suffers from its loss. Other than marine insurance, it is necessary for the all other insured to have insurable interest when the policy is purchased and also at the time of loss to get the claim under the policy. In nut shell, this principle implies that:

(i) The insured must have certain insurable interest in the subject matter of insurance.

(ii) In case of life insurance, it refers to the life of insured.

(iii) In fire and general insurance it must be present at the time of taking policy and also at the time of incidence of loss.

(iv) In marine insurance it is sufficient if the insurable interest exists only at the time of happening of loss.

(v) The owner of the property is said to have insurable interest as long as he is owner of the same and

(vi) Insurable interest is invariably applicable to all contracts of insurance.

(3) Principle of Indemnity:

To 'indemnify' may be understood as 'an assurance to make whole again, or to be reinstated to the position that one was in, to the extent possible, prior to the occurrence of a specified event or peril. Hence, life insurance is generally not deemed to be indemnity insurance, but fairly 'contingent' insurance. Accordingly, an 'indemnity' policy will never entertain any claims until the insured has paid out of pocket to third party. Take an example, in case inventory of any business entity is found lesser, the custodian or concerned employee will be asked to deposit the cost of material. In this case, after paying out of pocket he can raise the claim to insurer for recovery of loss if he acquires indemnity bond insurance from insurer.

An entity might be an individual, corporation or association seeking to transfer risk may be called 'insured' party; once risk is assumed by an 'insurer', known as the insuring party; by means of an agreement is called an insurance policy.

In case of Indemnity, only actual amount of loss not exceeding the amount of policy is reimbursed. Take another example — assuming that a person insured his house for A 25 lakhs against fire and the house is partially burnt and it is estimated that a sum of A 5 lakhs will be required for maintenance to restore it to the original condition. In this case the insurer is liable to pay A 5 lakhs only. On the contrary, exceptions to this rule are found in personal accident policies under general insurance, agreed value policies under marine insurance and reinstatement policies in engineering insurance. In these insurances, amount of indemnity is decided at the time of entering into the contract itself. The salient features of indemnity are listed below:

- Indemnity is a guarantee or assurance to reinstate the insured in the same position in which he was immediately prior to the happening of the uncertain event.
- The insurer takes liability to make good the loss.
- Indemnity is applied for fire, marine and other general insurance.
- Under this the insurer agrees to compensate the insured for the actual loss or maximum value of policy whichever is less.
- Prove that the event occurred and prove that a monetary loss has also occurred.

(4) Principle of contribution:

There is a certain values attached with each insured which is covered under insurance. When an insured obtains more than one policy on same risk, the principle of contribution comes into play. The basic purpose of contribution is to share the actual amount of loss among the different insurers who are liable for the same risk under different policies in respect of the same subject matter. It denotes that the insured may affect more than one policy to cover the same risk but in no case he can recover more than a full indemnity. In view of the above, the right of contribution arises when:

(i) More than one policy is related to the same subject matter.

(ii) The policies cover the same peril which caused the loss to insured.

(iii) All these policies are enforceable only at the time of the loss.

(iv) Under this principle the insured can claim the compensation only to the extent of actual loss and in this context he has an option that he can claim either from any one insurer or all the insurers.

(v) Total compensation received from different insurers should not exceed actual loss to insured and

(vi) Every insurer is individually liable maximum upto the amount indemnified.

However, the principle of contribution does not apply to life insurance.

(5) Principle of subrogation:

In the context of insurance, subrogation is a specific feature of indemnity principle and therefore it only applies to contracts of indemnity. Hence, it does not apply to life assurance or personal accident policies. Since the principle of subrogation is a result to the principle of indemnity and hence applied only to fire and marine insurance. According to this principle, when an insured has received full indemnity against his loss, all civil liberties and remedies which he has against third person will pass on to the insurer. In other words, right of subrogation is transferred to the insurer only when he has paid for the loss and this right is limited only to the rights and remedies available to the insured with reference to the belongings covered under insurance.

It aims to restrict an insured to recover more than the indemnity that he receives under his insurance against his loss and allows the insurer to recover or reduce the loss. Further, the doctrine of subrogation allows the insurance company to acquire the legal rights to pursue recoveries on behalf of the insured after settlement of insurance claim.

In instances, wherein the insured is in a position to recover the loss in full or partly from a third party due to whose negligence the loss may have been occurred, his right of recovery is subrogated or substituted to the insurer on payment of the claim. Subsequently, insurers can recover the claim from the third party and in case the lost property is recovered or the damaged property carries any value, the insurer will be its owner. Suppose, a bookstall is insured for A 2 lakhs against fire, the bookstall is damaged by fire and the insurer pays the full value of A 2 lakhs to the insured. Later on the damaged bookstall is sold for A 25,000. The insurer is entitled to receive the sum of A 25,000. Following conclusion can be drawn-up from above discuss:

- This principle is outcome of the principle of indemnity and is pertinent to all contracts of indemnity.
- According to this principle, once the insured is compensated for the loss due to damage to property insured, then the right of ownership of such property passes on to the insurer.

(6) Principle of proximate cause:

The principle of proximate cause states that the cause of the loss must be close or immediate and not distant. If the proximate cause of the loss is a risk which is covered in insurance, the insured can recover. In case the risk is the result of a remote cause which is not insured, in that case the insurer is not liable to pay compensation. Proximate cause means natural and uninterrupted series of events, which brings about a result, without interference of any force. However, proximate cause is the cause which in a natural and continuous series of events is accountable for a loss or damage.

It is believed that if there is a single cause of the loss, the cause will be proximate cause of loss and if the same cause was insured, insurer will liable to compensate for loss. When a loss has occurred due to more than one cause, the question arises as to which one is the proximate cause. If the causes recur in a series, they have to be viewed seriously. For the policy to cover the loss it must have an insured hazard that relates the proximate cause with the loss.

In nutshell, an insurer is responsible to pay a claim according to insurance contract only if the loss that created the claim was a proximate cause which is an insured peril. Thus the loss should be directly credited to an insured risk without any break in the chain of natural occurrence. It is elementary of this principle that:

- The loss of insured property can be caused by more than one cause in succession to another.
- The property may be insured against some causes and not against all causes.
- The proximate cause or nearest cause of loss is to be found out for ascertaining liability.
- If the proximate cause is the one which is insured against, the insurance company is bound to pay the compensation and vice-versa.

1.10 SUMMARY

- Insurance is a co-operative form of risk management mainly used to avoid against the risk of a contingent, uncertain loss. It may be defined as the reasonable transfer of the risk of a loss, from one body to another, in exchange for payment.
- An insurer is an Insurance company selling the insurance; the insured or policyholder is the person or entity buying the insurance policy. An amount to be charged by the insurer for a certain sum of insurance coverage is called the premium.

- Insurance is needed for social security, uncertainty, economic development, indemnity on loss, generation of employment, making available funds for investment, to educate the people about loss of prevention and reduction of worry and fear from risk.
- Insurance can be classified on the basis of its nature, business and risk.
- Providing protection and certainty as well as risk sharing are the primary functions of insurance. Whereas Prevention of loss, Providing of Capital, improvement of efficiency and helping in economic progress are the secondary functions.
- Basically, insurance is based on principle of co-operation and principle of probability. Besides, there are other allied principles *viz.* utmost good faith, insurable interest, principle of indemnity, principle of contribution, principle of subrogation and principle of proximate cause.

EXERCISES

(A) Long answer type questions:

1. What is insurance? Define the insurance and explain its need.
2. What is meant by insurance? Discuss its origin.
3. What do you understand by insurance? Explain its different functions.
4. Discuss the different types of insurance. Also explain that what is the difference between general insurance and life insurance?
5. Define the concept of insurance and discuss the principle of insurance.

(B) Short answer type questions:

1. Enumerate the needs of insurance.
2. 'Insurance transfers the risk'. Comment.
3. Explain the primary functions of insurance.
4. Explain the secondary functions of insurance.
5. What are the basic differences between general insurance and life insurance?
6. What do you mean by insured, insurer and policy?
7. Explain the principle of probability applied in insurance.
8. 'Insurance is based on a principle of co-operation'. Comment.
9. 'Subrogation transfers the rights and remedies to insurer.' Explain with suitable example.
10. 'Principle of indemnity plays vital role in insurance.' Discuss the statement.
11. Classify the types of insurance based on its nature.

(C) Write a brief note on following:

1. What is insurance?
2. Define insurance on the basis of functions.
3. Describe insurance from legal point of view.
4. General insurance.
5. Life insurance.
6. Principle of Indemnity in insurance.
7. Theory of probability applied in insurance.
8. Social insurance.
9. Classify the types of insurance on the basis of risk.
10. Miscellaneous insurance.
11. Insurable interest.

12. Principle of Proximate Cause.
13. Principle of Subrogation.

(D) Multiple type questions: (Choose any one of the options)

Que. (1) Life insurance underwrites different types of policies including

(a) Money back plan (b) Endowment policy
(c) Pension plans (d) all of these.

Que. (2) General insurance deals with all types of insurance excluding

(a) Health insurance (b) Science
(c) Life insurance (d) None of these.

Que. (3) 'Insurance is a device for the transfer to an insurer of certain risks of economic loss that would otherwise be borne by the insured.' This is definition is given by

(a) Thomas (b) Allen L. Mayerson
(c) Magee, D.H. (d) None of these.

Que. (4) The Babylonians developed a system of insurance in about 1750 BC, which was well known as

(a) Code of conduct (b) Babylonians Code
(c) Code of Hammurabi (d) None of these.

Que. (5) ULIP stands for

(a) Unit liability plan (b) Unit Linked plans
(c) Ultimate life plan (d) None of these.

Que. (6) Person or entity buying the insurance policy is well known as

(a) Policyholder (b) Insurer
(c) Both above (a) & (b) (d) None of these.

Que. (7) Which one of the following policies is not related to fire insurance

(a) Valued policy (b) Valuable policy
(c) Time policy (d) Average policy.

Que. (8) Which one of the following policies is not related to marine insurance

(a) Voyage policies (b) Valued policies
(c) Floating policies (d) Hull insurance policy.

[Answer: 1-(d), 2-(c), 3-(b), 4-(c), 5-(b), 6-(a), 7-(c), 8(c)]

(F) Match the pair:

(1) Comprehensive policy	(a) Marine Insurance
(2) Freight insurance	(b) Fire insurance
(3) Provides the benefits of saving and protection	(c) ULIP
(4) Plan helpful in speedy growth of money and in risk coverage	(d) Endowment type plans
(5) Plane provides saving, protection & liquidity of the investment	(e) Indemnity
(6) Principle is applied for fire, marine and other general insurance.	(f) Money back plus
(7) Cause of the loss must be close or immediate	(g) Subrogation
(8) It allows insurer to acquire the legal rights to pursue recoveries	(h) Proximate Cause

[Answer: 1- (b), 2-(a), 3-(d), 4-(c), 5-(f), 6-(e), 7-(h), 8(g)]

❑ ❑ ❑

CHAPTER 2

INSURANCE AGENT

Insurance Agent: Introduction, Meaning and Definition; and Characteristics of an Insurance Agent. Essential Qualification for an Insurance Agent. Types, Duties and Rights of an Insurance Agent. Workings of Insurance Agents; Essentials for a Successful Insurance Agent.

2.1 OBJECTIVES OF LEARNING

- *Understand role of insurance agents.*
- *Describe the working of an insurance agent.*
- *Explain the rights of an insurance agent, and*
- *Discuss the essentials for a successful agent.*

2.2 INTRODUCTION

Generally most of the people contact an insurance company through an insurance sales agent. These agents help individuals, families, and businesses in selection of insurance policies that provide the best protection for their lives, health, and property. Captive agents are those agents who work exclusively for one insurance company whereas independent insurance agents represent several companies and propose insurance policies for their customers with the company that offers the best rate and coverage. In both of the cases, agents are supposed to seek out new clients, prepare reports, maintain records and in the event of a loss to his policyholders, he helps in settling their insurance claims. Besides, agents use to offer their clients advice on ways the clients can minimize risk.

Insurance agents generally referred to as 'producers' in the insurance industry as they sell one or more types of insurance, for instance, life, health, disability, property and casualty and long-term concern. Property and casualty insurance is sold by the agents to protect individuals and businesses from financial loss resulting from fire, automobile accidents, theft, natural calamity and other events that can damage the property. Property and casualty insurance policies acquired for a business with specific term and condition can even cover compensation to injured workers and product liability claims.

2.3 MEANING AND DEFINITION OF INSURANCE AGENT

In general parlance, insurance agent is an authorized person of an insurance company who searches the potential customer for selling insurance as well as helps clients in choosing and obtaining insurance policies that suit their needs and in return he gets commission from the insurance company on insurance policies actually sold by him. In prospect of insurance, clients include individuals, families or any business entity. An insurance agent who works for a specific insurance company and only sells that company's product is called a *'captive agent'*. Whereas insurance agents or brokers, represent several companies and sell products of different insurance or finance companies are called *'independent agent'*. Apart from life and general insurance policies, many insurance agents also sell mutual funds, variable annuities and other securities. Thus, an insurance agent is a sales representative of an insurance company who looks for potential customers and thereafter sales, solicits, or negotiates insurance for compensation.

Definition:

(a) According to Section 2(10) of Insurance Act of 1938, Insurance agent' means *'an insurance agent licensed under Section 42 being an individual who received or agrees to receive payment by way of commission or other remuneration in consideration of his soliciting or procuring insurance business.'*

(b) Rule 2(d) of Insurance Regulatory and Development Authority (Licensing of Insurance Agents) Regulations, 2000 reads as *'Composite insurance agent means an insurance agent who holds a licence to act as an insurance agent for a life insurer and a general insurer.'*

2.4 CHARACTERISTICS OF AN INSURANCE AGENT

In view of the above discussion, characteristics of an insurance agent may be as follows:

(i) An insurance agent is a mediator to insured and insurer and works for the insurer.

(ii) Insurance agent is appointed by an authorized competent authority on behalf of Insurance Corporation.

(iii) Possession of license according to provisions of Section 42 of the Insurance Act, 1938 is must for insurance agents.

(iv) A person may be appointed as an insurance agent only if he possesses the minimum qualification as prescribed under the Insurance Agent regulation of 2000.

(v) The function of an insurance agent is not only to establish the relation between clients and insurance but its main function is to enhance the insurance business.

(vi) In addition to acquiring new business, taking care for continuity and renewal of existing policies is his primary function.

(vii) Insurance agents are compensated by commission or other means.

(viii) Insurance agents are not authorized to sanction any insurance proposal for insurer.

(ix) Insurance agents cannot offer any commission or other benefit to insured to acquiring business.

However, an insurance agent is not authorized to collect the premium behalf of insurer from insured and he is also not authorized to issue premium deposit receipt behalf of insurer.

2.4.1 Prospects of customers towards insurance agents:

In the matter of financial security and insurance protection, most of the people desire a long term relationship with a trusted consultant who will provide him long lasting services in the future. Study of independent insurance agents & brokers of America (IIABA) revealed that:

(a) Three out of four insurance consumers use an agent when purchasing personal insurance.

(b) More than half the respondents over 55 years of age have purchased insurance from the same agent for at least 20 years.

(c) More than 60 per cent accept value the opportunity to discuss insurance with a reliable person.

In view of the above, people want an agent with following characteristics:

(i) **Independent:** Independent agent represents several insurance companies and provide the facility to evaluate and compare the product of several insurance companies to find the right combination of coverage and value.

(ii) **Authorized:** Agent must be a license holder and he should be authorized by the company to sell the insurance.

(iii) **Experienced:** He must be well experienced. He must have a long working experience in the field of insurance and he must be capable to evaluate and compare the product of several insurance companies.

(iv) **Specialization:** Agents have experience in specialization in the relevant fields' viz. General insurance or Life insurance.

(v) **Customer oriented:** He must always be ready to provide service to his customers. He guides his policyholders on how to manage their accounts for routine update and transactions. He must be available easily and be helpful in making claim or final settlement.

2.5 ESSENTIAL QUALIFICATION FOR AN INSURANCE AGENT

Insurance companies usually prefer to hire insurance agents who have a degree, particularly in commerce, business or economics. They might consider hiring even a high school pass candidate who has demonstrated sales ability.

According to the provisions of the Insurance Act 1938, and the Insurance Regulatory and Development Authority (Licensing of Insurance Agents) Regulations, 2000, the essential qualification prescribed for an insurance agent is listed below:

(i) He must be a citizen of India.

(ii) He must attain minimum 18 years of age on the date of application.

(iii) He must not be convicted from any court of law for any of his illegal activities.

(iv) He must not be an offender of any illegal activity that is directly or indirectly related to insurance business.

(v) He must not be found guilty to the code of conduct prescribed by any of Insurance Authority.

(vi) He must not be appointed in any Govt. Service or public enterprises.

(vii) He must be mentally fit.

(viii) The applicant shall possess the minimum qualification of passing 12th Standard or equivalent examination conducted by any recognised Board/Institution, where the applicant resides in a place with a population of five thousand or more as per the last census, or he must pass 10th standard or equivalent examination from a recognised Board/Institution if the applicant resides in any other place.

(ix) According to regulation 5 of the Insurance Regulatory and Development Authority (Licensing of Insurance Agents) Regulations, 2000 *'the applicant shall have completed from an approved institution, at least, one hundred hours'* ***practical training*** *in life or general insurance business, as the case may be, which may be spread over three to four weeks, where such applicant is seeking licence for the first time to act as insurance agent.'*

(x) According to regulation 6 of the Insurance Regulatory and Development Authority (Licensing of Insurance Agents) Regulations, 2000, *"the applicant shall have* ***passed the pre-recruitment examination*** *in life or general insurance business, or both, as the case may be, conducted by the Insurance Institute of India, Mumbai, or any other examination body."*

2.6 TYPES OF INSURANCE AGENTS

According to nature of transaction in insurance business, there are two types of insurance sales agents:

(i) Captive agents: are insurance sales agents who work exclusively for a single insurer involved in life or general insurance business. They only sell policies provide by the company that employs them.

(ii) Independent insurance agents: work for insurance commissions, selling policies of several companies. They propose to sell insurance policies, including life and general insurance policies, of different companies to their clients according to their need.

Besides, the type of insurance agents, working for Life Insurance Corporation of India, can be categorized as follows on the basis of their mode of recruitment and their career prospects:

(i) Ordinary Agent: Any person possessing essential qualifications prescribed for an agent under section 42 of the Insurance Act, 1938, after obtaining prescribed license may become an insurance agent. Achieving of minimum prescribed target of insurance business is essential for such types of insurance agents. They are paid commissions at prescribed rate on total sum of premium received for policies sold by them.

(ii) Career agents: The candidates who are interested to build their career in insurance business and selected by the insurance corporation are called career agents. The career agents get a fixed amount as a stipend in first 3 years of their business career and during this period they are imparted rigorous practical training on insurance business by the well qualified trainers under the supervision of branch managers. Under this scheme following two subtypes of agents are appointed:

(a) Career agent working in urban areas and

(b) Career agent working in rural areas.

(iii) **Agents appointed by development officers:** These agents are appointed by their development officers. Concerned development Officer has the responsibility for imparting training and motivation to these agents.

2.7 DUTIES OF INSURANCE AGENTS

The relation between insurer and insurance agents is professional and typically based on mutual faith. In view of this, duty of insurance agents may be as follows:

(i) **To collect information regarding proposer:** Proposer is a person or potential client who seeks insurance. In this context, it is an important duty of the insurance agents to collect important information regarding proposer which directly or indirectly affect the risk of insurer. In view of this, information related to his health, age, business, habits, family background and risks involved in his job should be collected properly so that risk of insurers could be reduced.

(ii) **To inform the insurer about the risk factors:** It is the duty of an insurance agent to inform the insurer about the risk factors and provide all related information which may affect the degree of risk involved in the insurance contract.

(iii) **To solicit for procurement of new business:** Insurance agents should continue to try to solicit for procurement of new business and for this he should approach potential clients to expand customer base.

(iv) **To look after the existing business:** In addition to grasping new business, he should take utmost care of his existing business so that the same should be continued without any interruption.

(v) **Not to interfere in the business of other agents:** At the time of expanding business, an insurance agent should ensure that he is not misleading or trying to divert the clients of other agents as it is against the business ethics.

(vi) **To provide prompt and efficient services:** In this age of competition, customer satisfaction is very important. Therefore, it is the duty of insurance agents to provide prompt and efficient service assisting his clients in acquiring policy, remittance of premium, nomination, loan, surrender of policy and settlement of claims.

(vii) **To motivate the insured to pay premium timely:** The insurance agents should keep in touch with the insured and from time to time remind him to pay the premium so that policy does not lapsed.

(viii) **To co-operate with the insured in nomination:** It is the duty of insurance agents to help and guide the insured in getting registered the nomination timely so that in case of death problems to be faced by the family members could be avoided.

(ix) **To assist in getting payment of claims:** In both the circumstances i.e. death of insured or on normal maturity, it is the duty of insurance agents that he should actively help the insured or his nominee or succession in settlement of his claim. For this purpose he should assist him in completing of formalities required for claim.

(x) **To undergo training:** Training enhances the skill and performance of agents. Hence, it is expected from every agent that he should learn and acquire the knowledge about his business from his superiors *i.e.* Development officer and concerned Branch Manager.

(xi) To plan routine activities adequately: The agent is supposed to take care of time management and accordingly he should plan his activities daily to manage business effectively. Thus, he should maintain diary regularly and keep ready prospect guide, agent directory, commission register etc.

(xii) Miscellaneous duties: In addition to the above, an insurance agent is supposed to carry out some other miscellaneous duties as listed below:

- Read the notices, circulars and other means of information to update himself.
- Interview prospective clients to get data about their financial resources and discuss existing coverage.
- Grievance redressal of clients satisfactorily.
- Explain the features of various policies to clients according to his need.
- He should strictly follow the guidelines provided by the corporation from time to time to agents.
- Analyze clients current insurance policies and suggest additions or changes.
- He should follow the code of conduct prescribed by the associations for insurance agents.
- To make in the insurance programs and plans to suit individual clients.
- He should always maintain integrity and commitment in his business.

2.8 RIGHTS OF AN INSURANCE AGENT

The relation between the insurer and an insurance agent are the same as between an employee and his employer. An insurance agent enjoys almost all rights that are available for an employee from his employer. Being an important part of insurance business, insurance agents have following rights:

(i) Right to get remuneration: The insurance agent has the right to get remuneration at predetermined rate on his business from insurer for whom his is working for.

(ii) Right to be indemnified: When an insurance agent during his work suffers any loss, he has the right to recover such loss from the insurer if it is directly attributed to insurance business and he is not responsible for that loss. However, he has no right to seek compensation from his employer if the loss has arisen out of any unauthorized or illegal activity done by him.

(iii) Right to hold the agency: An insurance agent, by acquiring minimum requirement of business, can continue his agency as long as he wishes.

(iv) Right to ask for account: Every insurance agent has the right to ask for accounts related to his business from insurance company whenever he requires.

(v) Right to get bonus & commission: A permanent insurance agent is authorized to get bonus, commission in addition to his regular commission. Bonus commission is payable only to the eligible agents at a predetermined rate.

(vi) Right to get exemption to acquire minimum business requirement: According to section 9(4) of insurance Act 1938, an insurance agent can get exemption to acquire minimum business requirement in following conditions:

(a) If he has already served for more than 21 years for agency.

(b) If he has served for more than 15 years as an agent and has attained 55 years of age.

(c) After 15 years of service for as an agent, at any time if premium through renewal acquired by his business is reaches upto A 40,000/- per annum.

(vii) Right to receive gratuity and other benefits: According to Schedule-IV related to agent, a permanent insurance agent has the right to receive gratuity and other benefits from his employer.

(viii) Right to get other facilities: Insurance companies, from time to time, offer to give some extra benefits or facilities to their agents with certain terms and conditions under different schemes. These facilities include transportation allowance, loan for purchase of vehicle and home loan at lower interest rate. Every insurance agent fulfilling the terms and condition has right to avail these facilities.

(ix) Right to avail club membership: Life Insurance Corporation provides four level club memberships to agents. Membership of these clubs depends upon acquired volume of the business. When an agent acquires minimum business required for membership of a specific club, he becomes eligible to avail membership of the concerned club.

(x) Right to foreclose agency agreement: An insurance agent at any time, by serving one month advance notice, can foreclose his agency agreement.

(xi) Right to renewal of license: According to Section 42 of the Insurance Act, 1938, an insurance agent has the right to seek for renewal of his license.

(xii) Right to select commission rate option: Options for different periodic payment of commission rates are specified in Schedule IV of rules related to agent. A permanent insurance agent has right to select anyone.

2.9 WORKINGS OF INSURANCE AGENTS

Insurance agents work for insurance companies to generate new business by making contact with potential customers and sell different types of insurance. An agent explains various insurance policies and helps clients to choose plans that suit them. Insurance sales agents usually sell one or more types of insurance policies, such as property and casualty, life, health and long-term care. Agents may specialize in any one of these products or function as generalists providing multiple products. Many agents spend a lot of time for marketing their services and creating their own base of clients. Insurance agents sometimes find new clients through referrals by current clients. Keeping clients happy so that they recommend the agent to others is a key to success for insurance agents.

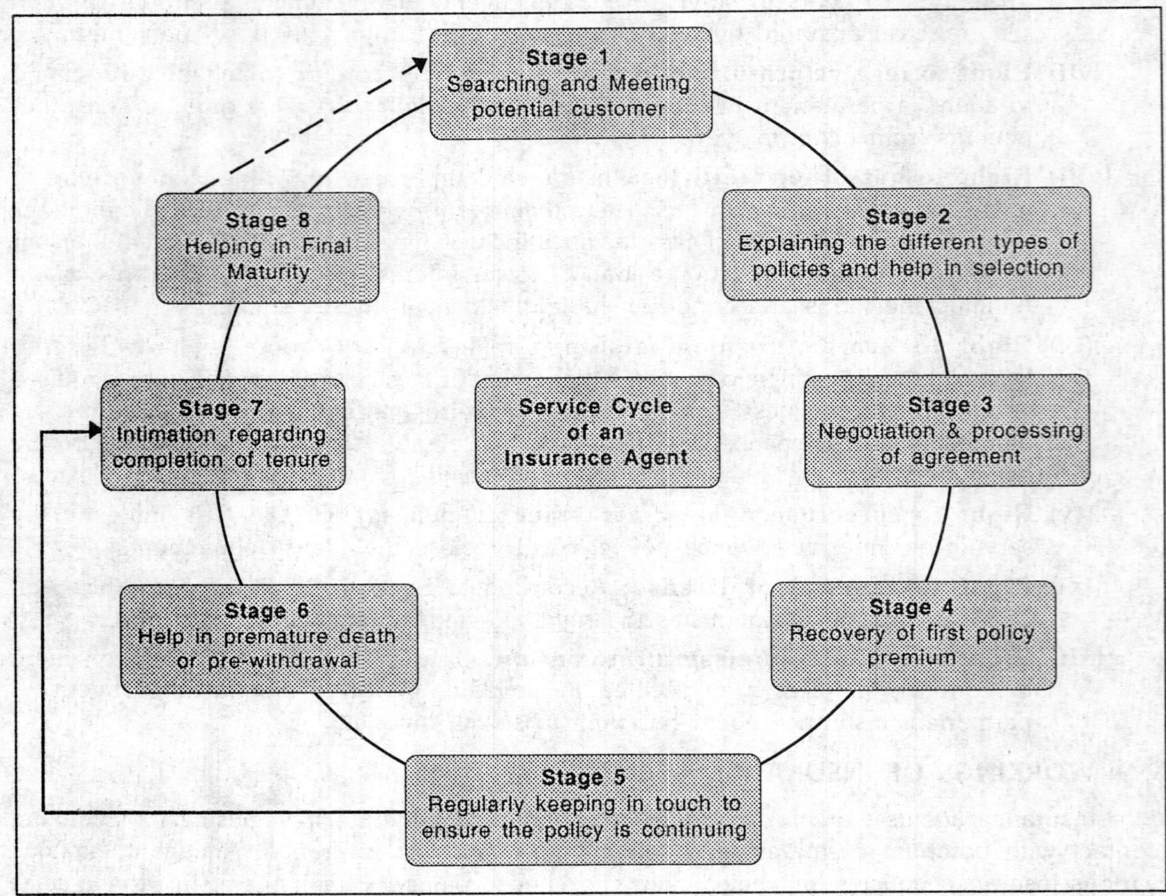

Fig. 2.1: Working Cycle of an Insurance Agent

The above figure depicts the functioning of life insurance agents. However, the workings of insurance may vary in case of different types of insurance.

An insurance agent maintains a long lasting relation with his clients being a creative sales agent. The duty of an insurance agent does not end by selling the insurance policy to clients; but follow-up sales service to clients is part of his workings. The working of insurance can be classified in the following two groups:

1. Workings prior to issue of insurance policy.
2. Workings after issue of insurance policy.

Workings prior to issue of insurance policy.

As per trend in insurance business, generally the following activities required to be carried out by the insurance agents prior to issue of insurance policy:

(i) **Searching for potential clients and making contact:** Insurance agents should continue search for new potential clients to sell the insurance policy. Persons engaged in different professions who have not yet acquired sufficient policies may be the potential clients. The agents should offer the insurance policies to different potential clients taking into consideration their background, necessity, family status and financial status etc., to suit individual clients. However, a single meeting for selling insurance may not suffice usually and hence insurance agents should consult the potential clients continuously to make them agree to procure the policy.

(ii) Motivating for procurement of policy: After general discussion and obtaining primary information about potential clients, if it appears that he is interested in insurance and raises different questions and doubts. All the doubts and queries of such client should be cleared by insurance agents and they should be motivated to procure the policy. During dealings with clients he should avoid to commit any fake assurance. Further, he should not encourage the patient, impassionate and criminal kind person to procure insurance.

(iii) Filling-up of proposal form: When a proposer decides to procure insurance policy, immediately the agent should get insurance proposal form filled by the proposer. The agent should help the proposer in filling-up the proposal form. In case proposer is not able to fill-up the form and requests the agent only then the agent should fill up the form after inquiring facts. After the form has been filled, all the facts should be read-out before the proposer and subsequently signature of the proposer should be obtained only if he is fully satisfied.

(iv) Age proof and payment of first premium: A valid proof of the proposer is enclosed along with proposal form. If proposer is not in a condition to provide the age proof immediately, the agent should collect it subsequently and produce it to the insurer at the earliest possible time. First installment of insurance premium is to be forwarded along with insurance proposal form. This payment can be made in cash or by cheque as per convenience of the proposer.

(v) Making of confidential report: While making confidential report regarding proposer, the agent should obtain required information/facts from the proposer. To reduce the risks involved in the proposal, the following facts should be taken care:

(a) Physical condition and health of proposer.

(b) Personal details of proposer mainly about any disease already suffered by him and his habits.

(c) Family particulars.

(d) Profession, living standard and working conditions of proposer.

(e) Possibility of increase or decrease in risks on life which is being proposed for insurance and

(f) Any other information related to proposal or proposer.

(vi) Submission of proposal: Agent should immediately submit the insurance proposal to the concerned branch/office along with confidential report and payment of first premium.

(vii) Removal of defect in insurance proposal: If there is any defect in the insurance proposal, immediately the agent should get it rectified from the proposer. After satisfying all the requirements, contract of insurance is executed by the insurer and accordingly policy is issued to the insured.

Workings after issue of insurance policy

Once the policy is issued thereafter, the second phase of agent's work starts. Services of agent are provided to the insured on different occasions. Post policy sales services of agents are as follows:

(i) **Help in nomination:** In case of death of insured, the claim of insurance is paid to his nominee or his successor in the absence of nomination. Hence, insurance agent should get filled-in nomination in proposal form from insured at the same time when the form is filled in. Agent should motivate and help the proposer to furnish the nomination.

(ii) **Conversion of policy:** Due to change in condition for insured, the policy can be converted/modified to suit the policyholder if he requests for the same. Agent should assist the policyholders if they seek for conversion/modification in their policies.

(iii) **Restoration of lapsed policies:** Due to nonpayment of premium, the policy is liable to lapse. Insurance companies, from time to time, offer various plans to the policyholder to restore his lapsed policies. Agents should motivate the policyholder to renew his policy availing relaxation offered by the insurer.

(iv) **Loan on policy:** In some specific cases, facilities of loan are also provided to the policyholders. Agents should help the policy holders who are seeking for loan on their policies.

(v) **Surrender of policy:** If the insured is not in a position to continue to pay premium due to his financial hardship, the insurance agents should help him in surrendering the policy.

(vi) **Settlement of claim:** Insurance agents should support the clients or their nominees (in case of death) in fulfilling the requisite formalities for speedy settlement of their claims. The insurance agents should be aware of rules, regulations and formalities applicable for claim so that he is able to help the claimants.

In view of the above, an insurance agent might perform some routine types of the following duties:

- Preparing reports and maintain records related to his business.
- Seek out new clients and solicit, negotiate, or motivate them for procurement of policy.
- In the event of a loss, he helps the policyholders to settle the claims.

2.10 ESSENTIALS FOR A SUCCESSFUL INSURANCE AGENT

The insurance business is filled with prospects; but this fact has a different reality that over more than 1/3rd of the new agents leave the industry within a year. Now the question arises that, what does it take for a new insurance to get success in the market? In response to the above, some important traits determine success in insurance business which are as follows:

(1) **Passionate:** Successful insurance agents are passionate regarding what they do and this helps in building honesty to the job. They get pleasure from helping others and prepare them for the unexpected, so they believe that they working for the welfare of the society. Leading insurance agents must be on a mission to improve the lives of their current and potential clients.

(2) **Friendly and sympathetic:** An Insurance agent must be friendly and be able to make potential clients satisfied during the sales process. They must be relaxed while starting discussions and have true interest in their client's safety and financial comfort.

(3) **Capable to handle rejections:** At the beginning of his career, an insurance agent faces a lot of rejection. Many potential clients attempt to avoid meetings, and some may even be annoyed on repeated approach for insurance. Successful agents accept this challenge. Hence, rejection is an important part of insurance business and it should be accepted willingly.

(4) **Goal oriented:** The insurance agents are fully responsible for their results. The capability to set short-term, mid-term, and long-term goals the insurance agents deal with daily business challenges. It is known to them that their actions determine the degree of their success and hence they do whatever is required to attain the outcome they desire. Insurance agents set their time schedule and concentration on potential customers according to their needs and expedite them at right time to procure the policy. It is their duty to ensure that they fully understand their customer's condition before offering any insurance. It is only feasible for them to formulate the best solution considering their customer's viewpoint and concern. This facilitates the insurance agents to successfully present the features and benefits of their product and service that are most pertinent to their customers. By cautiously fostering these qualities, aspirants can become very professional insurance agents with excellent sales performance.

(5) **Organized:** The successful insurance agents efficiently keep track of when to contact current and potential clients. Being organized and efficient, they have all the information related to their clients. Success in insurance requires determination. Their ability to do follow up with their clients helps them create referrals and repeat business. Keeping in touch with clients continuously lets agents provide better sales opportunities on different occasions, for instance, the birth of a child or the purchase of either a new vehicle or home.

(6) **Professionalism:** Successful insurance agents exhibit integrity, honesty and professionalism. They maintain their proficiency in their field of specialization. Their attitude towards research work makes them efficient to give quality advice to their customers. Applying the best sales practices, they call attention to ethical behaviour and can be exceptionally significant. They can cater to the sophisticated need of clients who demand professionalism. Their customers are not likely to turn to other insurance agents for counselling.

(7) **Good Listeners:** Potential clients express their areas of concern only if agents encourage them by listening patiently. Always keeping in mind the facts that opportunities should be exploited and service is rendered to the clients.

1.10 SUMMARY

- In general parlance, an insurance agent is an authorized person of the insurance company who searches the potential clients for selling insurance as well as helps clients in choosing and obtaining insurance policies that suit their needs and in exchange of this business he gets commission from the insurance company on insurance policies actually sold by him.
- People want an agent with characteristics such as an independent, authorized, experienced, specialist and customer oriented.
- Essential qualification for an agent is (i) He must be a citizen of India; (ii) He must attain minimum 18 years of age; and other qualification as prescribed in the Insurance Regulatory and Development Authority (Licensing of Insurance Agents) Regulations, 2000.

- *Mainly there are two types of insurance agents viz. (i) Captive agents; and (ii) Independent insurance agents. However in case of Life Insurance Corporation of India type of agents are:* (iii) ordinary agent; (iv) career agent; and (v) agents appointed by development officer.
- Duties of insurance agents include collection of information regarding proposer; informing the insurer about the risk factors; soliciting for procuring new business; looking after the existing business, not to interfere in the business of other agents, providing prompt and efficient services, motivating the insured to pay premium timely, co-operating with the insured in proceeding with nomination, assists in getting payment of claims, undergoes training and plans routine activities.
- Remuneration, indemnity, holding agency, enquiry for account, getting bonus commission, getting exemption to acquire minimum business requirement, gratuity and other benefits, getting other facilities, foreclosing agency agreement, right to renewal of license are some important rights of an insurance agent.
- The working of insurance can be classified two groups *viz.* (i) workings prior to issue of insurance policy; and (ii) workings after issue of insurance policy.
- Passion, friendliness, sympathetic, capable to handle rejections, goal orientation, organization, professionalism and good listeners are the essential features of a successful insurance agent.

EXERCISES

(A) Long answer type questions:

1. Who is an insurance agent? Describe the duties and rights of an insurance agent.
2. What do you mean by an insurance agent? Explain the working of an insurance agent.
3. What do you understand by insurance agent? Discuss his characteristics.
4. Describe the essential qualifications for an insurance agent. Also explain the types of agents.
5. Identify the rights and workings of an insurance agent.

(B) Short answer type questions:

1. What are the essential qualifications for an insurance agent?
2. Briefly discuss the characteristics of an insurance agent.
3. What are the duties expected from an insurance agent prior to issue of the policy?
4. Explain the duties of an insurance agent after issue of a policy.
5. Enumerate the rights of an insurance agent.
6. Describe the essentials for a successful insurance agent.
7. Define the prospects of customers towards insurance agents.
8. Enumerate the different types of Insurance agents.
9. What are the duties of Insurance agents?

(C) Write a brief note on following:

1. Customer's prospects towards insurance agents.
2. Definition of an insurance agent.
3. Qualifications for insurance agents.
4. 5 rights of insurance agents.
5. Difference between captive and independent agent.

6. Types of life insurance agents.
7. 5 essentials for successful agents.

(E) Multiple type questions: (Choose any one of given options)

Que. (1) IRDA stands for —

(a) Insurance Regulation and Development Authority
(b) Insurance Regulatory and Development Authority
(c) Insurance Registration and Development Authority
(d) None of these.

Que. (2) Possession of license according to Insurance Act, 1938 is must for Insurance agents. Under which section this provision has been made:

(a) Section 24 (b) Section 44
(c) Section 42 (d) None of these.

Que. (3) Insurance Regulatory and Development Authority (Licensing of Insurance Agents) Regulations, 2000 has been enacted on which of the following date:

(a) 04th July 2000 (b) 14th July 2000
(c) 12th September 2000 (d) None of these.

Que. (4) An insurance agent who works exclusively for a single insurance company is called:

(a) Independent agent (b) Career agent
(c) Captive agent (d) None of these.

Que. (5) Insurance agent who sells the insurance product of several companies is known as:

(a) Independent agent (b) Career agent
(c) Captive agent (d) None of these.

Que. (6) Rights of insurance agent includes:

(b) Gratuity (b) Normal Commission
(c) Bonus commission (d) All of these.

Que. (7) An insurance agent can get exemption to acquire minimum business requirement for holding the agency If he has already served for more than...........years for agency.

(a) 25 years (b) 21 years
(c) 33 years (d) None of these.

Que. (8) Insurance proposal form can be filled-up by:

(a) Proposer only (b) Insurance agents only
(c) Both "a" & "B" above (d) None of these.

[Answer: 1-(b), 2-(c), 3-(b), 4-(c), 5-(a), 6-(d), 7-(b), 8-(c)]

(F) Match the pair

(1) Insurance agent sells policy exclusively for a single insurer (a) Ordinary agent.
(2) Insurance agent sells policies of several companies (b) Carrier agent.
(3) Insurance agent who works after obtaining prescribed license (c) Captive agent.
(4) Insurance agent selected and appointed only by LIC (d) Independent agent.
(5) Section 42 of the Insurance Act, 1938 is related to (e) Entitlements of agent.
(6) Schedule IV of insurance act 1938 is related to (f) Renewal of license.

[Answer: 1-(c), 2-(d), 3-(a), 4-(d), 5-(f), 6-(e)]

❒ ❒ ❒

CHAPTER 3

LIFE INSURANCE

Life Insurance: Introduction, Meaning and Definition of Life Insurance; Types, Need and Importance of Life Insurance.

3.1 OBJECTIVES OF LEARNING

- *Understand the concept of life insurance;*
- *Discuss the need of life insurance;*
- *Explain the importance of Life insurance; and*
- *Illustrate various types of life insurance policies offered by insurance companies.*

3.2 INTRODUCTION

Insurance has become a vital part of our lives these days. Life insurance investment is seen as an added security to us and our family (dependent family members) in later years. When we buy an insurance policy we secure protection for our family even we are not alive. To cater to the need of people from various walks of life there are different life insurance plans. Insurance provides payment of a sum of money to the nominee upon the death of the insured or to the insured if he still living after reaching a specified age or on maturity of life insurance policy.

Every individual has got a definite economic worth attached to his life in the form of earning potential. If a person dies at a young age, his dependents suffer a financial loss as his death reduces regular earnings of the family. Besides, lots of his obligations towards the family remains unfulfilled due to his unexpected demise. This is the risks attached with the situation of early death. This risk can be covered by life insurance only.

It is human nature that one plans his life and his sources of income to the best of his capability considering his life expectation. Sometimes, even with the best of planning the individual is not capable of meeting different contingencies. Further, if a person survives beyond his predictable age, his former plan for securing sources of income till a certain age would become inadequate due to various reasons. It is seen that the expenditure on health care increases usually in the old age and this is the time when a person needs money. At this juncture, the person is in a position to go and earn the money and hence risk is attached with the situation. In such a contingent condition, life insurance policies will suffice the need in which withdrawals are possible as and when required. Besides, pension policies or annuities may also be helpful in overcoming such contingencies.

Therefore, life Insurance is beneficial for policyholders the cases of either 'dying in an early age as well as living so long' as it protects the individual against distinct risks attached in both the cases.

In a nut shell, life Insurance provides risk coverage to the life of policy holder. It is a tool of protection as well as investment. Life Insurance is a conditional agreement and not a contract of indemnity. In case of death of the assured the insurer provides protection against loss of income and compensates the nominee of the policy. Various life insurance policies are offered to take care of insurance requirements of persons in different situations and at different stages in life.

3.3 HISTORY OF LIFE INSURANCE

Life insurance emerged formally in 1818 with the establishment of the Oriental Life Insurance Company in Calcutta (now Kolkata). However, the Oriental insurance company failed in 1834. In 1829, the Madras Equitable started life insurance business in the Madras Presidency. With the enactment of British Insurance in 1870, the Bombay Mutual in 1871, Oriental in 1874 and Empire of India 1897 started their life insurance operations in the Bombay Residency. In Britishers regime, some of the foreign dominated insurance companies' *viz.* Albert Life Assurance, Royal Insurance, Liverpool and London Globe Insurance did good business India. On the contrary, the Indian insurance companies had faced tough competition from these foreign companies.

- *The Indian Life Assurance Companies Act, 1912* was the first statutory measure to regulate life business.
- *In 1928, the Indian Insurance Companies Act* was enacted to enable the Government to collect statistical information about both life and non-life business transacted in India by Indian and foreign insurers including provident insurance societies.
- In 1938, with a view to protecting the interest of the Insurance public, the earlier legislation was consolidated and amended by the *Insurance Act, 1938* with comprehensive provisions for effective control over the activities of insurers.
- *The Insurance Amendment Act of 1950* abolished principal agencies. However, there were a large number of insurance companies and the level of competition was high. There were also allegations of unfair trade practices. The Government of India, therefore, decided to nationalize insurance business.
- An Ordinance was issued *on the 19th January, 1956* nationalizing the Life Insurance sector and *Life Insurance Corporation* came into existence in the same year. The LIC absorbed 154 Indian, 16 non-Indian insurers, 75 provident societies, totally 245 Indian and foreign insurers in all. The LIC had monopoly till the late 90s when the Insurance sector was reopened to the private sector.

3.4 LIFE INSURANCE MEANING AND DEFINITION

Life insurance is an agreement under which an insurance company (also called insurer), in consideration of premium paid, agrees to pay a fixed sum of money (to designated beneficiary) on the death of the insured or on the expiry of a specified period of time whichever is earlier.

Since the subject matter of insurance is the life of a human being it is called 'Life insurance'. Life insurance provides risk coverage to the life of a person. The literal meaning of life insurance policy is safeguarding the family or dependents during the financial crisis.

(i) F.C. Oviatt, in his book titled *"Economic place of insurance and its relation to society"* described that *"The foundation of life insurance is the recognition of the value of a human life and the possibility of indemnification for the loss of that value.*

— *F.C. Oviatt*

(ii) ***Prof. John, H. Magee,*** has defined it as *"The life insurance contract embodies an agreement, in which, broadly stated the insurer undertakes to pay a stipulated sum upon the death of the insured or, at some designated time to a designated beneficiary."*

(iii) ***Federation of Insurance Institutes, Mumbai,*** has defined the life insurance as *"Life insurance is a contract whereby a person (insurer) agrees for a consideration that is payment of a sum of money or a periodical payment, called the premium, to pay to another (insured or his estate) a stated sum of the happening of an event dependent on human life."*

In view of the above definitions, it is evident that, life insurance is a contractual agreement made between the insurer and the insured. The insurer refers to the insurance company and the insuree is the insured person. In this agreement, the insurer (Insurance Company) undertakes to pay a sum of money to the nominated beneficiary upon the death of the insured or compensates the insured on other event, such as terminal illness or critical illness. In return, the policy holder or insured agrees to pay a specific periodical or lump sum payment (called the premium).

3.5 TYPES OF LIFE INSURANCE

Life insurance policies can be grouped into the following categories:

(i) Term policy

Term policy provides life insurance coverage for a specified period. It is a cheapest Insurance policy as the premium rates are comparatively lower than other policies. The policy does not accumulate cash value. In this policy, if the policyholder survives till the end of policy term, the risk cover lapses and no insurance benefit payment is made to him. However, a fixed sum of money is paid to the designated beneficiaries if the policyholder dies during the policy term. For instance, if an individual buys a term policy of A 5 lakh for a period of 10 years, his family will get a sum of A 5 lakh if he dies within that 10 year period; otherwise the premiums paid are not returned back. This plan is most suitable for those who are initially not capable to pay high premium but have need of life cover for a high amount.

(ii) Whole life policy

Whole life insurance provides lifetime death benefit coverage to the policyholder against death. The sum of amount assured becomes payable to the legal successor only on death of the assured. Hence, such policy does not expire until the death of the insured. The whole life policy can be of following three types:

(a) Ordinary whole life policy: In this case, the policyholder pays regular premiums until his death.

(b) **Limited payment whole life policy:** In this case, premium is payable for a specified period (20 years or 25 years) only and thereafter no premium is required to be paid.

(c) **Single premium whole life policy:** In this type of policy, a single premium is payable once in lump sum.

(iii) Endowment life policy

Endowment life policy is very popular among life insurance policies as it includes risk cover with financial savings. In this policy, the insurer undertakes to the policyholder to pay a particular sum of money to him or his successor on his death or on the maturity of the policy, whichever is earlier. Usually, the liability of insurer ends with the maturity of policy. In such policies, the premium is paid by the policyholder till the maturity of the policy or until the death of the assured whichever is first. The premium rate for endowment policy is comparatively higher than the whole life policy as it provides double benefit to the policyholder. In case of death during the term of policy, the beneficiary gets the sum assured. In other conditions, the policyholder himself gets back the premiums paid by him with other benefits like bonus.

(iv) Money-Back Plan

Money-Back Plan is best for the people who look for both insurance coverage and savings. It gives periodic part payments to the policyholders during the term of policy. In other words, a portion of the assured sum is paid out at regular intervals. The policyholder gets the balance sum assured with bonus (as admissible) if he survives till end of the term. In this policy, policyholders pay certain premiums for a fixed period and after completion of period they are benefited with reasonable rate of return along with the final lump sum return if insured is alive till maturity. However, a fixed lump sum is paid to the designated beneficiary in case death of insured occurs before end of term.

(v) Unit Linked Insurance Plan (ULIP)

Unit Linked Insurance Plan (ULIP) is well-liked by the investors; now-a-days as it provides the benefit of life insurance as well as mutual benefits to the policyholders. These are market-linked life insurance products and include life cover and fund accumulation option. In this plan, certain part of premium paid by the policyholder is invested in bonds, equities or debt funds for maximizing returns while the rest is used for risk coverage on life. However, if one applies for this plan then he should be ready for the risks related to the stock market. In this plan, buyers have liberty to choose the best option from a variety of fund options depending on their capacity to risk bear. ULIPs may be helpful for getting different long-term financial objectives such as planning for retirement, child's education, marriage etc.

(vi) Pension Plans

A good pension plan is a must for a respectful and independent retirement life. Pension plan is a kind of insurance policy which helps to provide better pension benefit to the policyholder in return of his savings. In such plans, the policyholder can pay either lump sum amount or premiums for definite years to get pension in later years.

(vii) Annuity policy

Annuity is same as pension plan. In this policy, the insurer pays a fixed amount to assured not in lump sum payment but in monthly, quarterly and half-yearly or yearly instalments after the assured attains a certain age. Annuity is paid till the assured survives. This is helpful to those who want to ensure a regular return after the expiry of a certain period.

(viii) Health Plans

Apart from risk to life, an individual is also uncovered from different uncertainties related to his health. Probability of suffering from ailments, diseases, disability caused by stroke or accident, cannot be overlooked. In case of any serious illness, the person is hospitalized and intensive medical treatment is given which can be very expensive. In such case, medical insurance is helpful in paying the expensive medical bills and reducing unexpected financial burden. At present, due to pollution in the environment and negligence in routine life, different diseases such as diabetes, heart, cancer, paralysis etc., are increasing rapidly. Thus, the probability of risk to health compels individuals to go for medical insurance cover.

(ix) Policies for children

Policies for children are designed for the different needs of the children such as education, marriage, security of life etc. Children endowment policy, marriage endowment, educational annuity plans, and Children's deferred assurances are some important policies especially designed for children.

(x) Policies for women

Life Insurance Corporation of India offers some policies such as Jeevan Sukanya and Jeevan Sathi, which are specially designed for women. Some of the features of these policies are as follows:

(a) ***Jeevan Sukanya*** is an endowment policy for the growing female child.

- Female child only within the age group of 1 to 12 years is covered in this plan.
- Risk of the child starts after 2 years of taking the policy or after age of 7, whichever is earlier.
- Premium is payable till child attains 20 years of age.
- On attaining age of 20 years, the assured is paid the sum assured as survival benefit and the thereafter policy continues to cover the life assured till maturity date when only bonus will be.
- In case the assured dies before maturity, the sum assured with bonus will be paid.

(b) ***Jeevan Sathi*** is an endowment policy, under which husband and wife both are covered. This policy is well known as Life Partner plan and provides a comprehensive family protection. Following benefits are provided in this policy:

- If both the husband and wife are alive on maturity, they will get a fixed full sum of amount as assured with bonus.
- In case of death of any one of the assured during the period of the policy, a fixed basic amount assured is paid to the surviving partner and surviving partner is not required to pay any further premiums.
- Insurance coverage for the full sum assured will remain available for surviving partner till maturity. In case she/he also dies before the maturity date, then the sum assured is paid to the nominee.

(xi) Group life insurance

Group life insurance is a unique plan of insurance under which the lives of a group of people are covered under single insurance policy. Usually this policy is opted by employers for benefit of the employees. Apart from this, a federation, union or association also secures this policy for benefit of their members. However, the insurance on every life is independent of that on the other lives. While underwriting the policy, insurer considers the size, turnover and financial position of the group instead of individual insurability. An individual is virtually insured till he is a member of that group. Therefore, under this policy, the insurer provides coverage for several people under a single contract.

3.6 NEED FOR LIFE INSURANCE

Life insurance is the best option of investment as it provides coverage of risks on life as well as helpful in economic growth. It is a form of security for the person who insures his life and his family. In larger scale, life insurance policies, by providing healthy and safe environment, have helped trade and other economic activities to grow efficiently. Further, it has generated a lot of job prospects with profitable career options. Thus, life insurance is beneficial for the entire society. Some of reasons to purchase a life insurance policy are as follows:

(i) Asset Protection

The fundamental advantage of life insurance is that the financial well-being of one's family remains protected from circumstances such as loss of income due to serious illness or death of the insured. Simultaneously, insurance policies also have a strong integral scheme for creation of wealth. Thus, the policyholders have dual benefit i.e. benefit of risk coverage and benefit of wealth creation.

(ii) Goal based savings

Everyone has some specific goals in his life and one tries to secure the same. The goals in life vary from time to time as per the requirement of the individual and his family. For example, a young newly employed person will set the goal to get married first; thereafter he would like to own a house followed by vehicle and other household requirements. After having children his goal shifts to planning for the education or marriage of his children. Before old age he starts planning to secure a source of regular income for his retired life.

Life insurance is the best investment option that offers specific plans especially for various needs of customer pertaining to his different life stages. Life insurance endeavors provide a well-suited plan to the customer as per his needs of that particular life stage. Accordingly, it ensures that the individual's financial goals of that particular life stage are met.

The table below gives a general guide to the plans that are appropriate for different life stages:

Life Stage	*Primary Need*	*Life Insurance Product*
Young & Single	Asset Creation	Wealth Creation plans
Young and Just married	Asset creation and protection	Wealth creation and mortgage protection plan
Married with kids	Children's education, Asset creation and protection	Education insurance, mortgage protection & wealth creation plans
Middle aged with grown up kids	Planning for retirement & asset protection	Retirement solution & mortgage protection
Across all life-stages	Health plans	Health Insurance

Source: http://www.iciciprulife.com

(iii) Early Deaths

It has been experienced that the mortality rate tends to decline due to increase in medical facilities. Concurrently, it has also been noted that the age at which people die is decreasing due to unhealthy living style, stress, pollution and other natural calamities. This compels people to secure a definite income for their family and dependents. This is the matter of great concern for the person who happens to be the single bread winner of his family. In these cases, only life insurance can fulfill the needs of his family.

(iv) Advancements in healthcare

Due to increase in average life span of human beings, the probability of healthcare in old age also increases. Due to advancement in medical science, most of all the treatments are available for different diseases. Some of the treatments are very costly and in a normal condition it is beyond the financial capacity of an ordinary person. It is a huge financial burden in the form of expensive medical bills. As there is no other option to overcome such encumbrance, people prefer to invest in Life insurance or other kinds of health insurance.

(v) Best option for salaried youth

Life insurance is normally looked upon as one of the savings scheme. In case of life insurance, the rate(s) of premium increases with the increase in age of the proposer. To get the benefit of less premium young people who are just employed see insurance as a gainful scheme to regulate their savings. Besides, tax benefits and additional benefits are also provided which are welcomed as they have a special attraction for the salaried youth.

3.7 IMPORTANCE OF LIFE INSURANCE

Life Insurance policies have dual benefits of savings and security. It is useful for all the individuals, groups, business community and the society. Life insurance policies provide us the strength to face the uncertainties and a guarantee towards financial stability for our family. In view of this, the life insurance has become an integral part of financial plans. Some of the important benefits of life insurance are given below:

(i) Risk Cover

Life today is full of uncertainties; in this situation life insurance provides protection to the dependents of insured in case of his early death. The dependents or designated beneficiaries get a fixed sum of money in case of death of the assured. Life Insurance guarantees that the insured's family continues to carry on its life in a normal manner.

(ii) Planning for life stage needs

Life Insurance not only provides protection against untimely death but also operates as a long term investment. Individuals can secure life insurance to meet the different goals at different stages of their life. These goals include different liabilities of an individual towards his family, such as children's education and their marriage, construction of house or securing annuities for relaxed retired life. As far as endowment plan in concerned, it offers in-built guarantees and definite maturity benefits through various policy options, for example, Money Back, Guaranteed Cash Values, and Guaranteed Maturity Values. At the time of maturity the policyholder will get a fixed lump sum amount as money back along with other additional benefits applicable in the respective plans.

(iii) Promotion of savings

Life Insurance is a long-term contract with the insurance company and thereby policyholders have to pay a fixed premium regularly at a defined interval. Consequently, life insurance encourages people to save money compulsorily. When a life policy is taken, the assured agrees to pay premiums regularly and if he fails to pay the premium regularly, his policy lapses. In case the policy lapses, the policyholder is not entitled for availing insurance benefit due to breach of contract in his part. Hence, it builds the habit of long-term savings in policyholders to meet financial needs at various life stages.

(iv) Initiates investments

Life insurance is recognized as an important mechanism for mobilizing people towards investment. Capital received in the form of premiums is reinvested in various investments by the Life Insurance Companies for the economic development of the country.

(v) Loan facilities

Policyholders have the option of taking a loan against the policy. It helps the policyholder to meet his unexpected life stage needs without adversely affecting the benefits of the policy they have bought. Loan amount is decided on face value of life insurance policy, premiums already paid and the overall term of respective policies. It also facilitates mortgage against loans taken by the policyholders in order that in case of any unanticipated event, the burden of repayment does not fall on the deceased family of the deceased.

(vi) Social Security

Life insurance is accepted as an important social security tool which helps in protection of lives and promoting investments thereby helpful in building a safe and protected climate for the society. Apart from these, life insurance provides different plans for different needs of a person such as financial assistance in education and marriage of children and for building a house. Thus, life insurance contributes to development of the nation in sharing the liabilities towards social security.

(vii) Tax Benefit

Premiums paid upto a maximum limit of A 1,00,000/- by the policyholders are deductible from the taxable income of the policy owner under section 80 (C) of Income tax Act, in India. Any earning from an Insurance Plan in form of maturity profits, claims, partial withdrawal is exempt from taxation under section 10 (10) D of Income Tax Act of India. Besides, death benefits or maturity benefits are also free from tax liabilities. In addition to these, income tax concessions are also available for corporate houses who take insurance policies. Most of the people and corporate houses make investments in insurance only for getting tax benefits. This, of course, enhances spending power of policyholders and promotes investments thereby promotes overall economic development of country. Hence, insurance plans provide attractive tax-benefits at the time of entry as well at exit.

(viii) Protection against rising health expenses

Life insurance is helpful not only in protection of life and accumulation of wealth, but it also provides health insurance plans by offering the benefits of protection against an unforeseen expenditure which occurs on hospitalization and treatment for serious diseases.

(ix) Assured income through annuities

Life Insurance is seen as one of the best mechanisms for planning retirement life. Even a small saving may secure source of regular income during the retired phase of life. Thus, an assured income through annuities is an important aspect of life insurance.

3.8 LIFE INSURANCE IN INDIA

Life Insurance in India was nationalized in 1956 by incorporating Life Insurance Corporation. All private life insurance companies at that time were taken over by LIC. Subsequently in 1993, the Government of India appointed R.N. Malhotra Committee to pursue the prospects of privatization of the life insurance sector in India. The committee has submitted its report in favor of privatization of the insurance sector in 1994. After a long debate on privatization, finally Insurance regulatory and Development Authority (IRDA) Act, amended Insurance Act 1938, has been passed in the year 2000. Immediately after enactment, the IRDA started issuing licenses to private life insurers.

Today Life Insurance has become a fastest growing sector in India. Since liberalization of insurance in 2000, the Government of India has allowed private corporate houses to operate their business in insurance sector thereafter competition is on increase. Apart from Life Insurance Corporation, the public sector life insurer, there are 23 other private sector life insurers, as listed below who are operating their business in India:

Life Insurer in Public Sector:

1. Life Insurance Corporation of India.

Life Insurers in Private Sector

1. Aviva Life Insurance.
2. AEGON Religare Life Insurance.
3. Bajaj Allianz Life.
4. Bharti AXA Life Insurance Co. Ltd.
5. Birla Sunlife.
6. CANARA HSBC Oriental Bank of Commerce LIFE INSURANCE.
7. DLF Pramerica Life Insurance.
8. Edelweiss Tokio Life Insurance Co. Ltd.
9. Future Generali Life Insurance Co Ltd.
10. HDFC Standard Life.
11. ICICI Prudential Life Insurance.
12. IDBI Fedaral Life Insurance.
13. India First Life Insurance Co.
14. ING Vysya Life Insurance.
15. Kotak Life Insurance.
16. Metlife India Life Insurance.
17. Max New York Life Insurance.
18. Reliance Life Insurance Co. Ltd.
19. Sahara Life Insurance.

20. SBI Life Insurance.
21. Shriram Life Insurance.
22. Star Union Dia-ichi Life Insurance Co. Ltd.
23. Tata AIG Life.

EXERCISES

3.9 SUMMARY

- Life insurance is an agreement under which an insurance company (also called insurer), in consideration of a premium paid, agrees to pay a fixed sum of money (to designated beneficiary) on death of the insured or on the expiry of a specified period of time whichever is earlier. Since the subject matter of insurance is life of a human being and hence, it is called "Life insurance".
- Life insurance policies can be grouped into categories such as (i) Term policy (ii) Whole life policy Endowment life policy, Money-Back Plan, Unit Linked Insurance Plans (ULIP), Pension Plans, Annuity policy, Health Plans, Policies for children, Policies for women, Group life insurance.
- Asset Protection, goal based savings, protection from early deaths, Advancements in healthcare, best option for salaried youth etc. are some basic needs for life insurance.
- Risk Cover, saving for old age, promotion of savings, building the habit of thrift, initiates investments, credit worthiness, social security, protection against rising health expenses , safe and profitable long-term investment , assured income through annuities etc. are some of the important benefits of life insurance.

(A) Long answer type questions:

1. What is meant by life insurance? Define the life insurance and explain its need.
2. What do you understand by life insurance? Discuss the history of life insurance in India.
3. Define life insurance? Also describe different types of life insurance policies.
4. Discuss the different types of life insurance. Describe the need of life insurance in present time.
5. 'Life insurance is an agreement'. Comment on it and specify its importance.

(B) Short answer type questions:

1. Specify the needs of insurance.
2. 'Life insurance is goal based investment'. Comment.
3. Discuss any 4 types of life insurance policy.
4. Explain the importance of life insurance.
5. Trace the emergence of Life insurance in India.
6. 'Life insurance has dual benefit'. Comments.
7. Differentiate between 'Term policy' and 'Whole life Policy'.

(C) Write a brief note on the following:

1. What is life insurance?
2. Term policy.
3. Whole life policy.
4. Endowment life policy.
5. Money-Back Plan.
6. Unit Linked Insurance Plans (ULIP).

7. Pension Plans and Annuity policy.
8. Health Plans.
9. Policy for Women.
10. Group Life Insurance.
11. Life insurance Vs. Goal base investment.

(D) Multiple type questions: (Choose any one of the given options)

Que. (1) In which city of India the Oriental life insurance company had been established:
(a) Madras (b) Kolkata
(c) Mumbai (d) None of these.

Que. (2) In which year Madras Equitable had started life insurance business:
(c) 1929 (b) 1818
(c) 1829 (d) None of these.

Que. (3) In 1956, how many foreign and Indian insurance companies have been absorbed in Life Insurance Corporation of India:
(a) 156 (b) 75
(c) 245 (d) None of these.

Que. (4) Jeevan Sukanya is an endowment policy for growing female child. It covers female child only within a age group of:
(a) 1 to 12 years (b) 3 to 12 years
(c) 3 to 20 years (d) None of these.

Que. (5) What is/are basic needs for life insurance:
(a) Assets protection (b) Goal based savings
(c) Both (a) and (b) above (d) None of these.

Que. (6) Which was/were the foreign dominated insurance company/companies in India:
(a) Albert Life Assurance (b) Royal Insurance
(c) Liverpool (d) All of these.

Que. (7) On which date an ordinance had been issued for the nationalization of Life Insurance sector in India:
(a) 19th January 1956 (b) 19th June 1956
(c) 17th July 1965 (d) None of these.

[Answer: 1-(b), 2-(c), 3-(c), 4-(a), 5-(c), 6-(d), 7-(a)]

(E) Match the columns:

(1) The Bombay Mutual Company established	(a) in 1994.
(2) The Indian Life Assurance Company's Act, enacted	(b) In 1928
(3) The Indian Insurance Company's Act was enacted	(c) in 1912
(4) The Malhotra Committee had submitted its report	(d) in 1871
(5) This policy includes risk cover with financial savings	(e) Money Back policy
(6) This policy does not accumulate cash value.	(f) Term policy
(7) It gives periodic part payments to the policyholders during the term of policy	(g) Endowment life policy

[Answer: 1-(d), 2-(c), 3-(b), 4-(a), 5-(g), 6-(f), 7-(e)]

❑ ❑ ❑

CHAPTER 4

ELEMENTS OF CONTRACTS

Elements of Contracts: Introduction, Definition, Types and Essentials of a Contract. Difference between Insurance Contract and other Contracts. Double Contract and Re-insurance and Differences between them.

4.1 OBJECTIVES OF LEARNING

- *Understand the concept of contract and insurance contract.*
- *Describe types and essentials of a contract as well as insurance contract.*
- *Discuss the double insurance and re-insurance, and*
- *Make distinguish between insurance and re-insurance.*

4.2 INTRODUCTION

Our entire financial system is based on the freedom of individuals to make a contract fulfilling their different interests. But a lot of people would be unaware about the essential elements require to make an enforceable contract. A contract is essential for any business operation. A contract should abide by the commonly recognized terms and conditions. Entering into business without a formal contract can be disastrous as it can deprive one or both parties of their privileges even it can yield a great loss to either party. To protect the interests of parties entering into contract, the Indian Contract Act was enacted in 1872. The objective of Indian contract law is to ensure fair business practices. The Indian contract Act laid the base of business laws. The Indian Contract Act provides general principles for forming, executing and implementing contracts.

With reference to successful operation of insurance business, the basic principles are required to be complied with. However, the insurance contract is same as other contracts. Therefore, all the characteristics and legal elements involved in valid contracts are also required essentially in the insurance contracts. Legal relation between insured and insurers are established and managed merely by insurance contract.

4.3 DEFINITION OF CONTRACT

In the Indian Contract Act, 1872, a contract has been defined from the legal point of view in following manner:

(i) Section 2(h) of the Act defines the term contract as *"any agreement enforceable by law". There are two essentials of this act, "agreement and enforceability."*

(ii) Section 2(e) defines agreement as *"every promise and every set of promises, forming the consideration for each other."*

(iii) Section 2(b) defines contract in these words: *"When the person to whom the proposal is made signifies his assent thereto, the proposal is said to be accepted. Proposal when accepted becomes a promise."*

(iv) *"An agreement between two or more parties for the doing or not doing of something specified in an agreement enforceable by law."* http://dictionary.reference.com.

(v) *"A binding agreement between two or more parties for performing, or refraining from performing, some specified act(s) in exchange for lawful consideration".* — www.investorwords.com

In the same way, some specific definitions of insurance contract defined by the different scholars are also specified below:

(i) ***Justice Tindal:*** *"Insurance is a contract by which a sum of money is paid to the assured in consideration of insurer's incurring risk of paying a large sum upon a given contingency."*

(ii) ***Justice Channell:*** *"A contract of insurance is a contract whereby one person, called the 'insurer' undertakes in return for the agreed consideration called the 'premium', to pay to another person call the 'insured', a sum of money or its equivalent, on a specified event."*

(iii) ***E.W. Patterson:*** *"Insurance is a contract by which one party for consideration called the premium, assumed particular risk of another party and promises to pay to him or his nominee a certain sum of money on a specified contingency."*

From the above definitions, we can say that in a contract:

- Both the parties must have capacity to contract.
- The purpose of the contract must be lawful.
- The form of the contract must be legal.
- The parties must intend to create a legal relationship and
- The parties must give their consent to the contract voluntarily.

In view of above definitions, it is understood that an agreement entered into voluntarily by two or more competent parties with the objective of creating a mutual legal obligation, which may have elements generally in writing is called a contract.

4.4 TYPES OF CONTRACT

For better understanding of the concept, the types of contracts can be classified on the basis of its validity, formation & performance. Thus, the types of contracts are discussed below:

(i) On the basis of validity:

(a) **Valid contract:** According to the Indian Contract Act, 1872, an agreement which comprises all the essential elements of a contract is called a valid contract. A valid contract is enforceable under law.

(b) **Void contract:** According to section 2(j) of *above Act,* a contract which ceases to be enforceable by law becomes void. It implies that a contract is valid until it is enforceable by law and after losing its legitimacy it has no values in the eyes of law and becomes void.

(c) **Voidable contract:** According to section 2(i) of the Act, *"an agreement which is enforceable by law at the option of one or more of the parties thereto, but not at the option of other or others, is a voidable contract."* It means, if the free consent of either parties entering into contract as an essential element is missing in a contract, the law confers liberty on the concerned party either to reject the contract or to accept it.

(d) **Illegal contract:** A contract is illegal if it is prohibited by law; or is of such nature that, if permitted, either may be harmful for society or would overwhelm the provisions of any law or is fraudulent; or involves or causes harm to a person or property of another, or any court of law regards it as morally wrong or opposed to community policy. However, these contracts are even punishable by law. Further, it can be understood that, all void agreements are not necessary illegal but all illegal agreements are absolutely void agreements.

(e) **Unenforceable contract:** Where a contract is good in matter but due to some technical defect, or reasons that is beyond control of either party, cannot be enforced by law is called unenforceable contract. However, such types of contracts are neither voidable nor void or illegal.

(ii) On the basis of structure:

(a) **Express contract:** Wherever the terms and conditions of the contract are expressly agreed upon in words (written or spoken) at the time of formation, the contract is called express contract.

(b) **Implied contract:** Wherein a proposal or acceptance is made otherwise than words, such agreement is said to be implied contract. However, the implied contract is one which is assumed from the acts or conduct of the parties or from the situation of the cases.

(c) **Quasi contract:** A quasi contract is formed by law. Since there is no aim of parties to enter into a contract in quasi contract and hence it is a non-intentional contract. Perhaps, it is the legal obligation which is imposed on a party who is bound to perform it. For example, compensating workmen who are injured in an accident while on duty by the employer is said to be a quasi contract.

(iii) On the basis of performance:

(a) **Executory contract:** Where one or both the parties enter into a contract have under liability to perform their obligations is called executory contract. Thus, a contract which is partially executed or completely unexecuted is termed as executory contract.

(b) **Unilateral contract:** Where only one party has to carry out his obligation at the time of the formation of the contract; whereas, the other party has fulfilled his obligation at the time of the contract or before the contract comes into existence is called unilateral contract.

(c) **Bilateral contract:** Where both the parties, entering in a contract, are mutually responsible to fulfill their obligations is called bilateral contract. It is also known as contract with executory consideration.

4.5 ESSENTIALS OF AN INSURANCE CONTRACT

Essential elements of a valid contract can be divided in two groups:

(i) General essential elements and

(ii) Special elements.

These essential elements can be described as follows:

[i] General essential elements

As stated above, an insurance contract is similar to a general contract and hence it has most of all the essential elements of a general contract. Section 2(h) and Section 10 of the Contract Act, 1872 defines these general elements which are follows:

(a) **Two or more parties:** In case of a general contract, at least two parties are required to enter into a valid contact. One party has to offer a proposal and the other must accept it. The person who offers the 'proposal' is called the 'promisor' or 'offeror' whereas the person to whom the offer of proposal is made is called the 'offeree' and the person who accepts this offer is called the 'acceptor'.

In the same way, at least two parties are required to enter into an insurance contract. The party who offers to assume the liability for compensation in the event of a loss is called 'insurer' whereas the other party to whom this promise is given is called 'insured'.

(b) **Proposal:** There must be a specific proposal to be offered by one party to other for creating a valid contract. Likewise, in life insurance contract the insurer party offers life coverage proposal to the insured party.

(c) **Acceptance and free consent:** The offer must be willingly accepted by the other party to execute the contract. The consent is said to be free if it is not induced by force, undue influence, fraud, misrepresentation or mistake. Legal enforceability of a contract is affected by lack of free consent. Similarly, there must be a free consent between the insurer and insured in case of life insurance contract. Therefore, only on free consent of insured to pay the prescribed premium, the insurance contract is deemed to be accepted.

(d) **Contractual competency of parties:** The parties entering into a contract must be legally competent. According to Section 11 of the Contract Act, a person is considered to be competent to contract if he satisfies the criterion such as (i) The person has reached the age of maturity (iii) the person is of sound mind; (iii) the person is not disqualified from entering into a contract by any law. An agreement by incompetent parties shall be a legal nullity. In the same tune, life insurance policy cannot be purchased by a minor. However, mother-father or any other legal guardian may purchase life insurance policy for minors. Besides, a mentally unfit person would not be a party for insurance contract.

(e) **Lawful consideration:** A contract is essentially a deal between two parties, where everyone receives 'something' of worth or benefit. This 'something' is described in law as 'consideration'. Consideration is a vital element of a legal contract. It is the worth for which the promise of the other is acquired. A contract with no consideration is annulled. This may be in any form of money, services renders, goods exchanged or a sacrifice which is of value to the either party. Consideration must be lawful.

In case of life insurance, considerations are present in the form of premium for insurer and an agreed compensation for insured.

(f) **Legal object:** The object of the contract must be legal. According to Indian Contract Act, an agreement is illegal, if it is: (i) illegal (ii) immoral (iii) fraudulent (iv) of a nature that, if permitted, it would defeat the provisions of any law (v) causes injury to the person or property of another (vi) opposed to public policy. Hence, for the valid life insurance contract the above facts are taken care to ensure legality of contract.

(g) **Legal formalities:** Usually, there are some legal formalities involved in a valid contract. In absence of these formalities, the contract can be enforced in the event of breach of contract by either party. Considering the legal importance of a contract, certain contracts are required to be in writing and may even entail registration. Hence, wherever law requires an contract to be put in writing or be registered, the same must be complied with. Similarly, legal formalities are also fulfilled in life insurance. Life insurance policy with duly affixed revenue stamp is issued to the insured and it acts as a legal contract.

[ii] Special elements of contract

In addition to the above general elements there are some special elements of contract. In this context, Utmost good faith, Insurable interest, Compliance of conditions and warranties, Doctrine of compensation or indemnity, applicability of doctrine of subrogation etc. may be included as special elements of a contract. The essential elements of an insurance contract are described as follows:

(a) **Utmost Good Faith:** According to this principle, both the insured (Policy holder) and the insurer (Insurance company) are bound by good faith to comply the honesty and fairness. Therefore, it is an important duty of the every individual, seeking for insurance, to disclose all the facts truly and fully as insurance shifts risk from one party (insured) to another (insurer). At any point of time breach of good faith renders the contract voidable at the discretion of the aggrieved party. The doctrine of utmost good faith is applicable to all contracts of insurance *i.e.*, life, fire and marine insurance. However, the principle of utmost good faith includes:

(i) The insured and the insurer, both the parties, should all the time have a good faith towards each other;

(ii) The insured should provide the complete, correct and clear information of subject matter to the insurer for assessing the factual risk;

(iii) The insurer should provide the complete, correct and clear information regarding terms and condition of the contract.

(b) **Insurable Interest:** Insurable interest must be present in all the insurances, irrespective it is property insurance, marine insurance or insurance on a person as the insured directly suffers from the loss. The concept implies that the insured has a risk in the loss or damage to the life or property insured. If an insured wishes to enforce an insurance contract before the Court of law, he must have an insurable interest in the subject matter of the insurance, which means that he has benefits from its preservation and that is why he suffers from its loss. Thus, insurable interest is invariably applicable to all contracts of insurance.

(c) Compliance of conditions and warranties: The terms and conditions stipulated in insurance policies are called assurance. It is compulsory for both the parties to follow these terms and conditions. If there is a breach of contract, the contract may be annulled and the responsible party cannot proceed for his claim. On the contrary, there are some implied assurances which are invariably followed by the parties and in case of non compliance the contract may also be deemed as void.

(d) Doctrine of indemnity: To "indemnify" may be understood as "an assurance to make whole again, or to be reinstated to the position that the things were in, to the extent possible, prior to the occurrence of a specified event or peril. Hence, life insurance is generally not deemed to be indemnity insurance, but fairly "contingent" insurance. According to this doctrine, only actual amount of loss, not exceeding the amount of policy, is reimbursed.

(e) Doctrine of Subrogation: Subrogation is a specific feature of indemnity principle and therefore it only applies to contracts of indemnity. Hence, it does not apply to life assurance or personal accident policies. According to this doctrine, once the insured is compensated for the loss due to damage to property insured, then the right of ownership of such property passes on to the insurer.

4.6 DIFFERENCE BETWEEN INSURANCE CONTRACT AND OTHER CONTRACT

Despite several similarities, there are some differences between an insurance contract and other contracts. Based on the nature of the contract, scope and characteristics these contracts can be differentiated as appended below:

DIFFERENCE BETWEEN INSURANCE CONTRACT AND OTHER CONTRACT

Sl. No.	*Basis of difference*	*General Contracts*	*Insurance Contract*
1.	Regulations	General contracts are governed under Indian Contract Act, 1872.	Apart from the Indian Contract Act, 1872, other relevant provisions of insurance regulations are enforceable in case of insurance contract.
2.	Purpose	The purpose of a general contract is usually related with the bindings of the parties to do or not to do something.	The purpose of an insurance contract is to provide a security against any uncertain/ probable loss.
3.	Insurable interest	Doctrine of insurable interest does not apply in general contract	While, insurable interest is must in a case of insurance contract.
4.	Breach of contract	In case of a breach of contract committed by either party in general contract, the party who suffers can proceed for compensation.	On the contrary, if breach of contract is committed by either party, another party can insist only for invalidation of contract in case of insurance.

4.7 DOUBLE INSURANCE

When a person is interested for more than one insurance policy for the same property or on his life irrespective from same insurer or different insurer is called *"double insurance"*. It is also called dual insurance. Double insurance may be preferred for homeowners, auto, health etc. In nut shell, double insurance means purchasing more than one policy for the same subject. However, liberty rests on a person that he can get two or more policies on his life or for his property. It is legal to get double insurance, and accordingly the insured can make claim to both insurers in the happening of a loss as both the insurers are liable for their respective polices. Therefore, the insured can claim the amount of all these policies.

The proposition of double insurance is dissimilar to fire and marine insurance. When a person gets more than one policies for the same property, he cannot claim the same amount as that of loss from different companies. He deserves to make claim of only total sum of loss from one or more companies. The loss will be contributed by the insurance companies in proportion to the policies issued by them. However, the insured cannot make profit, recovering over and above than the loss suffered by him, from this arrangement, because these insurers are liable only to distribute the actual loss in the same proportion as they share the total premium.

Supposing, "x" acquires 3 insurance policies for insuring his factory against fire from three different insurance companies *i.e.*, Company "A", "B" & "C" for ₹ 10,00,000/-, ₹ 9,00,000/- & for ₹ 6,00,000/- respectively. Unfortunately, due to fire in the factory he suffers a loss for an estimated value of ₹ 5,00,000/-. In this situation Mr. "X" can claim for compensation from any of the above insurance companies as the actual loss occurred is less than the assurance value of every insurer. Since the doctrine of contribution is applicable in this case as the same property is insured from three different companies hence the actual loss suffered by the insured would be shared by all the companies according to value of the policy issued by them proportionately. Thus the contribution of different insurance companies for compensation will be as follows:

$$\text{Formula: } \frac{\text{Insurance value for respective insurer} \times \text{Value of actual loss}}{\text{Sum of insurance value}}$$

(i) Contribution of Company "A" would be $= \dfrac{10,00,000 \times 5,00,000}{25,00,000} =$ ₹ 2,00,000

(ii) Contribution for Company "B" would be $= \dfrac{9,00,000 \times 5,00,000}{25,00,000} =$ ₹ 1,80,000

(iii) Contribution for Company "A" would be $= \dfrac{6,00,000 \times 5,00,000}{25,00,000} =$ ₹ 1,20,000

4.8 RE-INSURANCE

Whenever an insurance company insures the risk with some other insurance company it is called Re-insurance. It may be for the full amount of the policy or for a part of the policy. In case of loss the concerned insurance company will get compensation from the reinsurer company. However, the insured is concerned only with the company from which he purchased insurance policy. Re-insurances operate between insurance companies only. In India, the General Insurance Corporation is a re-insurer. For understanding the term better, some important definitions of reinsurance are as follows:

(i) *"Reinsurance is an arrangement whereby an insurer who has accepted an insurance transfers a part of the risk to another insurer so that his liability of any risk is limited to a figure proportionate to his capacity."*

— The Federation of Insurance Institute, Mumbai

(ii) *"Where the amount of any one risk from one hazard is such that it is beyond the limit prudent for one insurer to carry, it is necessary to effect re-insurance."*

— Dinsdale, W.A.

(iii) *"Reinsurance is the transfer by an insurance company of a portion of its risk to another company."* **— Reigel and Miller**

It is also termed as "insurance of insurance". It implies that an insurer who assumes an outsized risk may dispose it with another insurer to insure a share of the insured's risk. In the event of loss, if it is beyond the insurable capacity of the primary insurer then this reinsurance process is undertaken. In reinsurance, therefore, one insurer insures the risk which has been undertaken party or fully by other insurer. In the process of reinsurance, the original insurer who reallocates a part of the insurance contract is known as reinsured and the succeeding insurer is called reinsurer.

Obviously the reinsured has to pay reinsurance premium to reinsurer for risk shifted. Supposing, an individual wishes to insure his property for 20 lakhs, goes to an insurance company which will agree to the risk if it is satisfied as to the state of the property. In this condition, if original insurer has a maximum limit probably A 10 lakhs, it will dispose with another company to reinsure to take up that much of the risk as exceeds its limit, *i.e.* A 10 lakhs. As a result, if the house is destroyed in a fire the original insurer would pay A 20 lakhs to the insured. Subsequently insurance company would recover 10 lakhs, from the reinsurer.

In view of above analysis, the main characteristics of reinsurance can be described as under:

(i) The reinsurance is performed by two different insurance organizations for the same property or subject.

(ii) Since the reinsurance contract is same as insurance and hence all the laws applied in insurance contract is also applied to reinsurance.

(iii) The main objective of reinsurance is that risk beyond the limit sensible for one insurer is transferred to another insurer executing re-insurance.

(iv) Insured is directly related with original Insurer; whereas reinsurer has no liability towards the insured.

(v) Insurance contract and reinsurance contract both are two separate contracts. Insurance contract is executed between insured and insurer; whereas reinsurance contract is executed between original insurer and another insurance company.

DIFFERENCE BETWEEN DOUBLE INSURANCE AND REINSURANCE

Sl. No.	*Basis of difference*	*Double insurance*	*Reinsurance*
1.	Nature	In case of double insurance, the insured party acquires more than one insurance policy from different insurance companies.	Whereas in case of reinsurance, an insurance company insures the risks already assumed by him with some other insurance company.
2.	Contract	Different contracts are executed separately in between insured and different insurers.	Contracts executed in between Principal insurer and reinsurer in case of reinsurance.
3.	Compensation	In case of double insurance, the insured can claim for compensation from each of the insurers in the event of any loss to him. But the amount of compensation cannot exceed the actual loss.	The insured can prefer claim, in the event of loss, only to the principal insurer from whom the policy is purchased.
4.	Contribution	In double insurance, the loss of insured is shared by all the insurance companies in proportion to the policies issued by them.	In reinsurance, the reinsurer is liable to contribute for only a certain part of risk which is reinsured.
5.	Benefit to insured	In case of life insurance, insured or his nominee gets the amount of all insurance policies.	In case of reinsurance, the loss of insured is shared by both the insurer and reinsurer. However, insured has no any extra benefit from it.
6.	Purchase of policy	Insured purchases extra policies in double insurance.	In reinsurance, the insured purchases a single policy from principal insurer only.
7.	Purpose	Insured gets double insurance for the reason of getting extra benefits.	Reinsurance is done by insurer for the purpose of transferring extra risk to the reinsurer.
8.	Assured sum	In case of double insurance, assured sum increases with acquiring every additional policy.	In reinsurance, the assured sum does not increase. As already assured sum or its part is reinsured.

4.9 SUMMARY

- A contract is essential for any business operation. An agreement between two or more parties for the doing or not doing of something specified in an agreement enforceable by law. Entering into business without a formal contract can be disastrous as it can deprive one or both parties with their privileges, even it can yield a great loss to either party.

- Insurance contract is same as other contracts. Therefore, all the characteristics and legal elements involved in valid contracts are also required essentially in insurance contracts.
- The types of contracts can be classified on the basis of its validity as (i) Valid contract, (ii) Void contract, (iii) Voidable contract, (iv) Illegal Contract, or (v) Unenforceable contract or on the basis of its structure such as — (a) Express contract, (b) Implied contract, or (c) Quasi contract; and on the basis of performance, it can be classified as (i) Executory contract, (ii) Unilateral; and (iii) Bilateral Contract.
- Essential elements of contract can be divided in two groups such as (i) General essential elements; and (ii) Special elements. The general essentials elements include (i) Two or more parties; (ii) Proposal; (iii) Acceptance and free consent; (iv) Contractual competency of parties, Lawful consideration; (v) Legal object; Legal formalities etc. Whereas the special elements includes — Utmost good faith, Insurable interest, Compliance of conditions and warranties, Doctrine of compensation or indemnity, applicability of doctrine of subrogation etc.
- Double insurance means purchasing more than one policy for the same subject. The proposition of double insurance is dissimilar to fire and marine insurance. The loss will be contributed by concerned insurance companies in proportion to the policies issued by them.
- Whenever an insurance company insures the risk with some other insurance company it is called Re-insurance. Re-insurance operates between the insurance companies only. In India, the General Insurance Corporation is a re-insurer.

EXERCISES

(A) Long answer type questions:

1. What do you understand by contract? Differentiate between contract and insurance contract.
2. What is meant by insurance contract? Discuss its general and special essential elements with reference to a general contract.
3. Define contract. Also describe the different types of contracts.
4. What do you understand by double insurance and re-insurance? Distinguish between double insurance and re-insurance.
5. Discuss double insurance and re-insurance in detail with suitable examples.

(B) Short answer type questions:

1. Differentiate between contract and insurance contract.
2. What are the types of contracts?
3. Explain the general essentials of a contract with reference to insurance contract.
4. Explain the special essentials of a contact with reference to insurance contract.
5. What do you understand by double insurance?
6. What do you mean by re-insurance?
7. What are the differences between double insurance and re-insurance?
8. "The proposition of double insurance is dissimilar to fire and marine insurance than life insurance". Comments.

(C) Write a brief note on the following:

(a) Insurance contract.
(b) Types of contract on the basis of its validity.
(c) Types of contract on the basis of its structure.
(d) Types of contract on the basis of its performance.
(e) Double insurance.
(f) Re-insurance
(g) Doctrine of insurable interest in insurance contract.
(h) Doctrine of Subrogation in insurance contract.
(i) Discuss any 3 essentials of insurance contract.
(j) Explain any 3 differences between contract and insurance contract.

(D) Multiple type questions: (Choose any one of the given options)

Que. (1) To protect the interests of parties entering into contract, the Indian Contract Act was enacted in:

(a) 1872 (b) 1978
(c) 1972 (d) All of these.

Que. (2) Term as *"any agreement enforceable by law"* is stipulated for contract under which section of the Indian Contract Act:

(a) Section 12(h) (b) Section 21(h)
(c) Section 2(h) (d) None of these.

Que. (3) Under which section of the Indian Contract act agreement is defined as *"every promise and every set of promises, forming the consideration for each other"*:

(a) Section 2(h) (b) Section 2(e)
(c) Section 12(e) (d) None of these.

Que. (4) Which is not a type of contract is included in classification on the basis of its validity:

(a) Illegal contract (b) Expressed contract
(c) Valid contract (d) None of these.

Que. (5) Which one is not a type of contract according to classification on the basis of performance:

(a) Executory contract (b) Bilateral contract
(c) Voidable contract (d) None of these.

Que. (6) *"Reinsurance is an arrangement whereby an insurer who has accepted an insurance transfers a part of the risk to another insurer so that his liability of any risk is limited to a figure proportionate to his capacity."*

(a) Reigel and Miller (b) The federation of Insurance Institute, Mumbai
(c) Dinsdale, W.A. (d) None of these.

Que. (7) Special elements of an insurance contract includes:

(a) Utmost good faith (b) Doctrine of subrogation
(c) Insurable interest (d) All of these.

Que. (8) Who has defined the contract as "*Where the amount of any one risk from one hazard is such that it is beyond the limit prudent for one insurer to carry, it is necessary to effect re-insurance.*"

(a) Reigel and Miller (b) The Federation of Insurance Institute, Mumbai
(c) Dinsdale, W.A. (d) None of these.

[Answer: 1-(a), 2-(c), 3-(b), 4-(b), 5-(c), 6-(b), 7-(d), 8(c)]

(E) Match the pair:

(1) An agreement which comprises all the essential elements of a contract is called	(a) Voidable contract
(2) Which contract ceases to be enforceable by law called	(b) Illegal contract
(3) An agreement which is enforceable by law at the option is a	(c) valid contract
(4) A contract is illegal if it is prohibited by law and is said to be	(d) Void contract
(5) Such types of contracts which are neither voidable nor void or illegal	(e) Quasi contract
(6) Wherever the terms and conditions of the contract are specifically agreed upon in words (written or spoken) is called	(f) Implied contract
(7) Wherein a proposal or acceptance is made otherwise than words, such agreement is called	(g) Express contract
(8) There is no aim of parties to enter into a contract called	(h) Unenforceable contract

[Answer: 1-(c), 2-(d), 3-(a), 4-(b), 5-(h), 6-(g), 7-(f), 8-(e)]

❑ ❑ ❑

CHAPTER 5

FIRE INSURANCE

Fire Insurance: Meaning and Definition, Expected Hazards, Characteristics of Fire Insurance; Scope for Fire Insurance; Types of Fire Insurance Policies; and Claim Procedure for Fire Insurance.

5.1 OBJECTIVES OF LEARNING

- *Understand the meaning of the term 'fire' in viewpoint of fire insurance.*
- *Define the contract of fire insurance.*
- *Elucidate the characteristics of fire insurance contract.*
- *Describe the special policies under fire insurance.*
- *Discuss the procedures followed to settle a fire claim.*

5.2 INTRODUCTION

Fire accident is hazardous to human life as well as property. In case of life the loss due to fire is covered under Life insurance and in case the loss of property it is covered under fire insurance. Fire causes huge damage by physically reducing the materials to ashes. Further, due to fire accidents there can be indefinite loss to the property, buildings or industries besides the human lives. Various safety measures for reducing the cause and severity of fire accidents have been taken by man. But the human society is still uncovered from the probability of fire accidents. In this scenario, fire insurance is seen as paramount important for providing risk coverage to human life and their belongings from such unforeseen hazards.

In India, Fire Insurance comes under tariff class of business. All India Fire Tariff is the revised fire insurance tariff, which came into force on May 1st, 2001. The General Insurance Act (Tariff) determines the form of the contract in which a fire insurance is to be written. The fire insurance policy contains a preamble, operative clause, general exclusions and other general conditions. At present, single policy has been introduced to cover all property risks called "standard fire and special peril policy" in the place of three standard policies, *i.e.*, A, B&C.

5.3 MEANING AND DEFINITION

Fire insurance means insurance against any loss caused by fire. Fire insurance is a an agreement under which the insurance company in return for a consideration called premium undertakes to indemnify the insured for the financial loss which the latter may suffer due to damage of or damage to property or goods, caused by fire, during a particular period. In this contract a specific amount as an insured sum is agreed to by the parties at the time of the contract, which is payable to insured by the insurer in case of loss. The degree of loss can be ascertained only after the fire has occurred. The insurer is liable to make good the actual amount of loss not exceeding the maximum amount fixed under the policy.

'Fire insurance business means the business of effecting, otherwise than incident to some other class of insurance, business contracts of insurance against loss by or incidental of fire or other occurrence customarily included among the risks insured against in the fire insurance policy.' — ***Section 2 of the Insurance Act 1938***

A contract of fire insurance can be defined as an agreement whereby one party (the insurer) in return for a consideration (premium) undertakes to indemnify the other party (the insured) for the financial loss which the latter may suffer due to damage to the property insured against fire for a specified period of time and upto an agreed sum.

The document which contains the terms and conditions of the contract is called 'Fire Insurance Policy'. The policy contains important particulars of the contract such as name of the parties, description of the insured property, the sum for which the property is insured, amount of premium payable and the period for which insured. However, the premium may be paid either in single instalment or by way of different periodic instalments. Finally, the insurer is legally responsible to make good the loss only when loss is occur cause by actual fire. The phrase 'loss or damage by fire' also comprises the loss or damage caused even by efforts to extinguish fire.

5.3.1 Term 'fire' in relation to insurance:

Fire is not described in the fire insurance policy. It should therefore, be taken in the general sense as 'Fire' means the creation of light and heat by combustion or burning. Thus, there is fire when something burns. Consequently, fire, must result from actual ignition and the resulting loss must be proximately caused by such ignition. In view of the above, a claim for loss by fire must satisfy the following conditions:

(a) The loss should be caused by genuine fire or ignition and not just by high temperature. There must be rapid burning that produces ignition and may result in flames. That is why, the chemical action producing heat but not actual fire and damage caused by an acid is not considered as fire damage.

(b) The fire must be accidental, not incidental. If the fire is caused by an intentional act of the insured or his agents, the insurer will not be legally responsible for the loss. If a third party deliberately sets fire to the insured's property, in such cases the insurer is liable for loss caused by fire.

(c) The proximate cause of loss or damage to the insured property must be a fire.

(d) The loss or damage should be covered under the subject matter of the policy.

5.4 EXPECTED HAZARDS IN FIRE INSURANCE

It is essential for the insurer to evaluate all the probable risks attached with the property proposed for insurance in the primary stage of fire insurance. Insurance proposal to be accepted or not to be accepted is determined by the insurer considering the degree of risk involved in the insurance proposal. Accordingly, the premium is decided taking into account the volume of risk related to the property.

Hazard means all the causes that are responsible to increase in volume of risk attached to the properties. In insurance business, usually the hazards are divided in two groups viz. Moral hazards; and physical hazards.

1. Moral Hazards

Hazards or risk which is inherent to the character of responsible person concerned is called moral hazards. In this group the following hazards, which directly or indirectly are responsible for a fire accidents, are included:

(a) **Negligence:** In most of the case it is seen that due to carelessness of the person the fire has taken place.

(b) **Obstacles in industrial relation:** In industries where the relation between employer and employees is not healthy, it is seen that while demonstrations are done sometimes agitated employees damage the industrial properties.

(c) **Dishonesty/jealously:** Sometimes policyholder himself puts fire to his property and proceeds for false claims to recover fire insured amount from the insurer unethically.

(d) **Due to riots:** At the time of internal or external disturbance in law and order, some disruptive elements put fire to public properties such as vehicles, dwellings, factories etc. to create fear among the people.

(e) **Social misconduct:** some people are aggressive in nature and morally they are not capable to maintain the socially accepted conduct in adverse situations. In such cases, the distressed person damage the property of others making loss to them.

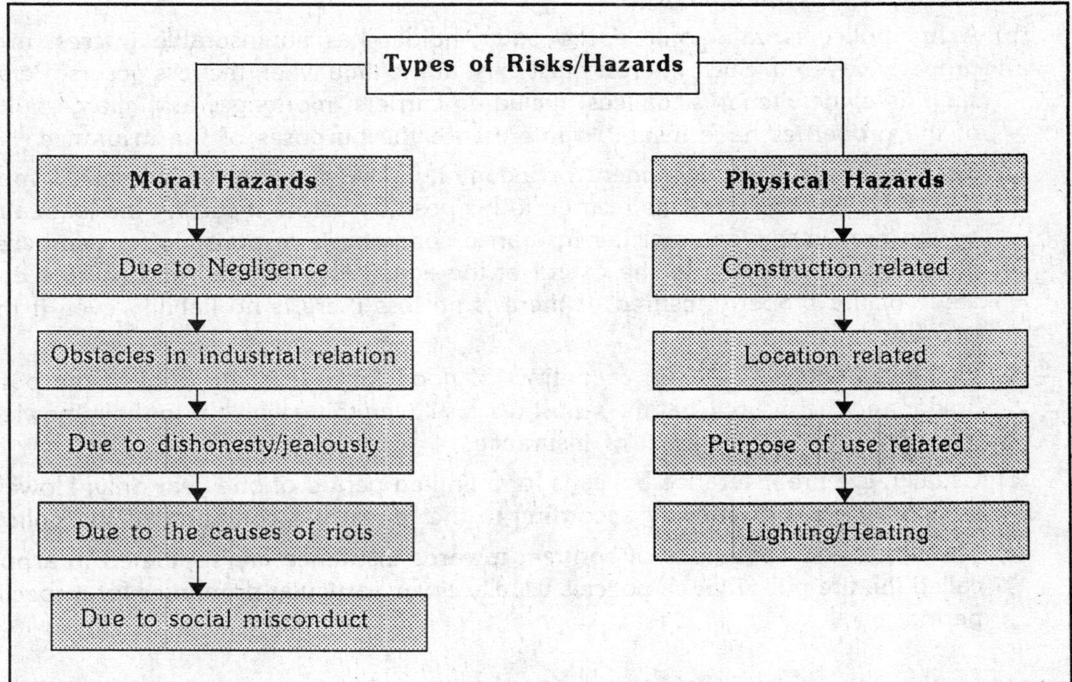

Fig. 5.1: Types of Risks/Hazards

(ii) Physical Hazards

The hazard/risk attached with the insured subject such as dwelling, shop, factory or godown etc. and have an effect on probability of loss to the subject property is called physical hazards. It includes:

(a) **Construction related:** Quality and manner of construction affects the degree and probability of risk. At the time of underwriting insurance, the quality of construction, life of building, having numbers of storey, condition of its wall and rooftop etc. are taken in consideration. For example, old building and multistory buildings have greater risk then a new and single story building.

(b) **Location related:** Degree of physical hazards also depends on location of building. Density of surrounding locality, location of fire/explosive plant and petrol pump etc. enhances the degree of risk.

(c) **Purpose of use related:** Quantum of physical hazards are also concerned with the premises used for certain purpose. The risk related to premises would be greater if it is used for chemical operations, petroleum products, production of fire crackers or production of explosives etc. On the contrary, risk will be the minimum if it is used as School, Hospital or general office.

(d) **Lighting/Heating:** At present, electricity, gas and inflammable items are used frequently in the houses, factories and production units. Electric sort-circuit, leakage of gages, ignition of inflammable items is major source of fire.

5.5 CHARACTERISTICS OF FIRE INSURANCE

The essential characteristics of the contract of fire insurance are as under:

(a) According to Indian Contract Act, 1872, fire insurance is a contract. Similar to other insurance contracts, it implies that fire insurance also has to satisfy the essentials of a valid contract.

(b) A fire policy is valid only if the policy-holder has an insurable interest in the property covered. Such interest must exist at the time when the loss occurs. Persons such as owner, tenants, bailees, including carriers, mortgages and charge-holders of the properties have insurable interest for the purposes of fire insurance.

(c) Fire insurance is an agreement of indemnity. The principal of indemnity implies that the insurer restores the insured to his position before incurring the loss caused by the fire. In this contract the insurance company is responsible for compensate the policy holder only to the extent of the actual loss suffered and not the entire value of the property insured. If there is no loss there is no liability even if there is a fire.

(d) Fire insurance is based on a contract of good faith. It is the duty of the policy-holder and the insurer that they must disclose everything which is in their knowledge that can affect the contract of insurance.

(e) Usually, the fire insurance policy is for a limited period of one year only. However, the policy can be renewed according to the terms and condition of the policy.

(f) The terms and conditions of contract towards insurance are stipulated in a policy called the fire policy. Such policies usually cover particular properties for a specified period.

(g) In general insurance, the fire insurance is called as 'An individual contract' as this type of insurance policy cannot be transferred without consent of insured.

(h) In there is more than one policy for the same property, each insurer is entitled to contribution from the others. At the time of loss and payment is made, the insurer is subrogated to the rights and interests of the policy-holder. However, an insurer can reinsure a part of the risk.

(i) Insurer is not liable for such loss where fire is caused by a deliberate act of policy-holder. In such cases, the policy-holder is liable to criminal prosecution

(j) Usually, fire policies contain a stipulation that the insurer will not be liable if the fire is caused by riot, civil disturbances, war and explosions. In the absence of such stipulations the insurer is liable for all losses caused by fire, whatever may be the causes of the fire.

(k) Insurable interest arises out of a pecuniary relationship between the insured and the subject matter of the insurance. It arises on account of (i) ownership, (ii) possession, or (iii) contract. Even if a person has a limited interest in a property or goods, he may insure them to cover not only his own interest but also the interest of others. The damage to property involves the insured in financial loss. Insurable interest should exist throughout the policy term.

Under fire insurance, the following persons have insurable interest in the subject matter:

(1) An individual has insurable interest in the property he owns.

(2) A partner has insurable interest in the property related of partnership.

(3) A businessman has insurable interest in his building, plant & machinery, stock, etc.

(4) A mortgagee has insurable interest in the property which is mortgaged.

(5) An official receiver or assignee in insolvency proceedings.

5.6 SCOPE FOR FIRE INSURANCE

The scope of fire insurance in present time is very vast. Accordingly, fire insurance policy is suitable for the owner of property, the persons who hold property in trust or in commission; individuals/ financial institutions as they who have financial interest in the property. The scope of cover in insurance policy is given below:

5.6.1 Scope of cover:

Standard fire and special peril policy usually cover loss due to the following perils:

- **Losses from fire:** Damage or destruction due to fire to the property insured. Besides, the property damaged or commodities spoiled by water used to extinguish the fire. However, natural heating or spontaneous combustion or drying process is not considered as damage due to fire.
- **Losses from Lightning:** Lightning has great intensity which can crack in a building. Such damage due to a lightning strike.
- **Storm, cyclone, typhoon, hurricane, tornado, and landslides:** These are all various types of natural calamities as a result of with thunder or strong winds or heavy rain fall etc. Loss or damage directly caused by these turbulences is covered. However, losses resulting from earthquake, volcanic eruption etc. is not covered.

- **Aircraft damage:** Loss, damage or destruction occurred due to aircraft, other aerial or space devices and articles dropped down from aircraft, incidents caused by pressure waves are not covered.
- **Riot, strike, malicious, and terrorism damages:** Any loss or damage to property insured caused by such activity or by the action of any lawful authorities in suppressing such disturbance is covered.
- **Bush fire:** Damage caused by burning of bush and jungles is covered under fire insurance; but it excludes destruction or damage caused by forest fire.
- **Overflowing of water tanks and pipes etc:** Loss or damage to property by water due to overflowing of water tanks and pipes is covered under this policy. Whereas bursting or accidental overflowing of water tanks, apparatus and pipes is not covered.
- **Loss due to fire fighting action:** Pulling down of adjacent premises by the fire brigade in order to prevent the progress of flame is covered. Besides, Breakage of goods in the process of their removal from the building where fire is raging e.g. damage caused by throwing furniture out of the window etc., are also covered in for insurance.

5.6.2 Exclusions:

On the other hand, standard fire and special perils policy usually does not cover the following perils:

1. In case of any loss arising out of "Act of god perils" such as Lightning, Landslide etc. the first 5% of each and every claim subject to a minimum of ₹ 10,000/- is not covered.
2. Loss due to fire caused by earthquake, invasion, act of foreign enemy, hostilities or war, civil strife, riots, mutiny, martial law, military rising or rebellion or insurrection.
3. Loss caused by subterranean (underground) fire.
4. Loss, damage or destruction caused to the insured property by pollution.
5. Loss by theft during or after the occurrence of fire.
6. Any Loss, destruction or damage to the stock in cold storages due to change in temperature.
7. Indirect losses such as loss of earnings, loss by delay, loss of market or any other kind whatsoever.
8. Any loss or damage caused directly or indirectly due to earthquake, volcanic eruption etc.
9. Loss or damage caused by lightning or explosion. However if it is actually ignites and spreads into fire then it is covered.
10. Loss by theft during or after the occurrence of any insured peril except as provided under riot, strike and terrorism damage cover.
11. Loss or damage to electrical devices, apparatus, fixture, or fitting caused by over-running, excessive pressure, short-circuits etc.
12. Expenses incurred on service charges paid to architect, surveyor and consulting engineers as fees for assessment.

5.6.3 Add-on Covers

At the option of the policyholders, the insurer can issue the standard fire policy with added benefits by charging additional premium. These added benefits are as follows:

(1) Fee paid to Architects, Surveyors and Consulting engineers (in excess of 3% claim amount).

(2) Worsening of stocks in cold storage due to failure of power.

(3) Forest fire.

(4) Spontaneous combustion.

(5) Earthquake as per minimum rates and excess applicable as specified in the tariff.

Therefore, the insurer is liable for specific perils as specified in the policy unless specifically provided for in the fire insurance policy. However, the insurer can issue the standard fire policy as per the New Fire Tariff adding benefits at the option of the policyholders by charging additional premium.

5.7 TYPES OF FIRE INSURANCE POLICIES

There may be various types of fire policies. These policies may be classified in 3 major groups such as (i) on the basis of the Indemnity; (ii) On the basis of stock; and (iii) on the basis of risk covered. The principal types of fire insurance policies are described below:

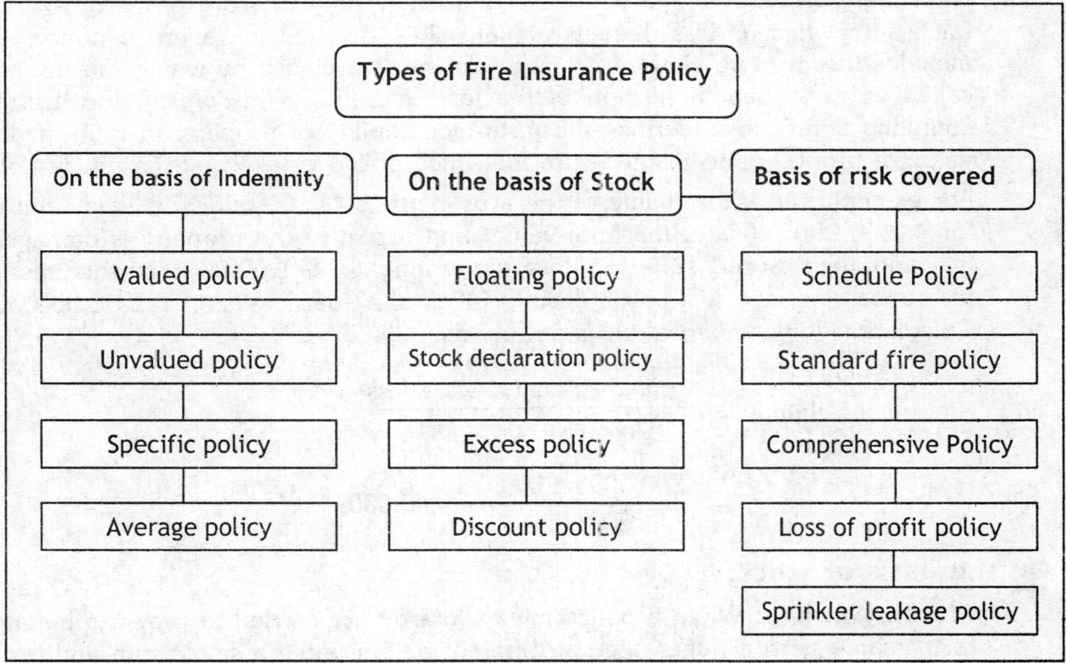

Fig. 5.2: Types of Fire Insurance Policy

(i) On the basis of indemnity:

(1) Valued Policy: Under this policy, the value of subject matter is declared and agreed at the time of contract of its insurance. In this policy, insurer will have to pay to the insured in the event of a total loss irrespective of the actual value of loss. Therefore, the policy violates the principle of indemnity. Agreed value of the subject matter as mentioned in the policy may not necessarily be the actual value of that property. It is issued merely only on artistic work, antiques and similar rare articles whose value cannot be determined easily.

(2) Unvalued policy: Under this policy, the value of the subject matter is not declared at the time of policy taken; but in case of loss the value is computed by assessment of actual loss to the property. Accordingly the insurer is liable only to the extent of actual loss not exceeding insured sum. This is also known as open policy.

(3) Specific policy: In this policy, the insurer undertakes to make good the loss to the insured upto the amount specified in the policy. In case of loss due to fire, the agreed sum will have to be paid to the policyholder irrespective of actual value of the property. In this policy, the actual value of subject matter is not relevant.

For example, if a policy is taken for ₹ 50,000 upon a shop whose actual value is ₹ 2,00,000 and a fire occurs causing the amount of loss ₹ 30,000. The insurance company will liable to pay the whole amount of loss, i.e., ₹ 30,000 irrespective of the fact that the building was insured for one-fourth of its actual value. Even if the loss is ₹ 50,000 the insurer will get the full amount. But if the loss is more than ₹ 50,000 then the insured will get ₹ 50,000 only. Therefore, the value of property is not relevant in determining the amount of indemnity in this policy. Such a policy is not subject to 'average clause'.

(4) Average policy: Average policy is enforceable only where a property is insured for a sum which is less than its actual value. It is called "average policy" as it includes the average clause. 'Average clause' is a clause by which the insured is called upon to bear a portion of the loss himself. In this policy, the insurance company agrees to undertake the insurance liability of property in ratio of actual value of property and insured sum for which policy is taken by the policy holder. For example the actual value of the a property is ₹ 5,00,000. If it is insured only for ₹ 2,00,000 (40% of the total value) and a part of the property is damaged in fire and the insured suffers a loss amounting to ₹ 1,00,000. In this case the insurance company will pay ₹ 40,000 (40% of actual loss, *i.e.*, ₹ 2,00,000) only. Calculation for compensation is as follows:

$$\text{Amount of claim} = \frac{\text{Insured amount} \times \text{Actual loss}}{\text{Actual calue of property}}$$

$$= \frac{2,00,000 \times 1,00,000}{5,00,000} = 40,000$$

(ii) On the basis of stock:

(5) Floating policy: When a policy covers loss by fire caused to property belonging to the same person but located at different places under a single sum and for one premium is called a floating policy. Floating policies are always subject to an average clause. It covers the fluctuating risk of several goods lying in different localities. For example - Such policy covers goods of the same person lying in two warehouses at two different locations. It is not easy for the owner to take a policy for a specific amount and hence the best way is to take out a floating policy for all the stock of goods.

(6) Stock declaration policy: This policy is taken for covering the loss for maximum expected value of stock in case where great fluctuations in the value can happen during the contract period usually for one year. For such policy 75% of the premium has to be deposited by the policyholder in advance. The maximum liability of insurance company is specified in the policy by the insured. At the end of the year the average stock and final premium is calculated and if it is less than already paid, the excess amount paid as premium is refunded to the policyholder.

(7) Excess policy: This policy is taken for covering the stock of merchandise whose value and quantity are constantly fluctuating. In such case, it is not appropriate to take one policy for definite sum. So the insured takes an ordinary policy for least value of the stock and another excess policy for excess value of the stock. Thus, two policies are issued under excess policy. The actual value of the stock will be reported periodically.

(8) Maximum value with Discount policy: This policy is taken for covering the maximum probable value of stock to be retained during the specific period. Under this policy, one third amount of the premium already paid is refunded to the insured on maturity of the policy. This policy is intended to cover the risk for maximum amount.

(iii) On the basis of risk covered:

(9) Schedule Policy: A schedule policy is one which covers many properties under combined terms and conditions. Particulars of the properties and their individual rates of premium are listed in same policy only for the convenience of the policyholder.

(10) Standard fire policy: This policy is taken for securing compensation on all direct loss or damage caused by lighting and burning. Such policy also covers damages and losses by other unforeseen events such as earthquake, flood, explosion, cyclone and riot.

(11) Comprehensive policy: This policy is taken for different commodities and hence is also known as 'all in one' or combined policy. A single policy covers the properties from different risks such as theft, burglary, third party risks, etc. besides fire. This policy may include loss of profits, *i.e.*, the insurer may undertake to indemnify the policy holder not only for the loss caused by fire but also for the loss of profits for the period during which the establishment concerned is kept closed owing to the fire.

(12) Loss of profit policy: This is also known as consequential loss policy. It is seen that the insured suffers a greater financial loss by dislocation of business for repair or maintenance after fire. During this intervening period some recurring expenses such as rent, salaries, taxes and other miscellaneous expenses are unavoidable. Such substantial loss to the insured is not covered by the ordinary fire policy. To facilitate the cover of such loss by fire, the 'consequential loss policy' is introduced. The loss so suffered is separately calculated from the loss actually suffered. Thus, the policy covers the loss of profit which sustains as a consequence of fire.

(13) Sprinkler leakage policy: This policy covers loss to the property arising out by the leakage of liquid or water. Besides, if fire takes place and in the course of fire fighting water is speared forcibly which causes any loss to properties is also covered in this policy.

5.8 CLAIM PROCEDURE FOR FIRE INSURANCE

In the event of fire, the following process is involved in settlement of claim:

(1) Intimation: First of all, the insured must immediately intimate the insurer about the loss caused by fire. In this context, a written claim should be given by the insured to insurer within 15 days from the date of loss.

(2) Furnishing of requisite documents: The insured is required to provide all plans, invoices, documents, proofs and other relevant information to the insurer for considering the claim. If the insured failed to submit these documents within 6 months from the date of loss, the insurer has the right to consider it as no claim.

(3) Verification of claim: Claim form provided by the insurer is returned by the insured after filled-in, duly signed declaration given in the form as to the truthfulness and accuracy of the information. On receipt of the claim form along with all relevant documents, the insurer verifies whether the essentials of a valid claim are satisfied or not. Thereafter, an official employed by the insurer investigates claims. In case of a large claim, the insurance company employs independent loss surveyor.

(4) Final settlement of claim: After satisfying as genuine claim, on the basis of the claim form and the investigation report, the company then settles the claim by paying the insured sum to the policyholder.

5.9 SUMMARY

- Fire insurance means insurance against any loss caused by fire.
- A contract of fire insurance can be defined as an agreement whereby one party (the insurer) in return for a consideration (premium) undertakes to indemnify the other party (the insured) for the financial loss which the latter may suffer due to damage to the property insured against fire for a specified period of time and upto an agreed sum.
- In the general sense as 'Fire' means the creation of light and heat by combustion or burning.
- Hazard means all the causes that are responsible to increase in volume of risk attached to the properties. In insurance business, usually the hazards are divided in two groups *viz.* moral hazards; and physical hazards.
- Moral Hazards includes — negligence, obstacles in industrial relation, dishonesty/ jealously, due to riots; social misconduct
- Physical hazards includes, perils related to construction, purpose of use, location and lighting/heating.
- Standard fire and special perils cover Losses from — fire, lightning, storm, cyclone, typhoon, hurricane, tornado, and landslides, aircraft damage, riot, strike, malicious, and terrorism damages, bush fire, overflowing of water tanks and pipes; and losses due to fire fighting action.
- Fire insurance policies may be classified in 3 major groups such as (i) on the basis of the Indemnity; (ii) on the basis of stock; and (iii) on the basis of risk covered.

- Policies on the basis of indemnity: valued policy, unvalued policy, specific policy, average policy.
- Policies on the basis of stock: floating policy, stock declaration policy, excess policy; and maximum value with discount policy.
- Policies on the basis of risk covered: schedule policy, standard fire policy, comprehensive policy, loss of profit policy; and sprinkler leakage policy.
- Claim procedure for fire insurance- Intimation to insurer, Furnishing of requisite documents, Verification of claim; and Final settlement of claim.

EXERCISES

(A) Long answer type questions:

1. What is fire insurance? Define fire insurance and explain expected hazards from it.
2. What is meant by insurance? Explain its characteristics.
3. What do you understand by insurance? Specify the scope for fire insurance.
4. Discuss the different types of fire insurance with suitable illustration.
5. Define the concept of fire insurance and discuss its claim procedure.

(B) Short answer type questions:

1. Describe the expected hazards in fire insurance.
2. Discuss the characteristics of fire insurance.
3. Explain the scope for fire insurance listing the perils covered or not covered under fire insurance.
4. Discuss the main fire insurance policies on the basis of the Indemnity.
5. Discuss the main fire insurance policies on the basis of stock.
6. Discuss the main fire insurance policies on the basis of risk covered.
7. Describe the claim procedure for fire insurance.

(C) Write brief note on following:

1. 'Fire' in relation to insurance.
2. Moral hazard of fire
3. Physical hazards of fire
4. Perils covered under fire insurance
5. Perils not covered under fire insurance
6. Valued Policy
7. Unvalued policy
8. Specific policy
9. Average policy
10. Floating policy
11. Stock declaration policy
12. Excess policy
13. Maximum value with discount policy
14. Schedule Policy
15. Comprehensive policy

16. Loss of profit policy
17. Sprinkler leakage policy

(D) Multiple type questions: (Choose any one of the options)

Que. (1) Fire is hazardous to —
(a) Human life (b) Property
(c) Both (a) and (b) above (d) None of these.

Que. (2) In which Section of the Insurance Act, 1938, fire insurance has been defined:
(a) Section 11 (b) Section 9
(c) Section 2 (d) None of these.

Que. (3) With reference to fire accidents, moral hazards includes —
(a) Negligence (b) Obstacles in industrial relation
(c) Social misconduct (d) All of these.

Que. (4) With reference to fire, which is not related to physical hazard —
(a) Construction related (b) Location related
(c) Riot (d) None of these.

Que. (5) Policies on the basis of indemnity includes —
(a) Valued policy (b) Specific policy
(c) Average policy (d) All of these.

Que. (6) Policies on the basis of stock includes —
(a) Floating policy (b) Value with discount policy
(c) Excess policy (d) None of these.

Que. (7) Which one of the following is also known as 'all in one' or combined policy —
(a) Schedule policy (b) Comprehensive policy
(c) Floating policy (d) None of these.

[Answer: 1-(c), 2-(c), 3-(d), 4-(c), 5-(d), 6-(d), 7-(b)]

(F) Match the pair

1. Valued policy, unvalued policy, specific policy, and average policy are grouped on the basis of: (a) Stock
2. Floating policy, stock declaration policy, excess policy; and maximum value with discount policy are grouped on the basis of: (b) Indemnity
3. Schedule policy, standard fire policy, comprehensive policy, loss of profit policy; and sprinkler leakage policy are grouped on the basis of: (c) Physical Hazards
4 Negligence is related to: (d) Risk coverage
5 Purpose of use of a specific premises is related: (e) Moral Hazards

[Answer: 1-(b), 2-(a), 3-(d), 4-(e), 5-(c)]

❒ ❒ ❒

CHAPTER 6

MARINE INSURANCE

Marine insurance: Introduction, Meaning and Definition, Main Clauses/ Terms Applied for Marine Insurance; Salient Feature of Marine Insurance, Marine Losses, Subject Matter of Marine Insurance; and Type of Marine Insurance.

6.1 OBJECTIVES OF LEARNING

- *Understand the meaning of the marine insurance;*
- *Elucidate the salient features of Contract of marine insurance;*
- *Details subject matter of marine insurance as well as types of marine losses; and*
- *Describe the different terms/clauses used in marine policies.*

6.2 INTRODUCTION

Marine insurance is one of the oldest type of insurance. It is an important element of general insurance. It provides insurance coverage on loss or damage of ships, cargo, terminals, and any transport or cargo by which property is transferred, acquired, or held between the starting point and final destination. The risks that marine insurance covers are fire, seizures, war, accidents or causalities which take place over the sea. Winds and waves are not included as risks in the marine insurance. However Marine insurance includes onshore and offshore uncovered property such as container terminals, ports, oil platforms, pipelines, hull, marine casualty and other marine liability.

It was the earliest well-developed kind of insurance, with origins in the Greek and Roman maritime loan. The origin of modern marine insurance is considered to be commenced in England in 1601 when a specialized chamber of assurance separately established from the other Courts. Thereafter, in 1906 the Marine Insurance Act was passed which included the previous common law. In India marine insurance is regulated by the Indian Maritime Insurance Act 1963. This Act is derived from the original English, Marine Insurance Act, 1906.

6.3 MEANING AND DEFINITION

1. According to the **Section 2 (13A) of the Insurance Act, 1938**, marine insurance business means *"the business of effecting contracts of insurance upon vessels of any description, including cargoes, freights and other interests which may be legally insured, in or in relation to such vessels, cargoes and freights, goods, wares, merchandise and property of whatever description insured for any transit, by land or water, or both, and whether or not including warehouse risks or similar risks in addition or as incidental to such transit, and includes any other risks customarily included among the risks insured against in marine insurance policies."*

2. According to **Section 3 of Marine Insurance Act, 1963,** the marine insurance is *'A contract of marine insurance is an agreement whereby the insurer undertakes to indemnify the assured, in the manner and to the extent thereby agreed, against marine losses, that is to say, the losses incidental to marine adventure.'*

From the study of above definitions it is understood that:

- Marine insurance is a valid agreement between the insurer and the insured.
- The insurer is known as the underwriter.
- The insured must be a cargo owner or a ship owner or a freight receiver.
- The document in which the term of contract is described is called "Marine policy".
- A particular sum paid by the insured is called premium, in return for an undertaking given by the insurer to indemnify the insured against loss or damage caused by certain specific perils.

6.3.1 Meaning of marine perils

According to **Section 2(e) of Marine Insurance Act, 1963, "maritime perils"** means *'the perils consequent on, or incidental to, the navigation of the sea, that is to say, perils of the seas, fire, war perils, pirates, rovers, thieves, captures, seizures, restraints and detainments of princes and peoples, jettisons, barratry and any other perils which may be designated by the policy.'*

In view of the above definition, maritime perils can be defined as an unexpected accident of the sea caused apart from the willful intervention of human beings. The perils are incidental that arises during the sea journey. There may be different forms of perils, out of these some are covered by insurance while others are not as mentioned below:

(i) Storm, tornado, burning and sinking of the ship, collision of one ship with another ship or against rocks, spoilage of cargo from sea water, piracy or willful destruction of the ship and cargo by the master (captain) of the ship or the crew, jettison etc. are covered under marine insurance as these are not considered as perils of sea.

(ii) Usual wear and tear of the vessel, breakage of goods due to bad movement of the ship, leakage if it is not caused by an accident, damage by rats and loss by delay etc. are not considered as peril of the sea and hence these are not covered under marine insurance.

6.4 MAIN CLAUSES/TERMS APPLIED FOR MARINE INSURANCE

A marine insurance policy may contain several terms and clauses. Some of these are common to marine policies whereas others are included to meet special requirements of the insured. Some of the important terms/clauses used in a marine policy are described below:

1. **At and From Clause:** The subject matter is covered under this clause while it is lying at the port of departure and until it reaches the port of destination. If the policy comprises of the word 'from' only instead of 'at and from', the risk is covered only from the time of departure of the ship. It is used in voyage policies.
2. **Barratry Clause:** Losses suffered by the ship owner or the cargo owner due to willful conduct of the master or crew of the ship is covered under this clause.
3. **Continuation Clause:** This clause authorizes the vessel to continue and complete her voyage even if the time of the policy has expired. This clause is used in a time policy. The insured has to give prior notice for this and deposit a monthly prorate premium.
4. **Contract of marine insurance:** means a contract of marine insurance as defined by section 3 of Marine Act.
5. **F.P.A. Clause:** The F.P.A. (Free of Particular Average) clause relieves the insurer from particular average liability.
6. **F.A.A. Clause:** F.A.A. (free of all average) relieves the insurer from liability arising from both particular average and general average.
7. **F.S.R. and C.C. Clause:** in this phrase, the each indicates as follows:

   F = Free,
   S = Strike,
   R = Riots,
   C.C. = Civil commotion.

   F.S.R. and C.C. Clause implies that if any loss is occurred due to strike, riots or civil commotion the insurer would not be responsible for compensate the losses.
8. **Free of Capture and Seizure Clause:** This clause relieves the insurer from the liability of making compensation for the capture and seizure of the vessel by enemy countries. The insured can insure such abnormal risks by taking an extra 'war risks' policy.
9. **Freight:** includes the profit derivable by a ship-owner from the employment of his ship to carry his own goods or other movables, as well as freight payable by a third party, but does not include passage money.
10. **Inchmaree Clause:** This clause covers the loss or damage caused to the ship or machinery by the negligence of the master of the ship as well as by explosives or latent defect in the machinery or the hull.
11. **Insurable property:** Means any ship, goods or other movables which are exposed to maritime perils.
12. **Jettison Clause:** Jettison means throwing overboard a part of the ship's cargo so as to reduce her weight or to save other goods. This clause covers the loss arising out of such throwing of goods. The owner of jettisoned goods is compensated by all interested parties.
13. **Lost or Not Lost Clause:** Under this clause, the insurer is liable even if the ship insured is found not to be lost prior to the contract of insurance, provided the insurer had no knowledge of such loss and does not commit any fraud. This clause covers the risks between the issue of the policy and the shipment of the goods.

14. **Maritime perils:** means the perils consequent on, or incidental to, the navigation of the sea, that is to say, perils, of the seas, fire, war perils pirates, rovers, thieves, captures, seizures, restraints and detainments people, jettisons, barratry and any other perils which are either of the like kind or may be designed by the policy
15. **Memorandum Clause:** this phrase is used for perishable goods.
16. **Movables:** Means any movable tangible property, other than the ship, and includes money, valuable securities and other documents.
17. **Running down Clause:** This clause covers the risk arising out of collision between two ships. The insurer is liable to pay compensation to the owner of the damaged ship. This clause is used in hull insurance.
18. **Ship:** includes every description of vessel used in navigation.
19. **Sue and Labour Clause:** This clause authorizes the insured to take all possible steps to avert or minimize the loss or to protect the subject matter insured in case of danger. The insurer is liable to pay the expenses, if any, incurred by the insured for this purpose.
20. **Suit:** includes counter-claim and set-off.
21. **Touch and Stay:** this phrase implies that the ship will travel via prescribed harbors (staying at these specific harbors). Insurance liability ceases if the journey of ship is performed from other than prescribed route. Therefore, the ship should not deviate from prescribed route.
22. **Touch and Stay Clause:** This clause requires the ship to touch and stay at such ports and in such order as specified in the policy. Any departure from the route mentioned in the policy or the ordinary trade route followed will be considered as deviation unless such departure is essential to save the ship or the lives on board in an emergency.
23. **Valuation Clause:** This clause states the value of the subject matter insured as agreed upon between both the parties.
24. **Waiver Clause:** This clause is an extension of the above clause. The clause states that any act of the insured or the insurer to protect, recover or preserve the subject matter of insurance shall not be taken to mean that the insured wants to forgo the compensation, nor will it mean that the insurer accepts the act as abandonment of the policy.
25. **Warehouse to Warehouse Clause:** This clause is inserted to cover the risks to goods from the time they are dispatched from the consignor's warehouse until their delivery at the consignee's warehouse at the port of destination.

6.5 SALIENT FEATURE OF MARINE INSURANCE

The salient features of a contract of marine insurance are as follows:

(i) **Insurable interest:** A marine insurance policy is valid only if the policy-holder has an insurable interest in the subject matter. Such interest must exist at the time when the loss occurs. It need not exist when the insurance policy is taken. Under marine insurance: (i) The owner of the ship; (ii) The owner of the cargo; (iii) Creditor who has advanced money on the security of the ship or cargo; (iv) The mortgagor and mortgagee; (v) The master and crew of the ship (due to his wages); and (vi) The person advancing the freight, have insurable interest for the purposes of marine insurance.

(ii) Utmost good-faith: Marine insurance is based on a contract of good faith. It is the duty of the policy-holder and the insurer that they must disclose everything which is in their knowledge and can affect the contract of insurance.

(iii) Indemnity: Marine insurance is an agreement of indemnity. The principal of indemnity implies that the insurer restores the insured to his position before incurring the loss. In this contract, the insurer is responsible for compensate the policy holder only to the extent of the actual loss.

(iv) Principle of proximate Clause: Marine insurance is subjected to the principle of proximate cause. Where a loss is occurred due to several causes in sequence to one another, the proximate or nearby cause of loss must be taken into account. Only then the insurance company will be liable to pay off the insured, if the proximate cause is covered under the policy.

(v) Right of Contribution: Section 80 of the Marine Insurance Act, 1963 read as *'Where the assured is over-insured by double insurance, each insurer is bound, as between himself and the other insurers, to contribute to the loss in proportion to the amount for which he is liable under his contract.'*

(vi) Warranties: Apart from these principles *i.e.,* good faith, indemnity, and insurable interest, it is obligatory that all the marine insurance contracts should fulfill the warranties also. Warrantee denotes the terms & condition which is indispensable to the contract of insurance. If it is not complied with by the insured, the contract comes to an end. However, two exceptions where the breach of warranty is exempted are: (i) Where owning to change in the circumstance the warranty is not applicable; and (ii) Where due to enactment of any subsequent law the warranty becomes unlawful.

There are two types of warranties *viz.* (i) Express; and (ii) Implied. An ***express warranty*** is that which is expressed or clearly stipulated in the contract and it can be easily established whether it has been fulfilled or not. For example, a marine policy usually contains the following express warranties: (i) Specific date on which the ship will sail; (ii) The ship is safe on a particular day; (iii) The ship will proceed to the port of destination without any deviation; or (iv) The ship is neutral and will continue so during the journey.

The ***implied warranty***, on the contrary, which is not expressly mentioned in the contract but the law takes it for granted. In other words, these do not appear anywhere in the policy, but are admitted without being put into words, and these are automatically applicable. For example, (i) The journey undertaken by the ship must be for legal purposes and if it is proven that it is used for carrying prohibited or smuggled goods, the insurer shall not be liable for the loss. As an another example, usually the ship should travel on specified route as stated in policy and if it is deviated from the route the insure will not liable for any loss.

(vii) Assignment: A marine insurance policy can be transferred to any other person(s) by executing assignment if the terms of the policy specifically not prohibit for the same. It may be assigned either before or after loss. The assignment may be made either by endorsement on the policy itself or on a separate document. It is not essential for insured to give a notice/information to the insurer about assignment. However, in case of death of the insured, a marine policy is automatically assigned to his successors.

(viii) Legality: Contract of Marine insurance contains all the essential requirements of a valid contract, *e.g.*, lawful consideration, free consent, capacity of the parties, etc.

6.6 MARINE LOSSES

Any incidental loss arising out from marine adventure due to perils of the sea is called marine loss. Under marine insurance, a loss may be either total or partial, as described below:

(i) Total loss: A total loss means the subject matter insured is fully destroyed or so damaged and is totally irretrievable to its owner. It may be *actual total loss* or *constructive total loss*. In actual total loss subject matter is completely destroyed or so damaged that it ceases to be a thing of the kind insured. In the case of an actual total loss no notice of abandonment need be given. Whereas, the constructive total loss is that in which the ship or cargo insured is not completely destroyed but is so badly damaged and the cost of repairing would be greater than the value of the property saved.

(ii) Partial loss: A partial loss is that where the subject matter is partially destroyed or damaged. Partial loss may be either general average or particular average. *General average* refers to the sacrifice made during extreme adverse circumstances for the safety of the ship and the cargo. This loss has to be shared by all the parties who have an interest in the marine adventure. For example, if the loss caused by throwing overboard of goods is considered as a general average and would be borne by various parties. Whereas, *particular average* loss arises from damage accidentally caused by the perils insured against. Such a loss is borne by the insurer.

6.7 SUBJECT MATTER OF MARINE INSURANCE

In case of marine insurance, the insured must either be an owner of the ship, owner of the cargo or the person interested in freight. Different types of sea perils affect these stakeholder while shipment. Besides, the income that the cargo would have made would also be lost. In view of this, the marine insurance can be classified in following three categories:

(i) Hull Insurance: Hull includes to the sea going vessels or ships as well as its machinery. The hull insurance also provides the coverage of the construction risk when the vessel is under construction. A vessel is uncovered to many perils or risks at sea during the voyage. An insurance which indemnifies the insured for such losses is called as Hull insurance.

(ii) Cargo Insurance: Cargo means the goods and commodities carried in the ship from one place to another. The cargo transported by sea is also subject to various risks at the port and during the voyage. It covers the transporter of the goods if the goods are damaged or lost. The cargo policy covers the risks connected with the transshipment of goods. The policy can be taken to cover a single shipment. An open cargo policy can be used in case of frequent shipments are made by the transporters, that insures the goods automatically when a shipment is made.

(iii) Freight Insurance: Freight means charges received for the carriage of goods in the ship. Usually the ship owner and the freight receiver are the same person. It can be recovered either in advance or after the goods reach the destination. In case the freight is charged in advance, the freight is secure. In other cases marine laws states that the freight is payable only when the goods safely reach the destination port. Hence if the ship is destroyed on the way the ship owner will suffer the loss of freight along with the ship. Meeting the above loss, the ship owner purchases freight insurance policy in addition to the hull policy.

(iv) Liability Insurance: Besides other insurances, this is purchased separately to meet the comprehensive liability insurance for property damage or bodily injury to third parties. It is called protection and indemnity insurance made for protecting the ship owner from miscellaneous liabilities such as for damage caused by the ship to docks, cargo, illness or injury to the passengers or crew, and fines and penalties.

6.8 TYPE OF MARINE INSURANCE

The subject of marine insurance is very wide and as per the needs, requirements and specifications of the transporter, an appropriate type of marine insurance can be opted for the best marine insurance plan. Since Marine Insurance is very vast, it provides for various types of insurance policy. Some of important types of marine insurance policies are as follows:

(a) **Single Vessel Policy:** Under this policy, only one vessel is covered by an insurance policy. If transporter has more than one vessel, in such condition he will have to buy separate insurance policy for each vessel.

(b) **Voyage Policy:** In this policy, the particular voyage is insured against risk while travelling from a port of departure to the port of destination. In this policy the risk starts from the departure of ship from the port and it ends on its arrival at the port of destination irrespective of the time factor. The policy is preferred mostly in case of cargo insurance.

(c) **Time Policy:** A marine insurance policy which is valid for a specified time period - generally valid for a year — is classified as a time policy. It is generally used in connection with the insurance of ship.

(d) **Mixed Policy:** A marine insurance policy which offers a client the benefit of both time and voyage policy is recognized as a mixed policy.

(e) **Un-valued Policy:** In this policy, subject matter insured is not fixed at the time of contract for insurance but it is ascertained wherever the subject matter is lost or damaged. Thus, the reimbursement is done only after the loss to the cargo and consignment is inspected and valued.

(f) **Valued Policy:** In this type of policy, the value of the cargo and consignment is ascertained at the time of effecting the policy and is mentioned in the policy document for specifying the value of the subject matter for reimbursements in case of any loss of it. The value which is agreed upon is called the insured value and the insured value is not necessarily the actual value. Therefore, a valued marine insurance policy is the opposite of an unvalued or open marine insurance policy.

(g) **Block Policy:** This policy provides risk coverage in addition to marine risks. In case where goods are to be transported by ship to the place of destination, this single policy covers all the risks including when the goods are dispatched by rail or road transport for shipment. This policy covers all the risks from the point of origin to the point of destination.

(h) **Port Risk Policy:** This policy is purchased to ensure the safety of the ship while it is stationed in a port.

(i) **Floating Policy:** In this policy, only the amount of claim is specified and all other particulars are omitted till the time the ship embarks on its journey, is known as floating policy. This policy is beneficial to the exporter who undertake frequent trips of cargo transportation through waters, this is the most ideal and feasible marine insurance policy. In case of floating policy, the insured takes a policy for a huge amount and on each occasion he informs the insurer about the shipment of goods. The insurer goes on recording the entries in the policy and when the sum assured is exhausted, the policy is called "fully declared" or "run off".

6.9 SUMMARY

- Marine insurance provides insurance coverage on loss or damage of ships, cargo, terminals, and any transport or cargo by which property is transferred, acquired, or held between the starting point and final destination.
- In India the marine insurance is regulated by the Indian Maritime Insurance Act 1963. This Act is derived from the original English, Marine Insurance Act, 1906.
- Insurable interest, utmost good-faith, indemnity, principle of proximate cause, right of contribution, warranties and legality are distinct characteristics of marine insurance.
- Any incidental loss arising out from marine adventure due to perils of the sea is called marine loss and it may be either total or partial.
- Marine insurance can be classified different categories such as (i) Hull Insurance; (ii) Cargo Insurance; (iii) Freight Insurance; and other (iv) Liability insurance.
- Marine Insurance provides various types of insurance policy. Some of important types of marine insurance policies are (i) Single vessel policy; (ii) Voyage Policy; (iii) Time Policy; (iv) Mixed Policy; (v) Un-valued Policy; (vi) Valued Policy; (vii) Block Policy; (viii) Port Risk Policy; and (ix) Floating Policy.

EXERCISES

(A) Long answer type questions:

1. What is marine insurance? Explain the different terms/clauses applied in marine insurance.
2. What is meant by marine insurance? Describe its salient features.
3. What do you understand by marine insurance? Specify probable loss and subject matter connected to marine insurance.
4. Discuss the different types of marine insurance with suitable illustration.

(B) Short answer type questions:

1. Describe the probable loss and subject matter of marine insurance.
2. Discuss the salient features of marine insurance.
3. Explain different clauses applicable in marine insurance.
4. Discuss different types of policies are available under marine insurance.

(C) Write a brief note on the following:

1. Warranties.
2. Total loss under marine insurance.
3. Partial under marine policies.
4. Single vessel policy.
5. Voyage Policy.
6. Time Policy.
7. Mixed Policy.
8. Un-valued Policy.

9. Valued Policy.
10. Block Policy.
11. Port Risk Policy;
12. Floating Policy.

(D) Multiple type questions: (Choose any one of the options)

Que. (1) It provides insurance coverage on loss or damage of:

(a) Ships (b) Cargo
(c) Terminals (d) All of these.

Que. (2) In which Section of the Marine insurance Act, 1963, the marine insurance has been defined:

(a) Section 13(A) (b) Section 3
(c) Section 2 (d) None of these.

Que. (3) In which section of the Marine Insurance Act, 1963, the "Maritime perils" have been described:

(a) Section 13(A) (b) Section 3
(c) Section 2(e) (d) None of these.

Que. (4) Under which clause, loss or damage caused to the ship or machinery by the negligence of the master of the ship as well as by explosives or latent defect in the machinery or the hull, is covered:

(a) "At and From clause" (b) Inchmaree clause
(c) Jettison clause (d) None of these.

Que. (5) Loss in which the ship or cargo insured is not completely destroyed but is so badly damaged and the cost of repairing it would be greater than the value of the property saved is called:

(a) Total loss (b) Partial loss
(c) Constructive loss (d) None of these.

Que. (6) Which policy provides coverage the ship while it is stationed in a port:

(a) Floating policy (b) Port Risk Policy
(c) Excess policy (d) None of these.

Que (7) A marine insurance policy which offers a client the benefit of both that the time policy and voyage policy is recognized as:

(a) Voyage policy (b) Time policy
(c) Mixed policy (d) None of these.

[Answer: 1-(d), 2-(b), 3-(c), 4-(b), 5-(c), 6-(b), 7-(c)]

(F) Match the pair:

1. Losses suffered by the ship owner or the cargo owner due to willful conduct of the master or crew of the ship is covered under this clause.	(a) Freight
2. This clause authorizes the vessel to continue and complete her voyage even if the time of the policy has expired. This clause is used in a time policy. The insured has to give prior notice for this and deposit a monthly prorate premium.	(b) Inchmaree clause
3. Includes the profit derivable by a ship-owner from the employment of his ship to carry his own goods or other movables, as well as freight payable by a third party, but does not include passage money.	(c) Barratry clause

4. This clause covers the loss or damage caused to the ship or machinery by the negligence of the master of the ship as well as by explosives or latent defect in the machinery or the hull.	(d) Continuation clause
5. Means any ship, goods or other movables which are exposed to maritime perils.	(e) Jettison clause
6. Jettison means throwing overboard a part of the ship's cargo so as to reduce her weight or to save other goods. This clause covers the loss arising out of such throwing of goods. The owner of jettisoned goods is compensated by all interested parties.	(f) Insurable property

[Answer: 1-(c), 2-(d), 3-(a), 4-(b), 5-(f), 6-(e)]

❒ ❒ ❒

CHAPTER 7

MISCELLANEOUS INSURANCE

Miscellaneous Insurance: Introduction; Personal Accident Insurance; Health Insurance; Motor Insurance; Burglary Insurance; Crop Insurance; Live Stock Insurance and Credit Insurance. Statutory Provisions for Insurance in India.

7.1 OBJECTIVES OF LEARNING

- Understand the concept of miscellaneous insurance;
- Discuss the insurance coverage provided under different miscellaneous insurance; and
- Describe the other salient features of these different miscellaneous insurance.

7.2 INTRODUCTION

The entire insurance business is divided in two groups namely (i) Life insurance; and (ii) Non-life or general insurance. As far as life insurance is concerned, that has already discussed in chapter 3 of this book. Further, there are varieties of insurances in non-life or general insurance. Fire and marine occupies major share of general insurance and hence these insurances have discussed separately in chapter-V & VI respectively. Except these the all other insurance falling under general insurance can be called as miscellaneous insurance. There are hundreds of miscellaneous insurance, out of these some important insurances are listed below:

1. Motor insurance;
2. Personal accident insurance;
3. Group insurance;
4. Burglary insurance;
5. Crop insurance;
6. Live stock insurance;
7. Export risk insurance;

8. Employer's liability insurance;
9. Mediclaim or Health insurance;
10. Fidelity insurance;
11. Third party public liability insurance;
12. Aviation insurance;
13. Insurance policy for bankers;
14. Insurance policy for professionals;
15. Insurance policies for shopkeepers of small institutions;
16. Family comprehensive policy;
17. Insurance policy for rural public;
18. Credit Insurance
19. Workmen's Compensation Insurance;
20. Travel Insurance;
21. Wedding Insurance;
22. Employee State Insurance Scheme;
23. Unemployment Insurance.

Besides, life, fire and marine insurance, several other general types of insurances are available now-a-days. The general insurance companies offers special schemes made for rural areas such as crop insurance, cattle insurance, insurance for huts, poultry etc. There is also a social security group accident scheme for providing insurance coverage to weaker sections of the society. Out of these, some importance insurance schemes are described below:

7.3 PERSONAL ACCIDENT INSURANCE

Accident means any sudden or unexpected event, which leads to a physical disability or accidental death. We all are always uncovered to the risk of accident, which is a hazard to our life as well as financial security, and therefore it is sensible to have sufficient personal accident cover to manage this unforeseen event. In India, personal accident policy, Janata personal accident policy and Gramin personal accident policies are available for managing an accidental risks.

An accident may include events like (i) Rail/ Road/Air Accident; (ii) Injury due to any collision/fall; (iii) Injury due to Bursting of gas cylinder; (iv) Snake-bite, Frost bite/Dog bite; or (v) Burn Injury, Drowning, Poisoning etc.

Scope of cover

Personal accident policy provides the benefit to the insured and his family in the event of following mishaps which may be selected by insured at the time of taking policy:

- On accidental death;
- On permanent total and partial disability and
- On temporary total disability
- Broken Bones, Burns due to an accident.
- It also provides benefit of Ambulance cost and hospital cash.

Type of disability:

(i) Permanently totally/partially disability: When an insured person sustains accidental injuries resulting in loss of limb and is certified by a medical specialist that the injury is of a permanent total or permanent partial nature, then only the insured shall deemed to be permanently totally/partially disabled.

(ii) Temporary total disability: Temporary total disablement arises when a person is not in a position to perform the duties that he performing immediately prior to the accident, which has to be certified by a medical professional.

However, injuries resulting out of self-inflicted injury, death due to war operations, attempted suicides, diseases or insanity, aircraft accidents, accidents due to nuclear weapons etc. are not covered under personal accident policy.

Documents required for claim:

(i) Claim form;

(ii) Police FIR or Police Panchnama;

(iii) Post-mortem report or Coroner's report;

(iv) Death Certificate;

(v) Succession certificate or notarized affidavit certifying legal heir status'

7.4 HEALTH INSURANCE

Due to technological advancement in medical science, the cost of medical treatment is also on increasing simultaneously. With rising health care costs, now it is not possible for an individual to spend a huge amount on medical treatment relating hospitalization. In view of this, health insurance has become vital for financing such medical expenses. It is an important and integral part of a risk management towards healthcare.

An insurance, which covers the financial loss arising out of ill health condition or due to temporary or permanent disability, which results in loss of income, may be called as health insurance. Like other insurance, it is a contract between an insurer and insured, in which the insurer agrees to provide specified health insurance in return of a consideration called premium. Health insurance claim is paid either in the form of direct payment or it is reimbursed to insured against the expenses already incurred by him on medical treatment.

7.4.1 Health insurance policies

A variety of health insurance policies exist for covering the health expenses in India are. Some of these are described below:

(i) Jan Arogya Bima Policy

(ii) Mediclaim policy;

(iii) Overseas mediclaim policy;

(iv) Cancer Insurance Policy

(v) Bhagyashree Child Welfare Policy

(i) Jan Arogya Bima Policy: This policy is especially designed for weaker section of the society to provide the medical insurance. This policy covers both the general purpose treatment and major illness like food poisoning, jaundice, heart attack, and accidents etc.

(ii) **Mediclaim Policy:** Mediclaim policy is accessible for individuals and groups exceeding 50 members. It covers the medical expenses in case of general purpose treatment as well as for major diseases and injuries. Special discount is allowed to groups exceeding 101 people under this policy. In this policy the medical expenses are reimbursable only if the insured is admitted in the hospital for a minimum duration of 24 hours. Cost of treatment includes consultation fee, cost of medicines and other hospitalization charges. Health insurance in India is offered at very cheap rates.

(iii) **Overseas Mediclaim Policy:** This policy covers the medical expenses incurred by Indians upto 70 years of age while traveling abroad. The premium is determined based on insureds age, purpose of travel, duration and plan opted by them under the policy.

(iv) **Cancer insurance Policy:** It is planned exclusively for cancer patients by Aid Association Members. This policy provides coverage to the insured in case he suffers cancer. All the expenses incurred for treatment of cancer not exceeding the sum insured will be paid directly to the insured person.

(v) **Bhagyashree Child Welfare Policy:** This policy is designed especially for single girl child aged upto 18 years. The age of the parents of the girls shouldn't exceed 60 years. It provides coverage to that girl in a family who loses her father or mother in an accident.

7.5 MOTOR INSURANCE

Motor insurance protects the policyholders against financial loss in the event of an incident involving a vehicle they own. For instance, motor insurance would normally cover both the property risk in case of theft or damage to the vehicle and the liability risk in case of legal claims arising from an accident.

In India, motor insurance covers for the loss or damage caused to the vehicle or its parts due to natural and man-made calamities. Accident cover is provided for individual owners of the vehicle while driving and also for passengers and third party legal liability. Motor Insurance in India is an essential requirement for all new vehicles used whether for commercial or personal use. The claims of motor vehicle Insurance can be accidental, theft claims or third party claims. The motor insurance generally includes:

(a) Loss or damage by accident, fire, lightning, external explosion, burglary, housebreaking or theft, malicious act.

(b) Loss/damage to electrical/electronic accessories; on payment of appropriate additional premium as prescribed by the insurer.

(c) Liability for third party injury/death, third party property and liability to paid driver.

The vehicle insurance does not include:

(a) Depreciation, mechanical and electrical breakdown, failure or breakage.

(b) When vehicle is used outside the geographical area.

(c) War or nuclear perils and

(d) Drunken driving.

Salient features of motor insurance

(i) In 1939, motor vehicle act came into force in India. Compulsory insurance was introduced by motor vehicle act to protect the pedestrians and other third parties.

(ii) Every owner of motor vehicle is required to take out an insurance policy to cover the third party risks under the Motor Vehicles Act, 1956. Such a policy is known as 'third party insurance or liability insurance'.

(iii) According to Section 24 of Motor Vehicles Act, *"No person shall use or allow any other person to use a motor vehicle in a public place, unless the vehicle is covered by a policy of insurance."*

(iv) As per the Motor Vehicles Act, private vehicles such as private cars, two wheeled, motorcycle/ scooters, commercial vehicles such as goods carrying vehicles, passengers carrying vehicles, miscellaneous & special types of vehicles are required to be insured.

(v) Like other insurances, Motor insurance being a contract also follows the principles of utmost good faith, insurable interest, indemnity, subrogation, contribution and proximate cause as it fulfills the all requirements as stipulated in the Indian Contract Act.

(vi) Transfer of insurance policy is allowed if the vehicle is sold by a person (existing policyholder) to another person (Future aspirant insured).

(vii) Section 110 of Motor Vehicle Act, 1939 confers the powers to the State Government for setting-up Motor Accidents claim tribunals. These tribunals help in sort-out the third party claims.

Claim settlement

If the vehicle damaged due to accident is reparable, it is repaired by the insured and cost of repairing is paid directly to the repairer (or insured if he had already paid the repairing charges) by if the insurer. In case, the damaged vehicle is beyond economy repair, the insured may claim for total loss or for a new vehicle.

Motor insurance claim usually includes following three phases:

(i) **Intimation:** At first, the insured will inform the insurer about loss. The loss is registered by the insurer.

(ii) **Assessment and verification of loss:** After registration, the automobile surveyor assesses the causes and extent of loss. He submits the assessment report showing the cost of repairs and replacement charges of spares etc.

(iii) **Payment of claim:** Finally, the claim is scrutinized on the basis of report and recommendations submitted by the surveyor. After being satisfied, the insurer permits the insured for repairing. After the vehicle is repaired, the insurer pays the repairing charges to the repairer or to the insured.

7.6 BURGLARY INSURANCE

This policy covers the property against loss/damage by burglary/house breaking. It also covers damage to our premises caused by burglars during burglary or attempts at burglary. The Policy pays actual loss/damage to your insured property caused by burglary/house breaking subject to the limit of Sum Insured. If Sum Insured is not adequate, Policy pays only proportionate loss. There is also a provision in the Policy to cover bulk items on 'first loss' basis wherein a percentage of total stock stored can be taken as that exposed to the risk of burglary and housebreaking. The premium is charged on this percentage selected only.

Risk covered

The Policy can be extended to cover riot, strike, malicious damage and theft. Further, policies can be issued on declaration basis and on floater basis for stocks.

Risks not covered

- The Policy will not pay for loss/damage.
- To goods held in trust/commission, jewellery, curios, title deeds, business books unless specifically insured.
- Recoverable under fire/plate glass insurance policy
- By abstraction from a safe using a key or duplicate key, unless it is obtained by violence or threat.
- Due to shop lifting, acts involving you/your family members/your employees.
- Due to War perils, Riot & Strike (covered by payment of additional premium), Acts of God, Nuclear perils.

There are three types of policies available:

- **Full Value Insurance:** The policy must be effected for the full value of the property to be insured.
- **First Loss Insurance:** In the event of improbability of total loss, proposer can opt for a percentage of total stocks to be insured
- **Stock Declaration Policies:** These policies are given where large stocks frequently fluctuate in quantity during the year. The sum insured is fixed at the maximum value of stocks which the insured anticipates he will hold at any one time. A deposit premium of 100% of the annual premium will be paid at the beginning of the insurance. Monthly declarations of value are to be sent to the company and the "deposit" premium will be adjusted at the end of the policy period based upon the average of the monthly declarations

Scope

1. Loss or damage to the property insured by theft following upon actual, forcible and violent entry into the premises.
2. Damage to the premises following upon entry as above or any attempt thereat.

The indemnity provided is to the extent of the intrinsic value of the property so lost or damaged, subject to the limit of the sum insured.

Exclusions

The company shall not be liable in respect of:

1. Gold, watches, jewellery, precious stones, plans, designs, money, business books etc. unless specifically insured.
2. Loss or damage where any insured or member of the insured's household or of his business staff is concerned in the actual theft or damage.

The policy shall cease to attach:

1. If the premises are left uninhabited for 7 or more consecutive days and nights.
2. In the event of material alterations to the premises whereby the risk is increased.
3. If the insurable interests has passed from the insured otherwise by will or operation of law

In event of claim:

1. The insured should give immediate notice to the police and also to the company and within 14 days submit to the company his claim in respect of loss or damage sustained.
2. The insured should also tender to the company all reasonable information, assistance and proofs in connection with any claim here under.

7.7 CROP INSURANCE

Crop insurance is taken by the agricultural producers and farmers to get protection from various types of risks associated with growing crops. Crop insurance covers risks related to crop loss or damage caused by weather, flood, drought, frost damage, insects, disease or the loss of revenue due to declines in the prices of agricultural commodities. Agriculture in India is highly subjected to risks like droughts and floods. Considering the risks associated with crops, the Government of India has introduced many agricultural schemes throughout the country.

Like other insurance, the principle of contribution is also followed in crop insurance. Accordingly, losses suffered by few are met from funds accumulated through small contributions made by many who are uncovered to similar risk. The sum insured is determined upto the total expenditure or a proportion of expected income from crop(s) for which premium is paid. Accordingly, in case of loss, the indemnity is paid on the basis of deficit in average yield from the guaranteed yield.

In this context, the Government of India was implemented a multi peril crop insurance called National Agriculture Insurance Scheme (NAIS). Agriculture Insurance Company of India, an Indian government owned company, implements this scheme. The scheme is compulsory for all the farmers who take agricultural loans from any financial institution. However, it is voluntary for other farmers. Special subsidy is provided to those farmers who own less than two hectares of land.

In this insurance, area base insurance coverage is provides. Area base insurance means that instead of individual farmers, a specific area is insured. The area may vary from one to another gram panchayat or block or district from crop to crop and state to state. The claim is calculated on the basis of crop cutting experiments carried out by agricultural departments of respective states. Any shortfall in yield compared to past 5 years average yield is compensated.

In this regard, the government of India has introduced various scheme. Out of these some important scheme is as under:

(i) Comprehensive Crop Insurance Scheme (CCIS): Under this insurance, a Comprehensive Crop Insurance Scheme (CCIS) has become operational in India since 1985 as an instrument of risk management in agriculture and as a measure of providing relief to farmers whose crops are damaged due to natural calamities. The sum insured is equal to crop loan disbursed subject to a maximum of A 10,000 per farmer. The premium is charged at the rate 1 per cent for pulses and oilseeds and of 2 per cent for rice, wheat and millets. Under this scheme, the losses incurred are met by the Central Government and respective States in the ratio 2:1.

(ii) Experimental Crop Insurance Scheme: This scheme was introduced by the Government of India during rabi 1997-98 season for covering small and marginal farmers growing specified crops in selected districts. The scheme could be implemented only in 14 districts of 5 States. The premium was totally subsidized was shared by the Central and State Governments in the ratio of 4:1. The Scheme has since been discontinued from 1998.

7.8 LIVE STOCK INSURANCE

This policy covers animals against death due to disease or accident arising out of fire, lightning, flood, cyclone, strike, riot and civil commotion etc. Under this Policy, coverage is provided for the sum insured or the market value of the animal at the time of death whichever is less. In this insurance animals are generally insured upto 100 per cent of their market value.

Salient feature of live stock insurance:

(i) Under live stock insurance, the pet animals such as, cows, bullocks, sheep, goats, buffaloes, camels, horses, ponies and mules etc. can be covered.

(ii) Assessment and valuation for insured sum will be as per the veterinary certificate and or declaration of the purchase committee.

(iii) Ear-tags will be supplied by the company.

(iv) Claims will be settled for the sum insured or market value prior to illness, whichever is less.

(v) Livestock Shield offers this cover at an reasonable premium of 4% per annum on the sum insured.

7.9 CREDIT INSURANCE

Credit Insurance policy is taken to recover the loss which may arise due to bad debts or non-payment of dues by the debtors. It provides protection to businessmen, who sell goods on credit terms while substantially reducing the overall risk of exposure to non-payment. It protects them against losses arising out of insolvency of their debtors. It thus enables a business to take advantage of peak and cyclical selling periods and to safely expand into new product lines or territories.

- **Credit Monitoring:** During life span of policy, the insurer collects monthly statements of client's sales and keeps a close observe on client-wise sales and their payment patterns. This practice helps in fixing clients future sales, buyer-wise.
- **Credit Control:** At the time of processing the proposal form, the insurers appraise a section of the client's buyers. This facilitates them to determine the credit limits.

This insurance is helpful to such businessmen who sell goods on credit as it protects them from loss arising out of bankruptcy of their debtors. In India, Export Credit and Guarantee Corporation (ECGC) provides credit insurance to exporters.

7.10 STATUTORY PROVISIONS FOR INSURANCE IN INDIA

Besides the above optional insurance, the Government of India made compulsory insurance for the employees to be provided by the employers. In this context, Workmen's (now employees) Compensation Act, and the Employee State Insurance Scheme are important milestones. These provisions are described below:

(i) Workmen's Compensation Insurance: In India, Workmen's Compensation Act was passed in 1934. This Act, made it obligatory for employers to pay compensation to the workers who died during duty or receive injuries or contract occupational diseases during the course of their duty. Employer may obtain insurance policy to cover such liability. It is also known as 'Employers Liability Insurance'. For seeking insurance for employees, the premiums are payable usually on the basis of wages. This policy is essential to every employer who employs 'workmen' as defined under the Workmen's Compensation Act in order to protect himself against the legal liabilities arising out of death or bodily injury to this workman. It also provides extended coverage through reimbursement of medical expenses, as surgical and hospitalization expenses including transportation costs on paying additional premium.

State owned insures such as the National Insurance Company Ltd, New India Assurance Company Ltd., Oriental Insurance Company Ltd, and United India Insurance Company Ltd, offer workmen's compensation policies.

(ii) Employee State Insurance Scheme: The Employee State Insurance Scheme (ESIS) is an insurance arrangement which provides both the cash and medical benefits to the beneficiaries. Employee State Insurance Corporation (ESIC), a wholly government-owned enterprise is responsible for managing this scheme. It was considered as a compulsory social security benefit for workers in the formal sector. The original legislation creating the scheme allowed it to cover only factories which has been using power and employing 10 or more workers. However, since 1989 the scheme has been expanded, and it now includes all such factories which are not using power and employing 20 or more persons. Mines and plantations are explicitly excluded from coverage under the ESIS Act.

7.11 SUMMARY

- Except Fire and Marine all other insurance falling under general insurance can be called as miscellaneous insurance.
- The general insurance companies offers special schemes made for rural areas such as crop insurance, cattle insurance, insurance for huts, poultry etc. There are also several social security schemes for providing insurance coverage to weaker sections of the society.
- *Personal accident policy* provides the benefit to the insured and his family in the event of accidental death or on accidental injuries/disabilities and other allied expenses as selected by insured at the time of taking policy.
- An insurance, which covers the financial loss arising out of ill health condition or due to temporary or permanent disability, which results in loss of income, may be called as *health insurance.*
- *Motor insurance* protects the policyholders against financial loss in the event of an incident involving a vehicle they own. It covers both the property risk in case of theft or damage to the vehicle and the liability risk in case of legal claims arising from an accident.
- *Burglary insurance* covers the property against loss/damage by burglary/house breaking.
- *Crop insurance* covers risks related to crop loss or damage caused by weather, flood, drought, frost damage, insects, disease or the loss of revenue due to decline in the prices of agricultural commodities.
- *Live stock insurance* policy covers the animal against death due to disease or accident arising out of fire, lightning, flood, cyclone, strike, riot and civil commotion etc.

- *Credit Insurance* policy is taken to recover the loss which may arise due to bad debts or non-payment of dues by the debtors. It is suitable for businessmen who sell goods on credit.
- The Government of India has made *compulsory insurance for the employees* to be provided by the employers. In this context, Workmen's (now employees) Compensation Act, and the Employee State Insurance Scheme are important milestones.

EXERCISES

(A) Long answer type questions:

1. What is miscellaneous insurance? Describe the personal accident insurance in detail.
2. What is meant by miscellaneous insurance? Explain the Statutory provisions for insurance in India.
3. What do you by miscellaneous insurance? Briefly discuss the health and motor insurance.
4. Discuss the different types of miscellaneous insurance.

(B) Short answer type questions:

1. What is personal accident insurance? Describe its scope.
2. What do you mean by health insurance? Discuss the different health insurance policies.
3. 'Motor vehicle insurance is compulsory for all the vehicle owners in India.' Comment on it.

(C) Write a brief note on the following:

1. Miscellaneous insurance.
2. Personal accident insurance.
3. Health insurance.
4. Motor insurance.
5. Burglary insurance.
6. Crop insurance.
7. Live stock insurance.
8. Credit insurance.
9. Statutory provisions for insurance in India.

(D) Multiple type questions: (Choose any one of the options)

Que. (1) Personal accident insurance covers due to injury caused in:

(a) Rail accidents (b) Road accidents
(c) Air accidents (d) all of these.

Que. (2) Health insurance covers the financial loss arising out:

(a) Only on permanent disability (b) Only on temporary disability
(c) Both (a) and (b) above; (d) None of these.

Que. (3) The vehicle insurance does not include:

(a) Depreciation (b) Drunken driving
(c) Both (a) and (b) above (d) None of these.

Que. (4) The crop insurance claim against shortfall in yield is determined comparing average yields of last:

(a) 5 years (b) 3 years
(c) 4 years (d) None of these.

Que. (5) The Employee State Insurance Scheme (ESIS) provides the benefits to its in the form of:

(a) Cash benefits (b) Medical benefits

(c) Both (a) and (b) above (d) None of these.

[Answer: 1-(d), 2-(c), 3-(c), 4-(a), 5-(c)]

(F) Match the pairs:

1. This policy is especially designed for weaker section of the society to provide the medical insurance. — (a) Overseas Mediclaim Policy
2. Mediclaim policy is accessible for individuals and groups exceeding 50 members for covering the medical expenses. — (b) Mediclaim policy
3. This policy covers the medical expenses incurred by Indians up-to 70 years of age while traveling abroad. — (c) Jan Arogya Bima Policy
4. In India, Comprehensive Crop Insurance Scheme was introduced — (d) In 1997-98
5. Experimental Crop Insurance Scheme was introduced by the Government of India during — (e) In 1985

[Answer: 1-(c), 2-(b), 3-(a), 4-(f), 5-(e)]

❑ ❑ ❑

CHAPTER 8

INSURABLE INTEREST

Insurable Interest: Meaning and definitions; Essentials to insurable interest; Significance of insurable interest; Types of insurable interest and what time the insurable interest must exist.

Procedure of Claims settlement: Meaning; Essential conditions of payment of claims; Maturity claim, Death Claims; and Various types of policy conditions and its implication.

8.1 OBJECTIVES OF LEARNING:

- *Understand the principle of insurable interest in insurance.*
- *Describe the significance, types and time for existence of insurable interest.*
- *Discuss the process for settlement of insurance claim, and*
- *Explain the rights of different beneficiaries for proceeding insurance claims.*

8.2 INSURABLE INTEREST

Insurable interest is an important principle of insurance contract. The concept of insurable interest is developed as a prerequisite for the purchase of insurance. Insurable interest enhances the industry's reputation and leads to greater acceptance of the insurance industry.

It is the insurer who can satisfy regarding insurable interest before issuing ones policy. In the absence of an insurable interest in the life or the thing insured, the insurance contract will simply be a wager and therefore will become void. Insurable interest is necessary for the validity of insurance policy.

8.3 DEFINITIONS:

(i) **The Webster's** (Third New International Dictionary) has defined Insurable interest *as the interest (as based on blood tie or likelihood of financial injury) that is judged to give an insurance applicant a legal right to enforce the insurance contract against the objection that is wagering contract.*

(ii) In the words of **Riegel and Miller**, *"An insurable interest is an interest of such a nature that the possessor would be financially insured by the occurrence of the event insured against."*

(iii) This term has been defined in **Section 7 of the Marine Insurance Act, 1963** as *"a person is interested in a marine adventure where he stands in any legal or equitable relation to adventure to any insurable property at risk therein, in consequence of which he may benefit by the safety or due arrival of insurable property, or may be prejudiced by its loss, or by damage there to, or by the detention thereof, or may incur liability in respect thereof."*

(iv) **www.wikipedia**, defines insurable interest as *"Insurance interest exists when an insured person derives a financial or other kind of benefit from continuous existence of the insured object (or in the context of living person, their continued survival).* A person has an insurable interest in something when loss or damage to it would cause that person to suffer a financial loss or certain other kinds of losses.

From the above definitions, it implies that insurable interest is a true, valid, determinable, and direct economic interest of an insurance policy holder or of the beneficiary of the policy in the continued existence or safety of the insured property or person. Thus, an insurable interest means that the policy holder or the beneficiary should be in position to suffer a direct financial loss if the event (against which the insurance cover was bought) does occur.

8.4 ESSENTIALS TO INSURABLE INTEREST

In any kind of insurance there are at least following four features which are essential to establish the insurable interest:

(i) There must be some subject-matter to insure, such as the life of a person, property like house, vehicle etc.

(ii) The relationship between the insured and the subject matter of insurance must be recognized by law.

(iii) The insurance policyholder must stand in a relationship with the subject matter of insurance somewhere by benefits from its safety, well being or freedom from liability and would be prejudiced by its loss, damage or existence of liability.

(iv) In case of property insurance, the Insured party has the legal right on that property which is insured.

(v) The subject-matter should be definite and it should be capable of being valued in terms of money.

8.5 SIGNIFICANCE OF INSURABLE INTEREST

Insurable interest is very important with reference to validity of an insurance contract, basis of compensation, control on gambling and security to property and lives. In view this some significance of insurable interest is as follows:

(i) Basis of a valid insurance contract: The insurance contract is recognized as a valid contract only when the insurable interest exists therein. In absence of it, the insurance contract is void and it has no legal validity. In Indian context, such contracts are treated as against public policy.

(ii) Basis of evaluation of compensation: The importance of insurance interest can be assumed with this fact that by applying this principle the probable loss or expected compensation can be predetermined in advance.

(iii) Control on gambling: Insurable interest restricts the practice of gambling. In case of non the legal aspect of insurable interest, anyone can acquire the insurance on other's life or on others property. In such condition the basic sense of insurance will be lost and this will encourage the tendency of gambling in society. Therefore, only those suffer who actually possesses the interest on insured object and is authorized for acquiring the insurance on it. This restriction prevents any gambling practice. Thus, insurable interest is one of the foundations of insurance because, in its absence, insurance would not be different from gambling and it would not constitute a binding agreement.

(iv) Security of life and property: Only when there is insurable interest one can secure insurance for any property or on life. If the essential condition of insurable interest is not imposed, then any person may acquire the insurance on others and thereby intentionally harm the property or life to get benefit of insurance. Hence, insurable interest is paramount while entering into contract of insurance for the security of insured.

8.6 TYPES OF INSURABLE INTEREST

Basically, insurance is divided in two categories *viz.*, (i) Life insurance; and (ii) Non-life insurance and accordingly insurable interests are also varied from nature of insured or object being insured. In view this, the insurable interests attached to the property insurance and life insurance are appended below:

(i) Property insurance

Every property has some value attached to it. The owner of the property is the person who directly suffers from the loss and damage of his property. Accordingly, every owner has an insurable interest in their property upto the value of the property. The principle of indemnity applied in insurance dictates that the insured be compensated for a loss of property, but not for more than what the property was worth. For example, a tenant who rented a house may not necessarily have a direct insurable interest in the rented house but the house owner may.

(ii) Life insurance

The policy holders must have certain insurable interest in the life assured. If the insurable interest is not present the contract of insurance is void. Hence the insurable interest must be present at the time of entering into contract with the insurance company for life insurance. Usually, life insurance is acquired by the insured to provide financial security and ensures continued well being to his family in case of his untimely death or disability which stops earnings of the house. It is imperative to mention here that it is not necessary that the assured should have insurable interest at the time of maturity also.

Therefore, every insured has an insurable interest in any property he owns or any property that is in his possession. For the purpose of life insurance, everyone is considered to have an insurable interest in their own lives as well as the lives of their spouses and dependents.

8.7 WHAT TIME THE INSURABLE INTEREST MUST EXISTS

As it has already mentioned that an insurable interest is must for a valid insurance contract. In absence of it the insurance contract is void and in such case the beneficiary cannot proceed for claim against loss. Now an important question arises that at what time the insurable interest must exist? In this context, the existence of insurance interest required for different time in different types of insurance may be as follows:

(i) In case of life insurance: In case of life insurance an insurable-interest must be present when the insurance policy is taken, but not essentially when a claim is preferred. For example, anyone who takes a life insurance policy on his or her spouse, and continues to pay premium even if they are separated by divorce, is entitled to have death benefits under the policy.

(ii) In case of marine insurance: In case of marine insurance, an insurable-interest must be present when a claim occurs, but not necessarily when the policy is taken; for example, a dealer may obtain a goods policy for the goods that is to be shipped in a year but must prove that the goods were actually shipped when making a claim for loss or damage, and

(iii) In case of other miscellaneous insurance: In case of other miscellaneous types of insurance especially in case of fire and auto, an insurance interest must be present, both at the time the policy is purchased as well as at the time when a claim occurs. For example, a vehicle owner who sells his vehicle on which fire insurance was taken, cannot collect on it in case of a fire once the vehicle is sold.

Therefore, for property and casualty insurance, the insurable interest must exist both at the time the insurance policy is purchased and when a loss occurs. Whereas, for life insurance the insurable interest need to exists only when the policy is purchased.

8.8 INSURANCE CLAIM

An insurance claim is the definite purpose for benefits provided by an insurance company. The effortless and speedy settlement of a valid claim is an important function of an insurance company. The benchmark to judge insurance company's efficiency is as to how quick the claim settlement is. The speed, kindness and fairness with which an insurer handles claims show the maturity of the company and may lead to great satisfaction of the customer. However, the insurance claim is the only way to formally apply for benefits under an insurance policy, but in anticipation the insurance company assesses the situation it will continue only a claim, not a pay-out.

8.9 ESSENTIAL CONDITIONS FOR PAYMENT OF CLAIM

Settlement of insurance claim is very vital for an insurance company. It is the liability of the insurance company to admit valid and legal claim. At the same time, the company must discover fake and invalid claim. A life insurance claim may arise in following conditions:

- On early death of policyholder before the maturity date.
- On maturity, *i.e.*, after expiry of the endowment period specified in the policy contract when the policy money becomes payable.

Some specific features are common to all life insurance claims. These are:

(1) Policy must be active at the time of claim.

(2) Insured must be covered by the policy.

(3) Nothing was outstanding to the insurer at the time of claim.

(4) Claim is secured by the policy.

8.10 CLAIMS PROCESS

The settlement of claim is a vital aspect of service to the policyholders. For this reason, the insurance company gives great emphasis on expeditious settlement of maturity as well as death claim. *According to the Life Insurance Council of India,* the following procedures are involved in settlement of maturity and death claims:

8.10.1 Filing a Claim

Claim settlement is one of the most important service that an insurance company can provide to its customers. Insurance companies have an obligation to settle claims promptly. The policyholder or the claimant (nominee or assigned) will need to fill a claim form and contact the financial advisor from whom he/insured bought the policy. He will be required to submit all relevant documents such as original death certificate and policy bond to the insurer to support the claim. Most claims are settled by issuing a cheque within 7 days from the time they receive the documents. However, if the concerned insurer is unable to deal with all or any part of the claim, the claimant will be notified in writing.

8.10.2 Types of claims

It has already stated that the insurance claims are usually preferred in two conditions such as on maturity and on untimely death of insured *i.e.*, prior to completion of term and hence the claims preferred in both the conditions are as follows:

(A) Maturity claims

If the policy holder survives the full term of policy, then basic sum is payable to him. This payment by the insurance company to the policy holder on the date of maturity is called maturity payment. The amount to be paid at the time of the maturity includes a sum assured and bonus/incentives as applicable. Usually insurance companies intimate the policyholders in advance with a blank discharge form for filling various details in it. It is to be returned to the office along with the original insurance policy and age proof if the same is not submitted by the policy holder.

As per the provisions of life insurance, no claim is acceptable in respect for a lapsed policy or death of the life assured happening within 3 years from the date of beginning of the policy. However, some concessions are given and payment of claims is made:

(a) If the policy holder had paid continuous minimum 3 years' premiums and after that did not pay the premium, the nominees/assured/policy holders get proportionate paid up value.

(b) In case of death of' the life assured within 3 years where policy is under the lapsed position, nothing is payable.

Procedure of the maturity claims

Settlement procedure for maturity claim is easier than death insurance claim. On receipt of duly completed and stamped discharge form along with original policy from policyholder, claim amount is paid by account payee cheque. However, some insurers make payment through ECS (Electronic clearance system) credit to the claimant's account on the maturity date.

(a) If the life assured is reported to have died later than the date of maturity but prior to the receipt of claim amount, the claim is to be treated as the maturity claim and in such a condition the claim is paid to the legal heirs. In this case death certificate and proof of title is required.

(b) Where the assured is detected to be mentally disturbed, an order from the court of law under the Indian Lunacy Act appointing a person to act as guardian to manage the properties is required.

In a nut shell, on the date of maturity life insured is required to send maturity claim/ discharge form and original policy bond well before maturity date to enable timely settlement. Most companies offer/issue post dated cheques and/ or make payment through ECS (Electronic clearance system) credit on the maturity date.

(B) DEATH CLAIMS

(i) Intimation of death

In case of the death of the assured, it has to be intimated in writing to the insurance company. Such intimation is done by the nominee or any other person assigned under the policy or from a person representing such assignee or nominee or in case there is no nomination or assignment it can be done by a relative of the life assured or any other person such as his employer, the agent or the development officer. The intimation of the death of the life assured by the claimant should include the following particulars:

(i) Name of the insured

(ii) Date of death

(iii) Cause of death

(iv) Place of death

(v) Name of claimant and his/her relationship with the insured.

(vi) Policy number(s).

If any of these information's are omitted the insurer may ask the claimant to furnish the same. These particulars must satisfy at-least two conditions (1) It must establish the identity of the deceased person as his life was assured under the policy of insurer; and (2) It must be authentic and provided by a concerned person.

(ii) Proof of death and other documents

In event of claim by death, on receiving the intimation of death the insurance company makes sure that the insurance policy has been in operation for the sum assured on the date of death and the intimation has been received from assignee, nominee or other claimant. The following documents are required for proceeding for claim in general case:

(i) Death certificate;

(ii) Original policy bond; and

(iii) Claim Forms issued by the insurer along with other supporting documents.

Whereas, if the claim has proceeded within three years from the date of commencement/ revival/reinstatement of the policy, the following additional documents/requirements may be called for:

(a) Certificate of Medical attendant (in case of out department patient) regarding his last illness

(b) Certificate issued from treating hospital, if the deceased had been admitted to hospital.

(c) Certificate of cremation or burial to be given by a person of known character and responsibility and who was also present at the cremation or burial of the body of the deceased.

(d) Certificate by employer if the deceased was an employee.

(e) Certified copies of the First Information Report, the Post-mortem report and Police Investigation Report if death was due to accident or unnatural cause.

These additional information are required to satisfy insurers on the genuineness of the claim, *i.e.*, no material information that would have affected their acceptance of proposal have been withheld by the deceased at the time of proposal. Further, these forms also help them at the time of investigation by the officials of the insurance company.

(iii) Net payable amount of claim

After having received the requisite documents, the insurance company calculates the amount payable against the policy. If a loan is drawn against the policy, then the outstanding loan and interest thereon is deducted from the gross amount. In the case of unpaid premiums, if any due before the assured's death with late fee where applicable and the premium falling due at the time of death is also deducted from the claim amount.

(iv) Contractual obligations for insurer

As per the regulation 8 of the IRDA (Policy holder's Interest) Regulations, 2002, the insurer is required to settle a claim within 30 days of receipt of all documents including clarification sought by the insurer. However, the insurance company can set a practice of settling the claim even earlier. If the claim requires further investigation, the insurer has to complete its procedures within six months from receiving the written intimation of claim.

Various types of policy conditions and its implication

In addition to above, there are different circumstances and conditions which direct or indirectly affect the settlement of insurance claims. In this context, *various types of policy conditions and its implication as stipulated by Life Insurance Corporation (LIC) of India, and available on its public portal* i.e. www.licindia.in, are listed below:

(i) Payment of Premiums: A grace period of one month but not less than 30 days is allowed where the mode of payment is yearly, half-yearly or quarterly and 15 days for monthly payments. If death occurs within this period, the life assured is covered for full sum assured.

(ii) Non-forfeiture regulations: If the policy has run for at-least 3 full years and subsequent premiums have not been paid the policy shall not be void but the sum assured will be reduced to a sum which will bear the same ratio as to the number of premiums paid bear to the total number of premiums payable.

(iii) Forfeiture in certain events: In case of untrue or incorrect statement contained in the proposal, personal statement, declaration and connected documents or any material information is recorded the policy shall be declared void and all claims to any benefits in virtue thereof shall cease.

(iv) Suicide: The policy shall be void, if the Life Assured commits suicide (whether sane or insane at the time) at any time or after the date on which the risk under the policy has commenced but before the expiry of one year from the date of commencement of the policy.

(v) Guaranteed Surrender Value: After payment of premiums for at least three years, the Surrender Value allowed under the policy is equal to 30% of the total premiums paid excluding premiums for the 1st year and all extra premiums.

(vi) Salary Saving Scheme: The rate of instalment premium shown in the schedule of the policy will remain constant as long as the employee continues with the employer given in the proposal. On leaving the employment of said employer the policyholder should intimate the Corporation. In case of the Salary Saving Scheme being withdrawn by the said employer, the Corporation will intimate the same to the policyholder. Thereafter 5% rebate given under Salary Saving Scheme will be withdrawn.

(vii) Alterations: After the policy is issued, the policyholder in a number of cases finds the terms not suitable to him and desires to change them. LIC allows certain types of alterations during the lifetime of the policy. However, no alteration is permitted within one year of the commencement of the policy with some exceptions.

(viii) Duplicate Policy: A duplicate policy confers on its owner the same rights and privileges as the original policy. The duplicate policy is issued only in specific cases after completion of requisite formalities by the policy holders.

(ix) Nomination: The nominee is statutorily recognized as a payee who can give a valid discharge to the Corporation for the payment of policy money. Nomination will be incorporated in the text of the policy at the time of its issue. After the policy is prepared and issued and if no nomination has been incorporated the assured can ordinarily affect the nomination only by an endorsement on the policy itself. A nomination made in this manner is required to be notified to the Corporation and registered by it in its records. A nomination is not required to be stamped. Any change or cancellation of nomination should be given in writing only by the Life Assured.

Nomination in favour of a stranger cannot be made as there is no insurable interest and moral hazard may be involved. Where the nominee is a minor, an appointee has to be appointed to receive the money in the event of the assured's death during the minority of the nominee.

(x) Assignment: An assignment has an effect of directly transferring the rights of the transferor in respect of the property transferred. Immediately on execution of an assignment of the policy of life assurance the assignor forgoes all his rights, title and interest in the policy to the assignee. The premium/loan interest notices etc., in such cases will be sent to the assignee. In case, the assignment is made in favor of public bodies, institutions, trust etc., premium notices/receipts will be addressed to the official who has been designated by the institutions as a person to receive such notice.

There are two types of assignments:

(a) **Conditional Assignment** whereby the assignor and the assignee may agree that on the happening of a specified event which does not depend on the will of the assignor, the assignment will be suspended or revoked wholly or in part.

(b) **Absolute Assignment** whereby all the rights, title and interest which the assignor has in the policy passes on to the assignee without reversion to the assignor or his estate in any event.

(c) **Re-assignment:** Status of a policy indicates if the policy is in force or has lapsed due to non-payment of premium. It also provides other important information with respect to the policy, for reference.

(xi)Concessions for claims during the lapsed period: The concessions for claims during the lapsed period as provided in following conditions:

(a) If the policyholder has paid premiums for at-least 3 full years and subsequently discontinued paying premiums, and in the event of death of the life assured within six months from the due date of the first unpaid premium, the policy money will be paid in full after deduction of the unpaid premiums, with interest up-to date of the death.

(b) If the policyholder has paid premiums for at-least 5 full years and subsequently discontinued paying premiums and in the event of death of the life assured within 12 months from the due date of first unpaid premium, the policy money will be paid in full after deducting the unpaid premiums, with interest up-to date of the death.

(xii) Revivals: If the premium under a policy is not paid within the days of grace the policy lapses. Revival is a fresh contract wherein the insurer can impose fresh terms and conditions. A policy can be revived under the following types of revival:

(a) ***Ordinary Revival:*** If a revival of the policy is effected within 6 months from the due date of first unpaid premium no personal statement regarding health is required and the policy is revived on collection of delayed premium plus interest. The rate of interest to be charged for such delayed premium will depend on the date of commencement of the policy.

(b) ***Revival on non-medical basis:*** For revival of the policy on non-medical basis the amount to be revived should not exceed the prescribed limit for non-medical assurance taken by the life assured.

(c) ***Revival on medical basis:*** If a policy cannot be revived under ordinary revival or revival on non-medical basis it can be revived with medical requirements. The medical requirements will depend upon the amount to be revived.

(xiii) Policy Loans: The maximum loan amount available under the policy is 90% of the Surrender Value of the policy (85% in case of paid up policies) including cash value of bonus. The rate of interest charged on loans is at 9% to be paid half-yearly. The minimum period for which a loan can be granted is six months from the date of its payment. If repayment of loan is desired within this period the interest for the minimum period of six months will have to be paid. In case the policy becomes a claim either by maturity or death within six months from the date of loan, interest will be charged only upto the date of maturity/death.

(xiv) Double Accident Benefit Claims: Double Accident Benefit is provided as an additional benefit with the life insurance cover. For this purpose an extra premium of A 1 per A 1000 sum assured is charged. For claiming the benefits under the Accident Benefit the claimant has to produce the proof to the satisfaction of the Corporation that the accident is defined as per the policy conditions. Normally for claiming this benefit documents like FIR, Post-mortem Report are insisted upon.

(xv) Disability Benefit Claims: Disability benefit claims consist of waiver of future premiums under the policy and extended disability benefit consisting in addition of a monthly benefit payment as per policy conditions. The essential condition for claiming this benefit is that the disability is total and permanent so as to preclude him from earning any wage/ compensation or profit as a result of the accident.

(xvi)Claims Review Committees: The Corporation settles a large number of Death Claims every year. Only in case of fraudulent suppression of material information is the liability repudiated. This is to ensure that claims are not paid to fraudulent persons at the cost of honest policyholders. The number of Death Claims repudiated is, however, very small. Even in these cases, an opportunity is given to the claimant to make a representation for consideration by the Review Committees of the Zonal office and the Central Office. As a result of such review, depending on the merits of each case, appropriate decisions are taken. The Claims Review Committees of the Central and Zonal Offices have among their members, a retired High Court/District Court Judge. This has helped providing transparency and confidence in our operations and has resulted in greater satisfaction among claimants, policyholders and public.

(xvii) Payment to minors: When a nominee is a minor, an appointee needs to be assigned by the policy holder. "In case the nominee is less than 18 years of age, the policy holder is required to provide an appointee as, legally, minors are considered incompetent to enter into a contract and therefore ineligible to receive claims directly.

(xviii) Policies without a nominee: In the absence of a nomination, the insurance company pays the claim amount to the Class I legal heir, that is, to son, daughter, spouse and mother. If insured have a will, the claim amount will be distributed according to the wishes that he has stated in his will. This is according to the Indian Succession Act, 1925. Otherwise, the insurance company asks for a succession certificate by the court of law, which will clearly state to whom the amount should be paid.

1.10 SUMMARY

- The Insurable interest is an important principle of insurance contract. The concept of insurable interest is developed as a prerequisite for the purchase of insurance. Insurable interest makes distance the insurance business from gambling, thereby enhancing the industry's reputation and leading to greater acceptance of the insurance industry.
- Thus, an insurable interest means that the policy holder or the beneficiary should be in position to suffer a direct financial loss if the event (against which the insurance cover was bought) does occur.
- Significance of insurable interest includes (i) Basis of a valid insurance contract (ii) Basis to evaluation of compensation (iii) Control on gambling; and (iv) Security of life and property.
- Basically, insurance is divided in two categories *viz.* (i) Life insurance; and (ii) Non-life insurance and accordingly insurable interests are also varied from nature of insured or object being insured.
- Settlement of insurance claims is very vital for an insurance company and insurance claim is preferred on early death of Policyholder or on maturity.
- Various types of policy conditions and its implications are related to claim of insurance. These are — payment of premiums, non-forfeiture regulations, forfeiture in certain events, claim in case of suicide, guaranteed surrender value, special provisions for salary saving scheme, alterations of policy scheme, issuance of duplicate policy, nomination, assignment including — conditional assignment, absolute assignment and re-assignment, concessions for claims during the lapsed period, revivals of policy, policy Loans, double accident benefit claims, disability benefit claims, payment to minors, etc.

EXERCISES

(A) Long answer type questions:

1. What do you understand by insurable interest? Describe its significance.
2. "Insurable interest is an important principle of insurance." Give your comments on this statement.

3. Define the insurable interest and also enumerate types of insurable interest with suitable examples.
4. What do you mean by insurance claim? Describe the essential conditions for payment of claim.
5. Explain the type of claims and necessary documents required for them.
6. Discuss the various types of policy conditions and its implication with special reference to Life insurance Corporation.

(B) Short answer type questions:

1. What is meant by insurable interest?
2. What are the essential conditions of insurable interest?
3. "There are different insurable interest in both the life and general insurance." Explain.
4. What do you understand by insurance claim?
5. Discuss the procedure of maturity claim in case of life insurance.
6. Describe the process of claim in case of death of insured.

(C) Write a brief note on the following:

1. Insurable interest
2. Essentials to insurable interest
3. Significance of insurable interest
4. Types of insurable interest
5. What time the insurable interest must exist
6. Insurance claim
7. Essential conditions of payment of claims
8. Filing a Claim
9. Maturity claim
10. Death claim
11. Nomination in life insurance
12. Assignment for life insurance
13. Concessions for claims during the lapsed period
14. Payment of claim in case of suicide
15. Payment of death claim to minor

(D) Multiple type questions: (Choose any one of the given options)

Que. (1) Insurable interest *"An insurable interest is an interest of such a nature that the possessor would be financially insured by the occurrence of the event insured against."* is defined by:

(a) The Marine Insurance Act (b) The Webster's dictionary

(c) Riegel and Miller (d) None of these.

Que. (2) In which section of the Marine Insurance Act, 1963, the insurable is defined as *"a person is interested in a marine adventure where he stands in any legal or equitable relation to adventure to any insurable property at risk therein, in consequence of which he may benefit by the safety or due arrival of insurable property, or may be prejudiced by its loss, or by damage there to, or by the detention thereof, or may incur liability in respect thereof."*

(a) Section 7 (b) Section 17

(c) Section 9 (d) None of these.

Que. (3) Insurable interest, as a direct economic interest of an insurance policy holder, is:

(a) True (b) Valid

(c) Determinable (d) All of these.

Que. (4) In case of life insurance an insurable-interest must be present:

(a) At the time of policy taken (b) Maturity

(c) Both (a) and (b) above (d) None of these.

Que. (5) In case of marine insurance, an insurable-interest must be present:

(a) At the time of policy taken (b) When claim occurs

(c) Both (a) and (b) above (d) None of these.

Que. (6) No claim is acceptable in respect for a lapsed policy or death of the Life assured happening within .... from the date of beginning of the policy:

(a) 3 years (b) 1 year

(c) 5 years (d) None of these.

Que. (7) ECS stands for:

(a) Electronic cash system (b) Electronic clearance system

(c) Electronic computer system (d) None of these.

Que. (8) The following documents are submitted by the policyholder for insurance maturity claim:

(a) Medical certificate (b) Death certificate

(c) Original Policy (d) None of these.

[Answer: 1-(c), 2-(a), 3-(d), 4-(a), 5-(b), 6-(a), 7-(b), 8-(c)]

(F) Match the pair:

(1) As per the regulation 8 of the IRDA (Policy holder's Interest) Regulations, 2002, the insurer is required to settle a claim	(a) not less than 30 days
(2) Minimum grace period allowed for premium on the basis of yearly, half-yearly or quarterly is	(b) 15 days
(3) In case of monthly premium, the minimum grace period allowed is	(c) within 30 days
(4) After payment of premiums for at least three years, Value the Surrender Value allowed under the policy is	(d) 90% of the Surrender
(5) The maximum loan amount available under the policy is	(e) equal to 30%

[Answer: 1-(c), 2-(a), 3-(b), 4-(e), 5-(d)]

❑ ❑ ❑

CHAPTER 9

GENERAL INSURANCE

General Insurance: Introduction, Organization of General Insurance Corporation and its Subsidiaries – (i) United India Insurance Company; (ii) National Insurance Company Limited; (iii) Oriental Insurance Company Limited; and (iv) The New India Assurance Pvt. Limited. Present status of General Insurance Companies in India.

9.1 OBJECTIVES OF LEARNING:

- *Understand the role of general Insurance in India.*
- *Discuss organization of General Insurance Corporation of India.*
- *Explain the establishment, function and organizations of subsidiaries of GIC; and*
- *Evaluate the present status of General Insurance companies of India.*

9.2 INTRODUCTION

At present, insurance requirements have expanded to maintain pace with the increasing risks. Today we find a wide variety of risk coverage available on every walk of life *viz.*, health insurance, crop and cattle insurance, property and vehicle insurance, travel insurance, theft, fire or accidental insurance and even a wedding insurance etc. With the progressive economic growth and development across the world there is a growing trend to cater to the needs of securing one's life and belongings.

General insurance companies have willingly fulfilled these increasing needs and have offered a variety of insurance covers that includes everything possessed by us. All the insurance other than 'Life Insurance' comes under the category of General Insurance. General insurance provides insurance coverage to:

(i) Property against fire, theft, burglary, terrorism, natural calamities etc.;

(ii) Persons against accident, health and liability insurance as well as legal liabilities etc.;

(iii) Professionals against credit insurance etc.;

(iv) Plant and machineries against breakdown or loss or damage due to fire, theft, burglary, terrorism, natural calamities or during transit;

(v) Marine insurance cover against any loss of goods while in transportation by sea, waterways, air, railways, Road and cover the hull of ships.

(vi) Motor vehicles against damage or accidents and theft.

(vii) Crops and cattle/live stock against any kind of loss.

Usually, the General Insurance Companies provide package policies particularly intended for householders, agriculturists, shopkeepers, industrialists, entrepreneurs, employees and for other professionals *viz.* doctors, engineers, chartered accountants etc., based on the individual requirements of the clients.

An appropriate general insurance cover is vital for every family to overcome unforeseen risks and uncertainties prevailing in life. Considering the complexity of insurance operations, it is advisable for prospective customers to carefully read and understand the terms and conditions of a policy before entering into an insurance contract. The proposal form must be filled in properly and completely with all truthful and relevant data by the client. Finally, customer must ensure that the insurance policy is sufficient and suitable for him as per his requirements.

9.3 GENERAL INSURANCE CORPORATION OF INDIA

General Insurance Corporation of India (GIC Re) is the sole reinsurance company in the Indian insurance market with over three decades of experience. GIC has its registered office and headquarters in Mumbai.

The General Insurance Corporation of India (GIC) was formed in pursuance of Section 9(1) of General Insurance Business (Nationalization) Act 1972. It was incorporated on the 22nd November 1972 under the Companies Act, 1956 as a private company limited by shares. GIC was formed to control and operate the business of general insurance in India. The Government of India (GOI) transferred all the assets and operations of the nationalized general insurance companies to GIC and other public-sector insurance companies. After a process of mergers and consolidation, GIC was re-organized with four fully owned subsidiary companies: National Insurance Company Limited, New India Assurance Company Limited, Oriental Insurance Company Limited and United India Insurance Company Limited.

GIC and its subsidiaries had a monopoly on the general insurance business in India until the landmark *Insurance Regulatory and Development Authority Act* (IRDA Act) of 1999 came into effect on the 19th April 2000. This act also amended the GIBNA Act and Insurance Act of 1938. The act alongwith the amendments ended the monopoly of GIC and its subsidiaries and liberalized the insurance business in India.

In November 2000, GIC was re-notified as India's Reinsurer, but its supervisory role over its subsidiaries ended. This was followed by the *General Insurance Business (Nationalization) Amendment Act of 2002*. With effect from 21st March 2003, this amendment ended GIC's role as a holding company of its subsidiaries. The ownership of the subsidiaries was transferred to the Government of India, which in turn divested its stake in the companies through listings on Indian stock exchange.

As a result of these reforms, GIC became the sole Re-Insurer in India, and is now called GIC Re. Indian insurance companies are required by law to cede 10% of every policy value to GIC Re, subject to some limitations and exceptions. GIC Re has diversified its operations and is now emerging as an important Re-Insurer in SAARC countries, Southeast Asia, Middle

East and Africa. GIC Re has also expanded its international operations through branches in London and Moscow.

The functioning of GIC is within the regulation of the following major acts:

- The Companies Act, 1956
- Insurance Act, 1938
- General Insurance Business (Nationalization) Act, 1972.
- General Insurance Business (Nationalization) Amendment Act, 2002.
- Insurance Regulatory and Development Authority Act, 1999

Vision of GIC:

"To be a leading Global Reinsurance and Risk Solution Provider"

Mission of GIC:

To achieve our vision by:

- *Building long-term mutually beneficial relationship with business partners.*
- *Practicing fair business ethics and values.*
- *Applying "state-of-art" technology, processes including enterprise risk management and innovative solutions.*
- *Developing and retaining highly motivated professional team of employees.*
- *Enhancing profitability and financial strength befitting the global position.*

Core Value of GIC:

- Trust and mutual respect
- Professional excellence
- Integrity and transparency
- Commitment
- Responsive service.

9.3.1 Main provisions of General Insurance Act, 1972

Some importance provisions of GIBNA is as follows:

(i) **Definition of General Insurance:** According to Section 3(G), *"general insurance business — means fire, marine or miscellaneous insurance business, whether carried on singly or in combination with one or more of them, but does not include capital redemption business and annuity certain business;*

(ii) **Authority for formation of GIC:** According to provisions in Section 9 of this Act, *the Central Government shall form a Government company in accordance with the provisions of the companies Act, to be known as the General Insurance Corporation of India for the purpose of superintending, controlling and carrying on the business of general insurance.*

(iii) **Transfer of share capital from Central Govt. to (GIC) Corporation:** As per Section 10 of Act, all the shares in the capital of every Indian insurance company which is to be acquired by the Central Government shall immediately be transferred to the Corporation.

(iv) **Functions of GIC:** has been enumerated under section 18 of the Act.

(v) **Authority for acquisition:** Section 19 of the Act, provides the authority to GIC to acquire all the companies engaged in General insurance business. It shall be the duty of every acquiring company to carry on general insurance business and to secure that it is developed to the best advantage of the community.

(vi) **Winding of companies:** It is specifically stipulated in Section 33 of the Act that no provision of law relating to the winding up of companies shall apply to the Corporation or to an acquiring company. However, the corporation or its subsidiaries/ acquiring companies can be winded up by the method prescribed in any specific orders of Central Government.

9.3.2 Function of GIC

According to Section 18 of the General Insurance Business (Nationalization) Act, 1972, the functions of the Corporation include:

(a) **To carry on General Insurance Business:** If the corporation thinks it desirable to do so, it may carry on any part of the general insurance business;

(b) **To set up standards:** Aiding, assisting and advising the acquired companies in the matter of setting up of standards of conduct and sound practice in general insurance business and in the matter of rendering efficient service to holders of policies of general insurance;

(c) **Controlling expenses:** Advising the acquired companies in the matter of controlling their expenses including the payment of commission and other expenses;

(d) **Investment of funds:** Advising the acquired companies in the matter of the investment of their funds ;

(e) **Customer service:** Issuing directions to the acquired companies in relation to the conduct of general insurance business.

9.4 ORGANIZATION STRUCTURE OF GIC

The structure of General Insurance Corporation can be classified in two parts *viz.* (i) Prior to liberalization era, consequent upon enactment of IRDA Act 1999, and followed by General Insurance Business (Nationalization) Amendment Act of 2002 (ii) Post Liberalization, especially after 21st March 2003 on enactment of above the Act and restructuring GIC as GIC Re.

9.4.1 Organizational structure of GIC prior to liberalization

Before liberalization, the General Insurance Corporation had been operating through its four subsidiary companies viz., National Insurance Company Limited, New India Assurance Company Limited, Oriental Insurance Company Limited and United India Insurance Company Limited till December 2000. General Insurance Corporation of India and its subsidiaries had a network of more than 4,200 offices across India and the GIC interacts with customers though agents, development officers and employees at different branch, divisional and regional offices of its four subsidiaries. The Corporation (including its subsidiaries) had a workforce of 85,000. GIC had also operated in the global markets of more than 30 countries, either through its own branches or subsidiaries. It offered a variety of non-life insurance policies in the fire, marine, theft, and other various segments including health insurance through its Mediclaim policy.

During this period, the Corporation did not propose any direct insurance policies except for the aviation insurance policies of Air India, Indian Airlines, Hindustan Aeronautics in addition to Crop insurance for rural areas. Besides, GIC has also set up the GIC Asset Management Company to manage the GIC Mutual Fund, GIC Housing Finance, and Export Credit Guarantee Corporation.

9.4.2 Organisational structure of GIC after liberalization

After enactment of IRDA Bill 1999, the insurance industry was opened for private players. This resulted in enhanced competition for all the public sector insurers including GIC. Therefore, the GIC was compelled to think for restructuring its organizational structure and business strategies. In January 2000, GIC took the initiative to deal with competition by deregulation of the insurance industry. Consultant firms viz (i) the global consultancy firm Price Waterhouse Coopers; and (ii) MP Chitale, a chartered accountancy, were appointed to consider the potential restructuring of the GIC and its subsidiaries.

Restructuring of GIC

The consultants appointed by GIC have suggested the following four options for its organizational restructuring:

- Either merge all the four companies or form two companies, with one exclusively conducting corporate business;
- Implement the recommendations of Malhotra Committee by detaching these four subsidiaries from GIC, and provide them operational independence;
- Allow equity cross holdings between the four subsidiaries; and
- Assign one geographical region to each of the four subsidiaries.

To make accurate understanding to the current business of GIC Re, the term ***'reinsurance'*** must be understand adequately. Reinsurance means *"A part of risk in insurance policies is transferred from a primary insurer to a reinsurer in exchange for a predetermined premium."* The *reinsurer* is paid a reinsurance premium by the insurers to buy reinsurance for transferring risk from the *insurer* to the *reinsurer*. However, *insurer* is issued insurance policies to its own policyholders.

On implementation of these reforms, General Insurance Company became the sole ***'Re-Insurer'*** in India, and is accordingly called as GIC Re. As per the provisions of law, all the Indian insurance companies are required to cede 10% of every policy value to GIC Re, except in exceptional cases. GIC Re has expanded its business and is now emerging as an vital Re-Insurer in SAARC countries including Southeast Asia, Middle East of Africa. Besides, it has also extended its international business in London and Moscow through their local branches.

9.5 UNITED INDIA INSURANCE COMPANY

United India Insurance Company Limited (UIICL) was incorporated as a Company on the 18th of February 1938. General Insurance Business in India was nationalized in 1972. 12 Indian insurance companies, 4 Cooperative Insurance Societies and Indian operations of 5 foreign insurers, besides General Insurance operations of southern region of Life Insurance Corporation of India were merged with United India Insurance Company Limited. After Nationalization, United India has grown by leaps and bounds and has workforce 18300 spread across 1340 offices providing insurance cover to more than 1 crore policy holders. The Company has a variety of insurance products to provide insurance cover from bullock carts to satellites.

United India has been in the forefront of designing and implementing complex covers to large customers, as in case of ONGC Ltd., GMR-Hyderabad International Airport Ltd., Mumbai International Airport Ltd Tirumala-Tirupati Devasthanam etc. UII has been also the pioneer in taking Insurance to rural masses with large level implementation of Universal Health Insurance Programme of Government of India and Vijaya Raji Janani Kalyan Yojana (covering 45 lakhs women in the state of Madhya Pradesh), Tsunami Jan Bima Yojana (in 4 states covering 4.59 lakhs of families) , National Livestock Insurance and many such schemes. UIICL has also made its presence in more than 200 tier II & III towns and villages through its innovative Micro Offices.

Introducing UIICL

- UIICL is a leading General Insurance Company.
- More than three decades of experience in Non-life Insurance business.
- Formed by the merger of 22 companies, consequent to nationalization of General Insurance.
- Head Quarters at Chennai.

Corporate Mission

- To provide insurance protection to all.
- To ensure customer satisfaction
- To function on sound business principles.
- To help minimize national waste and to help develop the Indian economy.

Citizens' charter

Its vision

- To become the most preferred insurer in India, with global footprint and recognition.
- To become a trusted brand admired by all stakeholders.
- To become the best-in-class customer service provider leveraging technology and multiple channels.
- To become the provider of a broad range of innovative products to meet the needs of all customer segments.
- To be a great place to work, with highly motivated and empowered employees.
- To be recognized for its contribution to the society.

Its commitments

It shall —

- Act courteously, fairly and reasonably in all its dealings with the customers.
- Make sure all its policy documents and claim procedures are clear and complete information is given about its Products and services.
- Deal quickly with the grievances of the customers and resolve them through nominated "Customer Care Officers" in all operating offices.
- Respond to all commercially viable general insurance needs of the citizens to provide new covers and promote insurance inclusion.

- Continue to provide customized insurance products for the rural and particularly for the weaker sections of the society at affordable prices.
- Continue to develop a professional workforce for execution of roles assigned to them.
- Has a regular consultative process with all our stakeholders and set up monitoring mechanism for delivery of promised services to its customers.

Standards for servicing

It shall —

- *Strive to carry out the timelines as prescribed by the Regulator in respect of policy holder's servicing.*
- *Be clear and transparent in seeking fulfillment of requirements for settling a claim or any other services to the customer.*

Standards of fairness and openness

It shall

- *Invite feedback from customers on services availed to suggest improvements.*
- *Review the standards of services offered, annually with a view to improve the benchmarks.*

Benchmarks for servicing

Decision on acceptance of proposal for:

- Motor, Individual Health, Personal Accident and Other Personal lines of Insurance - within 3 days of submission.
- Fire, Marine, Engineering and other commercial lines of Insurance — within 7 days of submission.
- Issuance of policies within 7 days of acceptance of premium.
- Issuance of Renewal Notice 15 days before expiry of policy.
- Appoint Surveyor/Investigator within 48 hours of intimation of claim
- Decide claims on Personal Line and Retail Insurances within 15 days and on Commercial Line Insurances within 30 days of receipt of required documents/clarifications.
- Provide claim status to the customers within 3 days of receipt of request by the policy issuing office.
- Make payment of claim within 3 days of receipt of discharge voucher.
- Inform the customer within 30 days of receipt of required documents if the claim is not admissible.
- Register grievances on the same day/monitor the grievances registered on Integrated Grievance Management System (IGMS) through the Company's Grievance Redressal System (UGMS) UGMS portal.
- Provide acknowledgement within 3 days of receipt.
- Resolve the grievances within 15 days of receipt.

Appeals on grievances not resolved, can be forwarded to Head office, Customer Care Department and resolution is provided in 15 days.

9.6 NATIONAL INSURANCE COMPANY LIMITED

National Insurance Company Limited was incorporated in 1906 with its registered office in Kolkata. Consequent to passing of the General Insurance Business Nationalisation Act in 1972, 21 Foreign and 11 Indian Companies were amalgamated with it and National became a subsidiary of General Insurance Corporation of India (GIC) which is fully owned by the Government of India. After the notification of the General Insurance Business (Nationalisation) Amendment Act, on 7th August 2002, National Insurance Company Ltd., has been de-linked from its holding company GIC and is presently operating as a Government of India undertaking.

National Insurance Company Ltd (NIC) is one of the leading public sector insurance companies of India, carrying out non life insurance business. Headquartered in Kolkata, NIC's network of about 1000 offices, manned by more than 16,000 skilled personnel, is spread over the length and breadth of the country covering remote rural areas, townships and metropolitan cities. NIC's foreign operations are carried out from its branch offices in Nepal.

Befittingly, the product ranges, of more than 200 policies offered by NIC cater to the diverse insurance requirements of its 14 million policyholders. Innovative and customized policies ensure that even specialized insurance requirements are fully taken care of.

The paid-up share capital of National is A 100 crores. Starting off with a premium base of 500 million rupees (50 crores rupees) in 1974, NIC's gross direct premium income has steadily grown to 4021.97 crores rupees in the financial year 2007-2008. It transacts general insurance business of Fire, Marine and Miscellaneous insurance. The Company offers protection against a wide range of risks to its customers.

The Company is privileged to cater its services to almost every sector or industry in the Indian Economy viz. Banking, Telecom, Aviation, Shipping, Information Technology, Power, Oil and Energy, Agronomy, Plantations, Foreign Trade, Healthcare, Tea, Automobile, Education, Environment, Space Research etc.

National Insurance is the second largest non life insurer in India having a large market presence in Northern and Eastern India.

The steady growth in premium income has been commensurately matched by profits over the years. As of March 2008, NIC's general reserve stood at 1457.25 million rupees (1457.25 crores rupees) with an asset value of 8867.99 million rupees (8867.99 crores rupees) signaling strong financial fundamentals.

It is:

- The fastest growing Non-life Insurance Company in India.
- The second largest Non-life Insurance Company in India.
- Internationally recognized as one of the top 5 General Insurance Companies in the Asia Pacific.

Customer service initiatives

- Establishing Connectivity among 1000 offices within the country.
- Facility to get Policy through NET soon.
- Tie-ups with leading Banks, Corporate Sectors, State Governments
- Conciliatory Forum for facilitating quick settlement of Motor Third Party claims, Compromise settlement, Lok Adalat and Jald Rahat Yojana.
- Zonal Advisory Committees set up to maintain progress.

- 'May I help you' counters set up at Head Office and all Regional Offices.
- Citizens Charter Commitments being implemented by all offices.

Product development

- More than 200 products available to cater to the needs of various sectors of the economy.
- Continuous product development to meet emerging needs of society and industry.
- R&D cell set up at Head Office for distinctive product innovation relevant to indigenous conditions and rural masses.
- New covers launched: PARIVAR - Mediclaim for Family, VIDYARTHI-Mediclaim for Students, UCO Medi + Care Bima Policy, Star National Swasthya Bima Policy, VARISTHA Mediclaim for Senior Citizens.

Marketing (intermediaries) department

As a major strategic initiative, National Insurance Company has tied up with commercial banks, Non Banking Financial Institutions, Automobile Manufacturers, NGOs and State Governments for marketing of its insurance services.

Marketing (I) Department has been established at the Head Office to provide the required thrust and direction to the business. Strategic Alliances Departments have been created at the Regional and Operating levels to exclusively cater to the Tie-Ups. The RO strategic alliances coordinator has the overall responsibility of servicing the tie-ups in the region. The total business from all alliances is budgeted to grow at the rate of 36% to A 1070 crores in 2006-07 and concerted efforts are being made in this direction. National Insurance Company Limited ranks among the top GLOBAL BUSINESS INSURERS. NIC has been awarded the 'AAA/STABLE' financial strength rating by CRISIL. It reflects the highest financial strength to meet policyholders' obligations.

Insurance coverage of National Insurance Company Limited are categorized in to the following categories:

1. Personal Line;
2. Industrial Line; and
3. Rural Line.

1. Policy — Personal Line:

(i) **Motor Policy:** Two Wheeler: Policy indemnifies bona fide owner of two wheelers, used for personal purposes against the loss due to damage/theft/burglary of vehicle or any part thereof, electrical accessories and also includes cover against liability towards third party personal injury and property damage.

(ii) **Householders Policy:** Policy covers risks of different types and protects the house as well as personal effects and household goods.

(iii) **Personal Accident Policy:** Policy compensates individuals against accidental injuries resulting in disability or death.

(iv) **Critical Illness Policy:** Policy provides exclusive benefit to individuals in the age group 20-65 years who are unexpectedly diagnosed for treatment of critical ailments like Coronary Artery Surgery, Cancer, Renal Failure, Major Organ Transplant, Stroke or Multiple Sclerosis.

(v) **NRI Accident Policy:** Policy covers Non-Resident Indians and family against loss arising from accidental injuries including death.

(vi) **Amartya Siksha Yojana Policy:** Policy covers cost of education of a student/ students in the age group of 4 to 25 years in the event of death of Parent/Guardian thus providing for continuation of studies.

(vii) **Rajrajeshwari Mahila Kalyan Yojana Policy:** Specially designed to protect the welfare of women mainly in rural and semi-urban areas.

(viii) **Bhagyashree Child Welfare Policy:** Policy provides protection to the girl child in the event of death of either or both the parents.

(ix) **Traffic Accident Policy:** Policy provides hospitalization expenses up to ₹ 1 lakh and Personal Accident Benefits up to ₹ 1 lakh in case of road/rail accidents resulting in injuries/death.

(x) **Niwas Yojana Policy:** Policy insures repayment of housing loan in case of accidental death/Permanent Total Disablement of loanee, also covers residential buildings owners permanent fixture and fittings against fire and allied perils including flood, storm, earthquake etc.

(xi) **Baggage Policy:** The policy indemnifies the individual or a party against loss/ damage to personal effects such as clothing, etc. carried as baggage during travel.

(xii) **Mediclaim Policy:** Provides protection to individuals, families, employers, employees and welfare bodies against heavy financial burden for treatment in hospitals for illness, disease or accident, whether involving surgery or not.

(xiii) **Motor Policy — Private Car:** The Policy indemnifies bona-fide owner of motor car, used for personal purposes against the loss due to damage/theft/burglary of vehicle or any part thereof, electrical accessories and also includes cover against liability towards third party personal injury and property damage.

(xiv) **Professional Indemnity for Doctors:** It covers liability on account of errors and omission of doctors while rendering professional services.

(xv) **Star National Swastha Bima Policy:** Star National Swasthya Bima policy is a unique Health Policy designed especially for the Account holders of Bank of India. The entire family consisting of the account holder, spouse and two dependent children upto the age of 21 years can be covered under this policy. This policy covers hospitalization expenses of the account holder and his family. In case of hospitalization expenses, the entire family is covered for the Floater Sum Insured as opted for, *i.e.,* either one or all members of the family, as stated above, can utilize the sum insured during the policy period.

(xvi) **Vidhyarthi-Mediclaim for Students:** VIDYARTHI-Mediclaim for students is a unique policy designed to provide health and personal accident cover to the students. It also provides for continuation of insured students education in case of death or permanent total disablement of the guardian due to accident.

(xvii) **UCO Medicare Bima Policy:** Uco Medicare Bima is a unique health cum accident policy designed especially for the a/c holders of Uco Bank. The entire family consisting of the account holder, spouse and 2 dependent children and two dependant parents can be covered under this policy.

(xviii) **Varishtha Mediclaim for Senior Citizens:** This policy has been designed to cater to the needs of our senior citizens. It covers hospitalization and domiciliary hospitalization expenses under Section I as well as expenses for treatment of critical illnesses, if opted for, under Section II. Diseases covered under critical illnesses are as under: • Coronary Artery Surgery • Cancer • Renal Failure, *i.e.*, Failure for both kidneys • Stroke o Multiple Sclerosis • Major Organ Transplants like kidney, Lung, Pancreas or Bone marrow • Paralysis and blindness at extra premium.

(xix) **BOI National Swastha Bima:** BOI National Swasthya Bima policy is a unique Health Policy designed especially for the Account holders of Bank of India. The entire family consisting of the account holder, spouse and two dependent children upto the age of 21 years can be covered under this policy. This policy covers hospitalization expenses for account holder and family. In case of Hospitalization Expenses, the entire family is covered for the Floater Sum Insured as opted for, *i.e.*, either one or all members of the family, as stated above, can utilize the Sum Insured during the policy period.

(xx) **Overseas Mediclaim:** Overseas Mediclaim policy covers medical expenses while travelling abroad for business/holiday. The policy will be valid only if the insured journey commences within 14 days of the first day of insurance as indicated in the policy schedule.

(xxi) **Baroda Health Policy:** Baroda Health policy is a unique health cum accident policy designed especially for the a/c holders of Bank of Baroda. The entire family consisting of the a/c holder, spouse and 2 dependent children can be covered under this policy. This policy covers Hospitalization expenses for a/c. holder and family. In case of hospitalization expenses, the entire family is covered for the floater sum insured as opted for, *i.e.*, either one or all members of the family can utilize the sum insured during the policy period.

2. Policies — Rural Line

(i) **Cattle/Livestock insurance:** Policy indemnifies against loss sustained due to loss of life of cattle/livestock.

(ii) **Sheep and Goat Insurance:** Policy indemnifies against loss sustained due to loss of life of sheep or goat.

(iii) **Elephant Insurance:** Policy provides indemnity to insured for the loss sustained by him due to death of his elephant used for commercial/religious purpose. Policy does not provide cover to circus elephants.

(iv) **Dog Insurance:** Policy covers death of pet dogs of cross-bred and exotic breeds between the age group of 2 months to 8 years.

(v) **Brackish Water Prawn Insurance:** Policy covers total loss of prawns, nursed seeds in hatcheries owned by state Government, FFDAS, State Fisheries Corporation, MPEDA or such other organizations.

(vi) **Silkworm (Sericulture) Insurance:** This policy covers total or partial loss due to death of silk worms of different varieties due to disease or accident.

(vii) **Janta Personal Accident Insurance:** Policy covers individuals in the age group of 10-70 years against death or total/partial disablement.

(viii) **Horticulture/Plantation Insurance:** Policy covers loss or damage to the Insured tree/plant due to fire/lightning/storm/hailstorm/cyclone/tempest.

(ix) **Kisan Agriculture Pump-set Insurance:** Policy covers centrifugal pump sets (Electrical and Diesel oil) submersible pump sets up to 25 HP used for agricultural purposes against electrical/mechanical breakdown, fire/lighting, theft and burglary, riot/strike/malicious damage etc.

3. Policies — Industrial Line

(i) **Erection All Risks Insurance (EAR):** Erection All Risk Insurance provides cover for projects involving equipment and other similar erections.

(ii) **Burglary (Business Premises) Policy:** Covers loss due to theft and burglary of movable properties like stock-in-trade, plant and machinery, furniture, fittings etc. followed by virulent and forceful entry or exit.

(iii) **Shopkeeper Policy:** This policy is specifically devised for small shopkeepers having building and stock value limited to less than or equal to rupees ten lacs. The policy covers a host of risks like stock in trade, building, furniture, money-in-transit, business interruption etc., and indemnifies the loss of the insured due to any of the perils covered.

(iv) **Bankers Indemnity Policy:** This Policy is specially designed for banks to provide indemnity against direct loss suffered by them (excluding Non-Banking Financial Institutions). The policy covers loss of money and/or securities inside the Bank or while in transit, forgery or alteration, dishonesty of employees etc.

(v) **Office Package Policy:** This policy provides a package of various covers required by an office establishment including cover for buildings, landlords fixture and fittings, boundary walls and fences, canteen etc. office contents, equipments, cover for employees, public liability etc. all built in one policy.

(vi) **Glass Insurance:** The policy covers loss due to accidental breakage of plain and ordinary glazed glasses without embossing, silvering, lettering, bending or ornamented fitted to doors, windows, show-cases, counters and shelves. Crockeries are not insurable under Glass Insurance.

(vii) **Money Insurance:** Policy indemnifies insured against loss of cash, currency notes, coins, securities, postal orders, stamps, cheques etc. while in transit or in locked safe.

(viii) **Jewellers Block Policy:** Covers loss or damage to the stock-in-trade and also cash and currency notes in the premises where the insured's business is carried on or at other premises where the property insured is deposited.

(ix) **Extended Warranty Policy:** Policy provides extended warranty to prospective buyers of vehicle, over and above the normal warranty provided by manufacturers /authorized dealers of vehicles like cars and two wheelers.

(x) **Directors and Officers Liability Policy:** Policy indemnifies legal liability to third party due to wrongful act by directors and officers of any company but excludes dishonest, fraudulent, criminal or malicious act, personal guarantee, libel and slander and damage to property and pollution damage.

(xi) **Fidelity Guarantee Policy:** The term fidelity guarantee insurance embraces policies indemnifying employers against financial loss on account of forgery, defalcation, embezzlement and fraudulent conversion by employees. The object is to provide protection in respect of the default of an individual acting in some capacity such as Cashier, Accountant, Store-keeper etc. The cover may be required in respect of a single employee or a number of employees.

(xii) Marine Cargo Insurance: The policy provides cover to cargo against risk of damage when it is exposed to maritime perils during transportation. The policy covers two categories of risk which are standard risks of transport and exceptional risks of transport (war, strike or similar).

9.7 ORIENTAL INSURANCE COMPANY LIMITED

The Oriental Insurance Company Limited was incorporated in Bombay on 12th September 1947. The Company was a wholly owned subsidiary of the Oriental Government Security Life Assurance Company Ltd. and was formed to carry out general insurance business. The Company was a subsidiary of Life Insurance Corporation of India from 1956 to 1973 (till the General Insurance Business was nationalized in the country). In 2003 all the shares of the company held by the General Insurance Corporation of India were transferred to the Central Government.

Oriental Insurance with its head Office at New Delhi, India has 23 regional offices and nearly 1000 operating offices in various cities of the country. The Company has overseas operations in Nepal, Kuwait and Dubai. The Company has a total strength of around 16, 000 employees. From less than a lakh at inception, the gross premium went up to A 58 crores in 1973 and during 2006-07 the figure stood at a mammoth A 4,020 crores.

The Company is a pioneer in laying down systems for smooth and orderly conduct of the business. The strength of the company lies in its highly trained and motivated work force that covers various disciplines and has vast expertise. Oriental specializes in devising special covers for large projects like power plants, petrochemical, steel and chemical plants. The company has developed various types of insurance covers to cater to the needs of both the urban and rural population of India. The Company has a highly technically qualified and competent team of professionals to render the best customer service. The goal of the Company was "Service to clients" and achievement thereof was helped by the strong traditions built up overtime. The Company has overseas operations in Nepal, Kuwait and Dubai.

Its Corporate Vision

'To be the most respected and preferred non-life insurer in the markets we operate'.

Its Corporate Objectives

To ensure that it —

(1) Acts as a financially sound corporate entity with high business ethics.

(2) Implements best human resource development practices to build a highly efficient, dedicated and motivated workforce with high morale and moral values.

(3) Optimally utilizes the information technology infrastructure.

(4) Provides excellent customer service.

(5) Runs the business profitably through prudent underwriting and efficient and proper claim management.

(6) Effectively manages its reinsurance operations.

(7) Effectively manage its investments for optimizing yield.

(8) Has effective risk management systems.

(9) Improves the penetration of non-life insurance by proper underwriting, innovation and marketing.

Management

Oriental Insurance is a professionally managed independent board-run company. Illustrious personalities like Shri T.A. Pai (who later became Cabinet Minister in the Union Government), Shri K.R. Puri, who rose to be the Governor of RBI and Shri B.D.Pande (who later became the Governor of West Bengal) were among the past Chairmen.

At present Dr. A.K. Saxena is the Chairman-Cum-Managing Director of this Company. The Board of Directors of this Company includes eminent personalities in various fields.

9.8 THE NEW INDIA ASSURANCE PVT LTD.

New India Assurance Company Limited (NIA) was established by Sir Dorab Tata on 23rd July 1919. New India is the first wholly Indian owned insurance company in India. New India was nationalized in 1973 with the merger of Indian insurance companies. New India is a pioneer among the Indian companies on various fronts right from insuring the first domestic airlines in 1946 to satellite insurance in 1980. With a wide range of policies New India has become one of the largest non-life insurance companies, not only in India, but also in the Afro-Asian region.

New India is a leading global insurance group, with offices and branches throughout India and various countries abroad. The company services the Indian subcontinent with a network of 1068 offices, comprising 28 regional offices, 393 divisional offices and 648 branches. With approximately 21000 employees, New India has the largest number of specialist and technically qualified personnel at all levels of management, who are empowered to underwrite and settle claims of high magnitude. New India has been rated "A-" (Excellent) by A.M. Best Co., making it the only Indian insurance company to have been rated by an international rating agency. Rating based on following factors:

- Superior Capital Position
- Strong Operating Performance
- Only Company to develop significant International operations, long record of successful trading outside India

Present Position

Gross Premium (in India) of ₹ 8,542.86 crores in the year 2011-2012, as against ₹ 7,097.14 crores in the year 2010-2011. It has assets worth ₹ 42,162.74 crores as on 31st March 2012, a network of offices-28 regional offices, 5 large corporate offices, 400 divisional offices, 588 branches, 26 direct agent branches and 149 micro offices. It has ranked 1st in the Indian market. It is the largest non-life insurer in Afro-Asia excluding Japan. First Indian non-life company to reach ₹ 10,073.88 crores gross premium. Global re-insurance facilities. It has over-seas presence in countries like Japan, U.K, Middle East, Fiji and Australia.

International Presence

Overseas operations commenced in 1920. It had operations in 20 countries in the year 2011-12 with a network of 9 branches, 7 agencies, 1 associate company and 3 subsidiary companies in the year 2011-12. Overseas premium of ₹ 1,531.37 crores was in the year 2011-12.

Pioneers

- First company to set up an Aviation Insurance Department in 1946.
- First company to handle the Hull Insurance requirements of the Indian Shipping Fleet.
- First company to establish its own training school.
- First company to introduce the concept of 'Model Office Training'.
- First company to create a department in engineering insurance.
- Pioneer in satellite insurance.

Vision NIA

"To be the most respected, trusted and preferred Non-life Insurer in the Global markets we operate."

Mission of NIA

- To develop general insurance business in the best interest of the community.
- To provide financial security to individuals, trade, commerce and all other segments of the society by offering insurance products and services of high quality at affordable cost.

Values of NIA

- Highest priority to customer's needs.
- High standards of public conduct.
- Transparency in operations.

Culture of NIA

- Courtesy and caring.
- Initiatives and innovation.
- Integrity, trustworthiness and reliability.

Commitments of NIA

It shall —

- Act courteously, fairly and reasonably in all its dealings with the customers.
- Make sure all its policy documents and claim procedures are clear and complete information is given about the products and services.
- Deal quickly and sympathetically with the grievances of the customer and resolve efficiently through nominated customer service officers in all operating offices. To educate the client about grievance redressal mechanism including the system of grievance redressal through Ombudsman.
- Respond to all commercially viable general insurance requirements of all categories including products for weaker section of the society at affordable price within 3 months from the date of such requirement.
- Continue to develop a dedicated, sensitized and professional workforce for efficient execution of roles assigned to them.
- Has a regular monitoring and consultative process with all our service providers and set up monitoring mechanism for delivery of promised services to our customers.

Standards for Servicing of NIA

It shall —

- Strive to achieve and excel the time lines/bench mark set forth by the regulator in respect of policyholders servicing.
- Be clear and transparent in seeking fulfillment of requirements for settling a claim or any other services to the customer.

Bench Marks for Servicing in NIA

Decision on acceptance of proposal for

- Motor, Individual health, personal accident and other personal lines of insurance - within 3 days of submission.
- Fire, marine, engineering and other commercial lines of Insurance - within 7 days of submission.
- Issuance of policies within 7 days of acceptance of premium.
- Issuance of Renewal Notice 15 days before expiry of policy.
- Appointing Surveyor/Investigator within 48 hours of intimation of claim.
- Decide claims on personal line and retail Insurances within 15 days and on Commercial Line Insurances within 30 days of receipt of required documents/clarifications.
- Provide claim status to the customers within 3 days of receipt of request by the policy issuing office.
- Make payment of claim within 3 days of receipt of discharge voucher.
- Inform the customer within 30 days of receipt of required documents if the claim is not admissible.
- Register grievances on the same day/monitor the grievances registered on Integrated Grievance Management System (IGMS) and those cases registered 'Online' through Company's Grievance Redressal System. Provide acknowledgement within 3 days of receipt and resolve the grievance within 15 days of receipt.

Financial Rating:

For the sixth consecutive year, the Company has been rated as "A" (Excellent) by M/s. A.M. Best Europe Ltd. The rating reflects Company's excellent risk adjusted capitalisation, prospective improvement in underwriting performance and its leading business profile in the direct insurance market in India.

Table 9.1

EMPLOYEE STRENGTH (as on 31-03-2012)

Category	*Number of Recruitments*	*Total Number of employees*	*Function*
Class I	322	6413	Supervisory
Class II (Marketing & Administration)	NIL	2292	Development Force
Class III	NIL	8358	Clerical/Secretarial
Class IV (Excluding Part Time Sweepers)	NIL	2047	Substaff/Drivers
Part Time Sweepers	NIL	218	—
TOTAL	322	19328	—

Products: The insurance products of New India has been categorized as follows:

Personal Insurance

- Pravasi Bharatiya Bima Yojana Policy
- Mediclaim 2007 Policy
- Family Floater Mediclaim Policy
- Janata Mediclaim Policy
- Senior Citizen Mediclaim Policy
- Personal Accident Policy
- Overseas Mediclaim Policy
- Householder's Policy
- Motor Policy
- Money Insurance
- Rasta Apatti Kavach (Road Safety Insurance)
- Suhana Safar Policy
- TV/VCR/VCP Insurance
- Mobile/Cellular Phone Insurance
- Other Personal Insurance
- Group Mediclaim Policy

Commercial Insurance:

- Jewelers Block Policy
- Bankers Indemnity Policy
- Shopkeeper's Policy
- Marine Cargo Policy
- Plate Glass Insurance
- Special Contingency Policy
- Neon Sign Insurance
- Multi Peril Policy for L.P.G. Dealers
- Fidelity Guarantee Insurance Policy
- Marine Hull Policy
- Aviation Insurance

Liability Insurnace:

- Public Liability Policy
- Products Liability Policy
- Professional Indemnity Policy
- Directors and Officers Liability Policy
- Lift (Third Party) Insurance
- Employers' Liability Policy
- Carrier's Liability Insurance
- Liability Insurance Act Policy
- Golfers Indemnity Insurance

Social Insurance:

- Universal Health Insurance Scheme for BPL families
- Universal Health Insurance Scheme for APL families
- Jan Arogya Bima Policy
- Raj Rajeshwari Mahila Kalyan Yojana
- Bhagyashree Child Welfare Policy
- Janata Personal Accident Insurance
- Student Safety Insurance
- Ashrya Bima Yojana
- Rural Insurance

Table 9.2: Performance of New India Assurance Company Limited, for last 14 years

Year	*Gross Premium (in India)*	*Gross Premium (Outside India)*	*Net Premium (Global)*	*Net Profit (Global)*	*Total Assets (Global)*	*Net Worth (Global)*
2011-2012	8542.86	1531.01	8771.21	179.31	42162.74	7057.61
2010-2011	7097.14	1128.37	7192.23	–421.56	39621.27	6890.47
2009-2010	6042.51	1056.63	6002.66	404.69	36832.91	7430.21
2008-2009	5508.82	946.96	5500.31	224.16	26931.58	7328.00
2007-2008	5276.91	874.55	4914.28	1401.13	31944.14	6972.80
2006-2007	5017.20	919.58	4751.76	1459.95	27444.57	5972.55
2005-2006	4791.49	884.05	4342.66	716.38	27025.58	4706.87
2004-2005	4210.81	892.35	3895.11	402.23	19827.19	4161.69
2003-2004	4045.68	875.79	3634.94	590.21	17510.44	3735.22
2002-2003	3921.24	891.55	3516.43	255.81	12984.75	3404.00
2001-2002	3512.33	685.73	3068.23	142.00	12273.02	3189.39
2000-2001	3041.17	451.88	2671.48	173.54	8292.00	3067.39
1999-2000	2979.53	327.00	2477.45	287.29	7664.71	2859.86
1998-1999	2729.48	283.16	2186.92	375.00	6727.72	2524.23
1997-1998	2433.73	254.04	1945.00	470.94	6071.67	1462.52

9.9 PRESENT STATUS OF GENERAL INSURANCE COMPANIES IN INDIA

The entire general insurance business of India had been nationalized on 22nd November 1972 with enactment of General Insurance Business (Nationalization) Act (GIBNA) of 1972, by the Government of India (GOI). After nationalization, the Government of India (GOI), took over the shares of 55 Indian Insurance Companies and the undertakings of 52 insured carrying on general insurance business.

General Insurance is well known as Non-Life Insurance in India. At present, there are 19 General Insurance Companies in India. These 19 General Insurance Companies can broadly be classified into following two categories:

(a) PSUs (Public Sector Undertakings); and

(b) Private Insurance Companies

PSUs (Public Sector Undertakings):

These PSUs insurance companies are wholly owned by the Government of India. There are absolutely 4 PSUs insurance companies in India namely:

(1) Oriental Insurance Company Limited;

(2) National Insurance Company Limited;

(3) The New India Assurance Pvt. Limited; and

(4) United India Insurance Company Limited.

(b) Private Insurance Companies:

There are 15 important private General Insurance companies in India namely:

(1) Bajaj Allianz General Insurance Co. Ltd.

(2) Cholamandalam MS General Insurance Co. Ltd.

(3) Future Generali Insurance Co. Ltd.

(4) HDFC Ergo General Insurance Co. Ltd.

(5) ICICI Lombard General Insurance Ltd.

(6) Iffco Tokio General Insurance Pvt. Ltd.

(7) Reliance General Insurance Ltd.

(8) Royal Sundaram General Insurance Co. Ltd.

(9) Tata AIG General Insurance Co. Ltd.

(10) Universal Sompo General Insurance Pvt. Ltd.

(11) Shriram

(12) Bharti AXA

(13) Raheja QBE

(14) SBI General

(15) L&T General

Table 9.3: Company Wise Gross Direct Premium Income in India: Non-life Insurers

Insurer	*Total Premium (crore)*		*Market Share (In per cent)*	
	2009-10	*2010-11*	*2009-10*	*2010-11*
National	4625.18	6220.70	13.36	14.61
New India	6042.51	7097.14	17.46	16.66
Oriental	4736.71	5457.33	13.68	12.82
United	5239.05	6376.66	15.13	14.98
Public-Total	20643.45	25151.83	59.63	59.07
Royal Sundaram	913.11	1144.00	2.64	2.69
Reliance	1979.65	1655.43	5.71	3.89
IFFCO Tokio	1457.84	1783.18	4.21	4.19
TATA AIG	853.80	1173.09	2.47	2.76
ICICI Lombard	3295.06	4251.86	9.52	9.99
Bajaj Allianz	2482.33	2869.96	7.17	6.74
Cholamandalam	784.85	968.00	2.27	2.27
HDFC Ergo	915.40	1279.91	2.64	3.01
Future Generali	376.61	600.15	1.09	1.41
Universal Sompo	189.28	299.10	0.55	0.70
Shriram	416.93	780.88	1.20	1.83
Bharti AXA	310.82	553.90	0.90	1.30
Raheja QBE	1.32	4.90	0.00	0.01
SBI General	—	43.02	—	0.10
L&T General	—	17.24	—	0.04
Private-Total	13977.00	17424.62	40.37	40.93
Grand Total	34620.45	42576.45	100.00	100.00

Source: Annual Report of IRDA, 2010-11.

According to this report, in case of public sector non-life insurers, all four companies expanded their business with an increase in respective premium collections. The market share of these companies, other than for National, however, declined from their previous year respective levels. National underwrote a premium of 6,221 crore in 2010-11 as against ₹ 4,625 crore in the previous year, which helped to improve its market share to 14.61 per cent in 2010-11 (13.36 per cent in the previous year). It reported a growth of 34.50 per cent, which is higher than the industry average for 2010-11. New India, with insurance premium of ₹ 7,097 crore, remains the largest general insurance company in India with market share of 16.67 per cent.

Segment wise premium

Table 9.4: Premium (Within India) Underwritten By Non-life Insurers — Segment Wise

Department	2009-10		2010-11	
	Premium (in crore)	Market Share (%)	Premium (in crore)	Market Share (%)
Fire	3869.27	11.18	4555.12	10.70
Marine	2167.59	6.26	2518.77	5.92
Motor	15047.00	43.46	18180.52	42.70
Health	7311.37	21.12	9944.03	23.36
Others	6225.22	17.98	7378.01	17.33
Total Premium	34620.45	100.00	42576.45	100.00

Source: Annual Report of IRDA, 2010-11.

IRDA has reported that, the Motor business continued to be the largest non-life insurance segment with a share of 42.70 per cent (43.46 per cent in 2009-10). It reported growth rate of 20.82 per cent (12.83 per cent in 2009-10). The premium collection in Health segment continued to surge ahead at ₹ 9,944 crore in 2010-11 from ₹ 7,311 crore of 2009-10, registering a growth of 36.01 per cent. This resulted in an increase in share of health segment to the total premium to 23.35 per cent in 2010-11 (21.12 per cent in 2009-10). The growth in the Health segment far out-paced the growth rate achieved by the non-life industry as a whole. The premium collection from Fire and Marine segments increased by 17.72 per cent and 16.20 per cent respectively in 2010-11 after remaining stagnant in 2009-10.

Premium Underwritten Outside India

Table 9.5: Ratio of Outside India Premium to Total Premium

(In per cent)

Insurer	2009-10	2010-2011
National Insurance	0.45	0.39
New India Insurance	14.88	13.71
Oriental Insurance	2.43	2.02

*United Insurance of India — ceased operations in 2003-04.

According to IRDA, all public sector insurers (except United India) are underwriting non-life insurance business outside India. United India ceased its operations outside India in 2003-04. The total premium underwritten outside the country by the three public sector insurers stood at ₹ 1,265 crore in 2010-11 as against ₹ 1,195 crore in 2009-10 registering growth of 5.86 per cent (11.04 per cent in the previous year). The premium underwritten outside India accounted for 2.89 per cent of total premium underwritten.

Comparison of PSUs insurers

The following table contains the information related to year of establishment, situation of head quarters, No of unit/branch offices, workforce employed, premium received during 2010-11 and market share of public sector companies of India engaged in general insurance:

Table 9.6: Comparison of PSU's Insurers

Insurers (Public Sector)	***Established in year***	***Head Quarter***	***Unit/ Branch Office***	***Work-force***	***Premium Received in 2010-11 (in crores)***	***Market Share (%)***
National Insurance	1906	Kolkata	1000+	16,000+	6220.70	14.61
The New India Assurance	1919	Mumbai	1068	20000+	7097.14	16.66
United India	1938	Chennai	1340	18300	6376.66	14.98
Oriental Insurance	1947	Delhi	1000+	16,000+	5457.33	12.82

It is evident from above data that the head quarters of these companies are situated in all the four metro cities of the India. It is evident that even after the intervention of numbers of private players; the public sector general insurance companies are performing well and collectively occupy more than 59% of market share. It is also noted that the New India Assurance company ltd. acquiring 16.66% market share, it is in top rank in general insurance business of India.

9.10 SUMMARY

- The General Insurance Corporation of India (GIC) was formed in pursuance of Section 9(1) of General Insurance Business (Nationalization) Act 1972. It was incorporated on 22nd November 1972 under the Companies Act, 1956 as a private company limited by shares. GIC was formed to control and operate the business of general insurance in India.
- The Government of Indian (GOI) transferred all the assets and operations of the nationalized general insurance companies to GIC and other public-sector insurance companies. After a process of mergers and consolidation, GIC was re-organized with four fully owned subsidiary companies *viz.* (i) National Insurance Company Limited; (ii) New India Assurance Company Limited; (iii) Oriental Insurance Company Limited; and (iv) United India Insurance Company Limited.
- In November 2000, GIC was re-notified as India's Reinsurer, but its supervisory role over its subsidiaries was ended. This was followed by the General Insurance Business (Nationalization) Amendment Act of 2002. Coming into effect from 21st March 2003, this amendment ended GIC's role as a holding company of its subsidiaries.
- United India Insurance Company Limited was incorporated on 18th February 1938 and nationalized in 1972. 12 Indian Insurance Companies, 4 Cooperative Insurance Societies and Indian operations of 5 Foreign Insurers were merged with United India Insurance Company Limited. It's headquarter is Chennai, 1340 regional/Branch Offices; employing 17322 employee; has earned ₹ 6,376.66 crores as premium in 2010-11 and holds 14.98% of market share in insurance sector.
- National Insurance Company Limited was incorporated in 1906. Consequent to passing of the General Insurance Business Nationalisation Act in 1972, 21 Foreign and 11 Indian Companies were amalgamated with it and National Insurance became a subsidiary of General Insurance Corporation of India (GIC) which is fully owned by the Government of India. Its headquarter is Kolkata, more than 900 regional and Branch offices; employs more than 16000 employees; it earned ₹ 6,220.70 crores as premium in 2010-11 and holds 14.61% market share in insurance sector

- The Oriental Insurance Company Ltd. was incorporated on 12 September 1947. The Company was a wholly owned subsidiary of the Oriental Government Security Life Assurance Company Ltc and was formed to carry out General Insurance business. The Company was a subsidiary of Life Insurance Corporation of India from 1956 to 1973 (till the General Insurance Business was nationalized in the country). Its headquarter is situated in Delhi, employing more than 16000 employees, collected ₹ 5,457.33 crores as premium in 2010-11 and acquires 12.82% market share of general insurance.
- New India Assurance Company Limited has Incorporated on July 23rd, 1919 Founded by the House of Tata Founder member — Sir Dorab Tata. Nationalized in 1973 with merger of Indian insurance companies. Headquarter — Mumbai, employing more than 20000 employees, earned ₹ 7,097.14 crores as premium in 2010-11 and acquires 16.66% market share of general insurance.

EXERCISES

(A) Long answer type questions:

1. What do you mean by General Insurance? Describe the main provisions of General Insurance Business (Nationalization) Act, 1972.
2. What are the risks covered under General Insurance? Explain the functions of General Insurance Corporation of India.
3. Write an essay on organizational structure of General Insurance Corporation of India.
4. Write an essay on United India Insurance Company.
5. Write an essay on National Insurance Company Limited.
6. Write an essay on Oriental Insurance Company Limited
7. Write an essay on the New India Assurance Pvt. Limited.
8. Discuss the present status of general insurance companies in India with special reference to PSUs insurers.

(B) Short answer type questions:

1. Describe the main provisions of General Insurance Act, 1972.
2. Discuss any four functions of General Insurance Corporation.
3. What do you understand by nationalization of Insurance Business?
4. Explain the organizational structure of General Insurance Corporation of India.
5. Describe about any two subsidiaries companies of General Insurance Corporation of India.
6. Explain the Vision and Mission of any two insurers in your own language.

(C) Write a brief note on the following:

1. Star National Swastha Bima Policy;
2. Fidelity Guarantee Policy
3. General Insurance
4. Objectives of General Insurance Business (Nationalization) Act, 1972.
5. Discuss any two provisions of General Insurance Business (Nationalization) Act, 1972.
6. Any two functions of General Insurance Corporation.

(D) Multiple type questions: (Choose any one of the given options)

Que. (1) The General Insurance Corporation of India (GIC) was formed in pursuance of which section of General Insurance Business (Nationalization) Act, 1972:

(a) Section 19(1) (b) Section 1(9)

(c) Section 9 (1) (d) None of these.

Que. (2) When was the General Insurance Company incorporated:

(a) 30th June 1972 (b) 22nd November 1972

(c) 12th November 1972 (d) None of these.

Que. (3) General Insurance has been defined in which Section of General Insurance Business (Nationalization) Act, 1972:

(a) Section 13(G) (b) Section 18(a)

(c) Section 3(G) (d) None of these.

Que (4) Insurance Regulatory and Development Authority Act (IRDA Act) of 1999 came into effect from:

(a) 19th April 2000 (b) 01st January 2000

(c) 01st April 2000 (d) None of these.

Que (5) Section 18 of General Insurance Business (Nationalization) Act, 1972 is related to:

(a) Objectives of GIC (b) Formation of GIC

(c) Functions of GIC (d) None of these.

Que (6) Consequent to nationalization of General Insurance, how many companies were merged with the United India Insurance Company:

(a) 24 (b) 22

(c) 23 (d) None of these.

Que (7) Consequent to nationalization of General Insurance, totally how many companies were merged with the subsidiaries companies of General Insurance Corporation:

(a) 107 (b) 99

(c) 170 (d) None of these.

Que (8) "Amartya Siksha Yojana Policy" covers cost of education of students of which age group:

(a) 4 to 18 years (b) 4 to 25 years

(c) 5 to 25 years (d) None of these.

[Answer: 1-(c), 2-(b), 3-(c), 4-(a), 5-(c), 6-(b), 7-(a), 8-(b)]

(F) Match the pairs:

(1) National Insurance has been incorporated in the year	(a) 1938
(2) New India Assurance has been established in	(b) 1947
(3) United India has been established in which year	(c) 1906
(4) Oriental Insurance was incorporated in which year	(d) 1919
(5) Head quarter of National Insurance	(e) Chennai
(6) Head quarter of The New India Assurance	(f) Delhi
(7) Head quarter of United India	(g) Kolkata
(8) Head quarter of Oriental Insurance	(h) Mumbai

[Answer: 1-(c), 2-(d), 3-(a), 4-(b), 5-(g), 6-(h), 7-(e), 8-(f)]

References:

1. http://www.gicofindia.com
2. http://www.uiic.co.in
3. http://www.nationalinsuranceindia.com
4. http://www.orientalinsurance.org.in
5. http://www.newindiainsurance.org.in
6. IRDA annual report 2010-11.

❑ ❑ ❑

CHAPTER 10

EMERGING TRENDS IN INSURANCE SECTOR

New emerging trends in Insurance Sector: Introduction, Historical background of Life Insurance and General Insurance. Insurance sector reforms, The Malhotra Committee, IRDA Bill, Liberalisation of Insurance Markets, and Current Scenario of Insurance Sector.

10.1 OBJECTIVES OF LEARNING

- *Trace the emergence of insurance business in India.*
- *Discuss the present status of Life and General Insurance in India.*
- *Describe the insurance sector reform in India, and*
- *Explain the liberalization of insurance business in India.*

10.2 INTRODUCTION

The entire insurance business industry in India is basically divided in two divisions *viz.* (i) General insurance or non-life insurance; and (ii) Life insurance. Both the above divisions are further divided in various sub subdivisions depending upon nature of insurances. The following figure depicts the in general classification of Indian Insurance Industry:

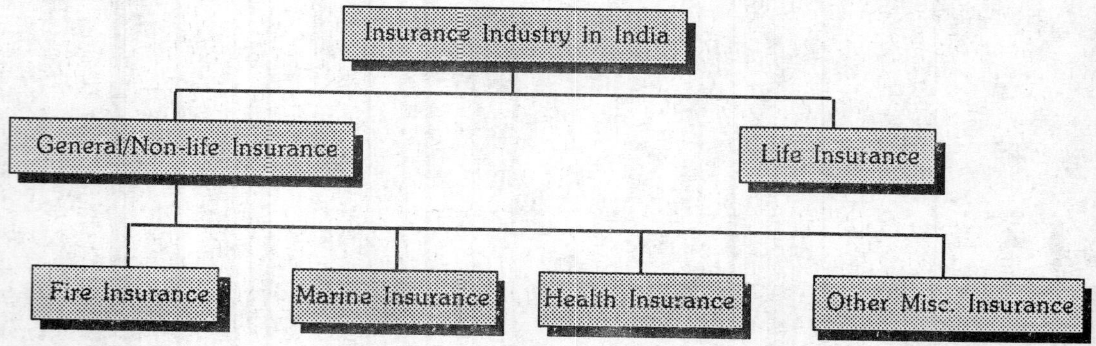

Fig. 10.1 Classification of Indian Insurance Industry

For study of new emerging trend of insurance industry in India, it is imperative to discuss it in two ways — its historical background and its present state. The insurance industry had its origin in the early 19th century with the coming of British enterprise in India. Insurance, particularly non-life remained an urban oriented business of the Insurance companies operating through their agencies. Whereas, the life insurance has wide coverage throughout the country. The developments of general insurance and life insurance have run concurrently. In view of the above statement, it becomes necessary to study the historical background of general insurance and life insurance independently.

10.3 HISTORICAL BACKGROUND OF LIFE INSURANCE

The formal life insurance business started for first time when an insurance company, the Oriental Life Insurance Company, was established in 1818, at Calcutta by Bipin Behari Dasgupta and others. Subsequently, Bombay Life Assurance Company in 1823 and Madras Equitable Life Assurance Society in 1829 were established. The Bombay Mutual Life Assurance Society, formed in 1870, was the first native insurance provider. The Indian Life Assurance Companies Act was the first statute in India, it was enacted in 1912 to regulate the life insurance business. Thereafter, in 1928, the Indian Insurance Companies Act was passed to facilitate the Government of India to gather statistical information about both life and non-life insurance businesses. Finally, the Insurance Act was subsequently reviewed and a complete legislation called the Insurance Act was enacted in 1938.

Consequently, Parliament of the India passed the Life Insurance Act on 19th June 1956, whereas nationalisation of life insurance business took place in 1956. 245 Indian and foreign insurance and provident societies were initially merged and then nationalized. According to the provisions of Act, the Life Insurance Corporation of India (LIC) has come into existence with effect from 1st September 1956 with a capital contribution of ₹ 5 crores from the Government of India. The company from the time of its inception started its operations with 5 zonal offices, 33 divisional offices and 212 branch offices throughout the country. At present it has 7 zonal offices, 100 divisional offices located in different parts of India, and about 2048 branches located in different cities and towns of India, and has a wide network of around 10 lakh agents for seeking life insurance business from the public. In view of the above, important milestones in the life insurance business in India are as follows:

- In 1912, The Indian Life Assurance Companies Act was enacted as the first statute to regulate the life insurance business.
- In 1928, The Indian Insurance Companies Act was enacted to facilitate the government to collect statistical information about both life and non-life insurance business.
- In 1938, earlier legislation consolidated and amended by the Insurance Act with the objective of protecting the interests of the insuring public.
- In 1956, 245 Indian and foreign insurers and provident societies were taken over by the central government and were nationalized. LIC incorporated by an Act of Parliament [LIC Act 1956].

10.4 HISTORICAL BACKGROUND OF GENERAL INSURANCE

The General insurance business in India, conversely, can trace its roots to the Triton Insurance Company Ltd., the first general insurance company established in the year 1850 in Calcutta by the British.

Some of the important milestones in the general insurance business in India are:

(i) In 1907, the first company the Indian Mercantile Insurance Ltd. had been set up, to carry out all classes of general insurance business.

(ii) In 1957, General Insurance Council, a wing of the Insurance Association of India, has been established for framing the code of conduct for ensuring fair conduct and sound insurance business practices in India.

(iii) In 1968, the Insurance Act has been amended to regulate investments and set minimum solvency margins and the Tariff Advisory Committee had also been set up in the same year.

(iv) In 1972, the General Insurance Business (Nationalisation) Act, 1972 has been passed for nationalization of general insurance business in India and this act was enacted with effect from 1st January 1973.

The General Insurance Corporation of India was incorporated on 22nd November 1972 to control and operate the business of general insurance in India. After merger and consolidation of 107 insurers, GIC was re-organized with four fully owned subsidiary companies: National Insurance Company Limited, New India Assurance Company Limited, Oriental Insurance Company Limited and United India Insurance Company Limited.

GIC and its subsidiaries had a monopoly on the general insurance business in India until the landmark *Insurance Regulatory and Development Authority Act* (IRDA Act) of 1999 came into effect on 19 April 2000. This act also amended the GIBNA Act and Insurance Act of 1938. The act along with the amendments ended the monopoly of GIC and its subsidiaries and liberalized the insurance business in India. However, under the provisions of the Insurance Act, 1938, the General Insurance Corporation of India has been designated as the 'Indian reinsurer' which entitles it to receive obligatory share of 10 per cent from all the direct non-life insurers. The limits have been laid down in consultation with the Reinsurance Advisory Committee.

10.5 INSURANCE SECTOR REFORMS

Consequent upon the nationalisation of the life insurance industry in 1956 and the general insurance industry in 1972, the insurance industry of India was limited only to the operations of Life insurance Corporation for life insurance business and General Insurance Corporation and its four subsidiaries viz. National Insurance Company Limited, New India Assurance Company Limited, Oriental Insurance Company Limited and United India General Insurance Company Limited for non-life insurance. Over the years, this state monopoly resulted in lethargic, self-contentment, use of old-fashioned technologies, inefficient and inadequate customer services and non-coverage of the potential market. Due to this attitude, the Indian economy was unable to take full advantage of insurance services for the nation. Due to sluggish attitude and bankruptcy, the restructuring of insurance sector has been felt by the government of India. Constitution of Malhotra committee and subsequent enactment of IRDA were the landmark for reformation of insurance sector.

10.5.1 Malhotra Committee

Considering the need of time, the Government of India set-up a high-powered committee headed by Mr. R.N. Malhotra in 1993. The committee was headed by the former Finance Secretary and RBI Governor, was constituted to evaluate the present status of Indian insurance industry and recommended its future direction. The committee was set up with a purpose of harmonizing the reforms in the Indian financial sector. The reforms were concentrated towards *'creating a more efficient and competitive financial system suitable for the requirements of the economy keeping in mind the structural changes currently underway and recognizing that insurance is an important part of the overall financial system where it was necessary to address the need for similar reforms.'*

Further, the Malhotra committee was directed by the Government to make recommendations for changing the arrangement of insurance industry, to make specific suggestions regarding how to improve the performance of LIC and GIC and to submit the proposal on regulation and supervision of the insurance sector in India. Further, the committee was also requested to evaluate the strengths and weaknesses of the existing insurance industry and to make recommendations for changes in its operation and the general policy framework keeping in mind the reforms ongoing in other parts of the financial sector.

After a thorough study of issue, the Malhotra committee has submitted its report in 1994, with the following recommendations:

Structure:

(i) Government's stake in the insurance companies to be brought down to 50 per cent.

(ii) Government should take over the holdings of GIC and its subsidiaries so that these subsidiaries can act as independent corporations.

(iii) All the insurance companies should be given greater freedom to operate.

Competition

(i) Private Companies with a minimum paid up capital of ₹ 1 billion should be allowed to enter the insurance sector.

(ii) No Company should deal in both Life and General Insurance through a single entity.

(iii) Foreign companies may be allowed to enter the industry in collaboration with the domestic companies.

(iv) Postal Life Insurance should be allowed to operate in the rural market.

(v) Only one State Level Life Insurance Company should be allowed to operate in each state.

(vi) Entry of private sector companies within well defined parameters of nature of business.

(vii) The insurance Act should be amended.

(viii) An autonomous authority *viz.*, Controller of Insurance should be appointed.

(ix) A strong and effective Insurance Regulatory Authority (IRA) as a statutory autonomous board should be established.

Investments

(i) Mandatory Investments of LIC Life Fund in government securities to be reduced from 75 per cent to 50 per cent.

(ii) GIC and its subsidiaries are not to hold more than 5 per cent in any company.

Customer Service

(i) LIC should pay interest on delays in payments beyond 30 days.

(ii) Insurance companies must be encouraged to set up unit linked pension plans.

(iii) Computerisation of operations and updating of technology to be carried out in the insurance industry.

On the whole, the committee strongly felt that to facilitate and improve customer services and increase the coverage of the insurance policies, industry should be opened up to competition. But simultaneously, the committee felt the need to exercise caution as any failure on the part of new players could ruin the public confidence in the industry. Consequently, it was decided to allow competition in a limited way by stipulating the minimum capital requirement of ₹ 100 crores.

The committee suggested to provide greater autonomy to insurance companies in order to improve their performance and enable them to act as independent companies with economic motives. For this purpose, it had wished-for setting up an autonomous regulatory body- The Insurance Regulatory and Development Authority. The recommendations of the committee were discussed at length in different forums. The recommendations to set up an autonomous IRA had been widely supported by the different forums. Since enacting legislation for setting-up the statutory Insurance Regulatory Authority (IRA) had to take time, then government constituted an interim IRA, awaiting the enactment of comprehensive legislation.

Reforms in the Insurance sector were the first move with the passage of the IRDA Bill in Parliament in December 1999. The IRDA since its incorporation as a statutory body in April 2000 has promptly come into action to framing regulations and registering the private sector insurance companies. Right from its set-up as an independent statutory body the IRDA has put in a framework of globally well-suited regulations. The other decision taken, at the same time, to provide the supporting systems to the insurance sector and in particular the life insurance companies were the launch of the IRDA online service for issue and renewal of licenses to agents. The approval of institutions for imparting training to agents has also ensured that the insurance companies would have a trained workforce of insurance agents to sell their products.

On the basis of recommendations of Malhotra committee, the then Finance Minister of India proposed the opening up of insurance to the private sector, including multinational companies.

10.5.2 IRDA Bill

Keeping in view the recommendations of Malhotra Committee, the IRDA Bill was drafted and consequently the government has allowed the privatisation of public sector insurance companies, LIC and GIC. The bill did not provide for any dilution of 100 per cent government equity in the two premier companies.

The IRDA bill wanted to provide a statutory status to the interim Insurance Regulatory Authority and amend the 1938 Insurance Act, the 1956 Life Insurance Corporation Act and the 1972 General Insurance Business (Nationalisation) Act to open up the sector. It provides for a nine member regulatory body with statutory powers. The bill also fixed minimum capital requirement for life and general insurance at ₹ 100 crores and for reinsurance firms at ₹ 200 crores. The Malhotra Committee Report justified the entry of foreign insurance companies by arguing that if it is permitted, it should be done on selective basis preferably through joint venture with Indian partners. In 1999, the bill was finally passed and IRDA was formed to regulate and promote insurance business in India. The IRDA Act confers the authority with powers to frame different regulations, issue licenses, set capital requirements and solvency margins, prepare investment norms, inspect the books of private insurers independent of the government.

In November 2000, GIC was re-notified as India's Reinsurer, but its supervisory role over its subsidiaries ended. This was followed by the General Insurance Business (Nationalisation) Amendment Act of 2002. Coming into effect from 21st March 2003, this amendment ended GIC's role as a holding company of its subsidiaries. The ownership of the subsidiaries was transferred to the Government of India, which in turn divested its stake in the companies through listings on Indian stock exchanges.

As a result of these reforms, GIC became the sole Re-Insurer in India, and is now called GIC Re. Indian insurance companies are required by law to cede 10 per cent of every policy value to GIC Re, subject to some limitations and exceptions. GIC Re has diversified its operations and is now emerging as an important Re-Insurer in SAARC countries, Southeast Asia, Middle East and Africa. GIC Re has also expanded its international operations through branches in London and Moscow.

10.6 LIBERALISATION OF INSURANCE MARKETS

Usually, liberalisation refers to a relaxation in previous government restrictions, generally in areas of social or economic policy. However, economic liberalisation is often associated with privatisation. Liberalisation of Insurance entails shifting of the insurance industry from a Government monopoly to a competitive environment. Open market policy allows for better resource allocation and creation of wealth and prosperity of people and the country. It facilitates development of health care, education and infrastructure of the country. In a liberalised insurance market, consumers have the facility to choose from different insurance providers having a wide range of products.

A liberal insurance market is one in which the market decides who should be permitted to sell insurance, what, how and the prices at which these insurance products should be sold.

There are certain prerequisites to formulate liberalisation of insurance:

- Sound competition law.
- Efficient and reliable regulation.
- Phased liberalisation.
- Reliability and impartiality among competitors.
- Optimum quantum of guidelines.
- Efficient disclose and spreading of information to the society.

Insurance markets in India possess certain flaws justifying the need for competition as well as regulation.

10.7 CURRENT SCENARIO

Considering the second largest population of the world, life insurance happens to be a mega opportunity in India. As on date, nearly 80 per cent of Indian population is without life insurance cover while health insurance and non-life insurance continues to be below international standards. Further, this part of the population is also subject to weak social security and pension systems with hardly any old age income security. This, itself is an indicator that growth potential for the insurance sector in India is immense.

A perceptive and advance insurance sector is required for economic development as it provides long-term funds for infrastructure development and at the same time strengthens the risk taking ability. It is anticipated that over the next ten years India would require investments of the order of one trillion US dollar. The Insurance sector, to some extent, can make possible investments in infrastructure development to continue economic growth of the country.

10.7.1 Indian insurance sector:

According to IRDA report 2011, the number of insurance companies stood at 48 at the end of 2010-11, consisting of 23 life insurers, 24 non-life insurers and a reinsurer. Edelweiss Tokio Life Insurance Company was granted registration in the year 2011-12, leading to total number of insurance companies increasing to 49 as on September 2011.

Table 10.1: Registered Insurers in India

(As on 30th September 2011)

Type of Business	*Public Sector*	*Private Sector*	*Total*
Life Insurance	1	23	24
General Insurance	6	18	24
Re-insurance	1	0	01
Total	8	41	49

Source: IRDA Report 2011.

The first year premium, which is a measure of new business secured, underwritten by the life insurers during 2010-11 was 1,26.381 crore as compared to 1,09,894 crore in 2009-10 registering a lower growth of 15 per cent against 25.84 per cent of 2009-10. In terms of linked and non-linked business during the year 2010-11, 37.38 per cent of the total premium was underwritten in the linked segment while 62.62 per cent of the business was in non-linked segment (43.52 and 56.48 per cent respectively in 2009-10). The total premium underwritten by the life insurance sector in 2010-11 was 2,91,605 crore as against 2,65,447 crore in 2009-10 exhibiting a growth of 9.85 per cent (19.69 per cent in 2009-10).

The non-life insurers underwrote premium of 42,576 crore in 2010-11, as against 34,620 crore in 2009-10 registering a significantly higher growth of 22.98 per cent against growth of 14.06 per cent in the previous year. In the non-life lines of business, the Health segment continued to rise in terms of its share to the total non-life premium. The share of health segment rose further to 23.35 per cent in 2010-11 (21.12 per cent in 2009-10 and 20.06 per cent in 2008-09).

10.7.2 Indian Insurance in the global scenario

According to IRDA report 2011, in life insurance business, India ranked 9th among the 156 countries, for which data are published by Swiss Re. During 2010-11, the estimated life insurance premium in India grew by 4.2 per cent (inflation adjusted). However, during the same period, the global life insurance premium expanded by 3.2 per cent. The share of Indian life insurance sector in global market was 2.69 per cent during 2010, as against 2.45 per cent in 2009.

The non-life insurance sector witnessed significant growth of 8.1 per cent during 2010. Its performance is far better when compared to global non-life premium, which expanded by 2.1 per cent during the same period. The share of Indian non-life insurance premium in global non-life insurance premium increased slightly to 0.58 per cent, thereby improvising its global ranking to 19th in comparison to 26th in last year.

10.8 SUMMARY

- The formal life insurance business started for the first time when insurance company, the Oriental Life Insurance Company, was established in 1818, at Calcutta by Bipin

Behari Dasgupta and others. Life Assurance Company (1823), Madras Equitable Life Assurance Society in 1829 were established. The Indian Life Assurance Companies Act as the first statute in India was enacted in 1912 to regulate the life insurance business. Thereafter, in 1928, the Indian Insurance Companies Act was passed to facilitate the Government of India to gather statistical information about both life and non-life insurance businesses. Finally, the Insurance Act was subsequently reviewed and a complete legislation called the Insurance Act was enacted in 1938.

- Life Insurance Corporation incorporated in 1956 by an Act of Parliament- LIC Act 1956 and the General Insurance Corporation of India was formed in 1972.
- Constitution of Malhotra committee and subsequent enactment of IRDA were the landmark for reformation of insurance sector.
- The Malhotra committee strongly felt that to facilitate improvement in the customer services and increase in coverage of the insurance policies, the industry should be opened up to competition.
- Enactment of the Insurance Amendment Act ended GIC's role as a holding company of its subsidiaries.
- According to IRDA report 2011, in life insurance business, India ranked 9th among the 156 countries. The non-life insurance sector witnessed significant growth of 8.1 per cent during 2010.

EXERCISES

(A) Long answer type questions:

1. Trace the historical background of Life insurance and General insurance in India.
2. Describe the insurance sector reforms in India. Also discuss the recommendations of Malhotra committee.
3. Discuss the constitution of Malhotra Committee and its recommendations. Also explain its impact on IRDA Act.
4. What do you understand by liberalisation? Explain liberalisation of insurance sector in India.

(B) Short answer type questions:

1. Trace the emergence of life insurance in India.
2. Discuss the historical background of general insurance in India.
3. Describe the insurance sector reforms in India.
4. Explain the impact of liberalisation on insurance business in India.
5. Elucidate the objectives of Malhotra committee and its recommendations.

(C) Write a brief note on the following:

1. Historical background of Life insurance.
2. Malhotra Committee.
3. IRDA Bill.
4. Insurance sector reforms.
5. Liberalisation in insurance sector.
6. Present scenario of insurance sector.

(D) Multiple type questions: (Choose any one of the given options)

Que. (1) R.N. Malhotra committee to evaluate the present status of Indian insurance industry had been constituted in:

(a) 1939 (b) 1993
(c) 1957 (d) None of these.

Que. (2) R.N. Malhotra submitted its report in:

(a) 1949 (b) 1994
(c) 1956 (d) None of these.

Que. (3) In its report, the Malhotra committee had recommended for Government stake in the Insurance Companies to be brought down to:

(a) 30% (b) 40%
(c) 50% (d) None of these.

Que. (4) According to Malhotra committee report, private Companies should be allowed to enter in the insurance sector with a minimum paid up capital of:

(a) A 10 billions (b) 10 millions
(c) A 1 billion (d) None of these.

Que. (5) Malhotra Committee has suggested that Postal Life Insurance should be allowed to operate in the:

(a) Urban market (b) Rural market
(c) Both "a" and "b" above (d) None of these.

Que. (6) According to the Malhotra committee, GIC and its subsidiaries are not to hold stake of any company of ....in any company:

(a) more than 50% (b) more than 25%
(c) more than 5% (d) None of these.

[Answer: 1-(b), 2-(b), 3-(c), 4-(c), 5-(a), 6-(c)]

(F) Match the pairs:

(1) Indian Life Assurance Companies Act was enacted as the first statute in	(a) 1907
(2) Indian Insurance Companies Act was enacted to facilitate the government to collect statistical information about both life and non-life insurance businesses in	(b) 1956
(3) LIC incorporated by an Act of Parliament- LIC Act in	(c) 1928
(4) The Indian Mercantile Insurance Ltd. had been set up in	(d) 1912
(5) The General Insurance Council, a wing of the Insurance Association of India, has been established in	(e) 1972
(6) The Insurance Act has been amended to regulate investments and set a minimum solvency margin and the Tariff Advisory Committee has also been set up in	(f) 1968
(7) General Insurance Business (Nationalisation) Act, 1972 has been passed for nationalisation of general insurance business in India in	(g) 1957

[Answer: 1-(d), 2-(c), 3-(b), 4-(a), 5-(g), 6-(f), 7-(e)]

❑ ❑ ❑

CHAPTER 11

LIFE INSURANCE CORPORATION OF INDIA

Life Insurance Corporation (LIC) of India: Brief History of Life Insurance, Establishment, Objectives, Functions, Salient Feature of Life Insurance Corporation and its Deve opment and Evaluation.

11.1 OBJECTIVES OF LEARNING

- *Trace the history of l fe insurance.*
- *Describe the establishment, objectives, functions of Indian Life Insurance Corporation.*
- *Discuss the salient features of Life Insurance Corporation of India; and*
- *Evaluate the development and present status of Indian Life Insurance Corporation.*

11.2 BRIEF HISTORY OF LIFE INSURANCE

Life Insurance in its modern form came to India from England in the year 1818. Oriental Life Insurance Company was started by Europeans in Calcutta. It was the first life insurance company on Indian soil. All the insurance companies established during that period were brought up with the purpose of looking after the needs of European community and Indian natives were not being insured by these companies. However, later with the efforts of eminent people like Babu Muttylal Seal, the foreign life insurance companies started insuring Indian lives. But Indian lives were being treated as sub-standard lives and heavy extra premiums were being charged on them.

Bombay Mutual Life Assurance Society heralded the birth of first Indian life insurance company in the year 1870, and covered Indian lives at normal rates. Starting as Indian enterprise with highly patriotic motives, insurance companies came into existence to carry the message of insurance and social security through insurance to various sectors of society. Bharat Insurance Company (1896) was also one of such companies inspired by nationalism.

The Swadeshi movement of 1905-1907 gave rise to more insurance companies. Insurance companies such as the United India in Madras, National Indian and National Insurance in Calcutta and the Co-operative Assurance at Lahore were established in 1906. In 1907, Hindustan Co-operative Insurance Company took its birth in one of the rooms of the Jorasanko, house of the great poet Rabindranath Tagore, in Calcutta. The Indian Mercantile, General Assurance and Swadeshi Life (later Bombay Life) were some of the companies established during the same period.

Prior to 1912 India had no legislation to regulate insurance business. In the year 1912, the Life Insurance Companies Act, and the Provident Fund Act were passed. The Life Insurance Companies Act, 1912 made it necessary that the premium rate tables and periodical valuations of companies should be certified by an actuary. But the Act discriminated between foreign and Indian companies on many matters, putting the Indian companies at a disadvantage.

The first two decades of the twentieth century saw lot of growth in insurance business. From 44 companies with total business-in-force as ₹ 22.44 crore, it rose to 176 companies with total business-in-force as ₹ 298 crore in 1938. During the mushrooming of insurance companies many financially unsound concerns were also floated which failed miserably.

The Insurance Act 1938 was the first legislation governing not only life insurance but also non-life insurance to provide strict state control over insurance business. The demand for nationalization of life insurance industry was made repeatedly in the past but it gathered momentum in 1944 when a bill to amend the Life Insurance Act 1938 was introduced in the Legislative Assembly. However, it was much later on the 19th of January, 1956, that Life Insurance in India was nationalised. About 154 Indian insurance companies, 16 non-Indian companies and 75 provident fund companies were operating in India at the time of nationalisation.

11.3 ESTABLISHMENT OF LIC

Nationalisation was accomplished in two stages; initially the management of the companies was taken over by the Ordinance, and later, the ownership too by means of a comprehensive bill. The Parliament of India passed the Life Insurance Corporation Act on the 19th of June 1956, and the Life Insurance Corporation of India was created on 1st September, 1956, with the objective of spreading life insurance much more widely and in particular to the rural areas with a view to reach all insurable persons in the country, providing them adequate financial cover at a reasonable cost.

LIC had 5 zonal offices, 33 divisional offices and 212 branch offices, apart from its corporate office in the year 1956. Since life insurance contracts are long-term contracts need was felt in the later years to expand the operations and place a branch office at each district headquarter. Re-organization of LIC took place and large numbers of new branch office were opened. As a result of re-organization, servicing functions were transferred to the branches, and branches were made accounting units. It worked wonders with the performance of the corporation. It may be seen that from about 200.00 crores of new business in 1957 the corporation crossed 1000.00 crores only in the year 1969-70, and it took another 10 years for LIC to cross 2000.00 crore mark of new business. But with re-organization happening in the early eighties, by 1985-86 LIC had already crossed 7000.00 crore sum assured on new policies.

11.4 OBJECTIVE OF LIC

- Spread Life Insurance widely and in particular to the rural areas and to the socially and economically backward classes with a view to reaching all insurable persons in the country and providing them adequate financial cover against death at a reasonable cost.
- Maximize mobilization of people's savings by making insurance-linked savings attractive.

- Keeping in mind welfare of the community as a whole to provide attractive return to the investors.
- Conduct business with care emphasizing the fact that the money belongs to the policyholders.
- Act as trustees of the insured public in their individual and collective capacities.
- Meet the various life insurance needs of the community that would arise in the changing social and economic environment.
- Involve all people working in the Corporation to the best of their capability in furthering the interests of the insured public by providing efficient service.
- Promote amongst all agents and employees of the Corporation a sense of participation, pride and job satisfaction through discharge of their duties with dedication towards achievement of corporate objective.

Mission

- *'Explore and enhance the quality of life of people through financial security by providing products and services of aspired attributes with competitive returns, and by rendering resources for economic development'.*

Vision

- *'A trans-nationally competitive financial conglomerate of significance to societies and pride of India'.*

11.5 FUNCTIONS OF LIC

According to Section 6 under chapter III of Life Insurance Corporation Act, 1956, the functions of LIC are as follows:

(1) Subject to the rules, if any, made by the Central Government in this behalf, it shall be the general duty of the Corporation to carry on life insurance business, whether in or outside India, and the Corporation shall so exercise its powers under this Act as to secure that life insurance business is developed to the best advantage of the community.

(2) Without prejudice to the generality of the provisions contained in sub-section (1) but subject to the other provisions contained in this Act, the Corporation shall have power-

(a) To carry on capital redemption business, annuity certain business or reinsurance business in so far as such reinsurance business appertains to life insurance business.

(b) Subject to the rules, if any, made by the Central Government in this behalf, to invest the funds of the Corporation in such manner as the Corporation may think fit and to take all such steps as may be necessary or expedient for the protection or realization of any investment; including the taking over of and administering and property offered as security for the investment until a suitable opportunity arises for its disposal.

(c) To acquire, hold and dispose of any property for the purpose of its business.

(d) To transfer the whole or any part of the life insurance business carried on outside India to any other person or persons, if in the interest of the Corporation it is expedient so to do.

(e) To advance or lend money upon the security of any movable or immovable property or otherwise.

(f) To borrow or raise any money in such manner and upon such security as the Corporation may think fit.

(g) To carry on either by itself or through any subsidiary any other business in any case where such other business was being carried on by a subsidiary of any insurer whose controlled business has been transferred to and vested in the Corporation under Act.

(h) To carry on any other business which may seem to the Corporation to be capable of being conveniently carried on in connection with its business and calculated directly or indirectly to render profitable the business of the Corporation.

(i) To do all such things as may be incidental or conducive to the proper exercise of any of the powers of the Corporation.

(3) In the discharge of any of its functions the Corporation shall act so far as may be on business principles.

On perusal of above provisions, the functions of Life Insurance Corporation can be summarized as follows:

1. It is the general duty of the Corporation to carry on life insurance business, whether in or outside India to the best advantage of the community.
2. Protection or realization of any investment made by the public.
3. Carry on its business by itself and a subsidiary of any insurer.
4. Carry on other business profitable to the corporation.

11.6 SALIENT FEATURES OF LIFE INSURANCE CORPORATION

Indian Life Insurance Corporation operates following plans for insurance and investment:

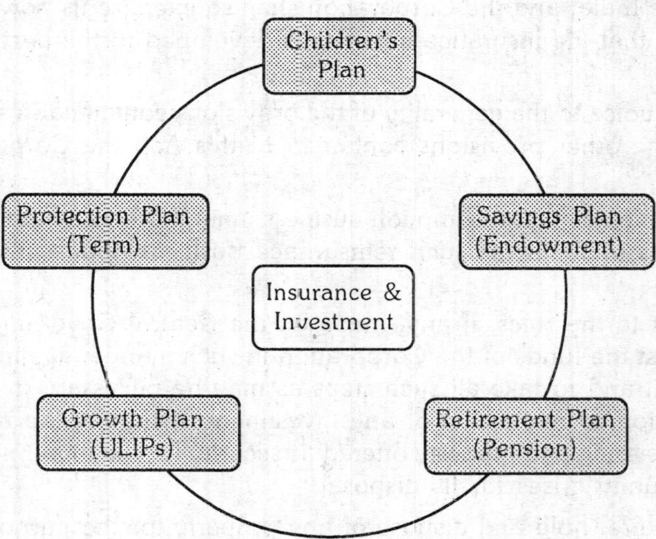

Fig. 11.1: Insurance and Investment

(1) **Growth Plan (ULIP):** Unit linked Insurance Plan is a mixed product of insurance and investment which offers flexibility in making choice in terms of investment proportions. An investor can opt to invest certain percentage in equity whereas balance in debt funds or besides he can invest in 100 per cent equity or 100 per cent debt funds. Therefore Choice depends on investor's risk profile.

(2) **Retirement Plan (Pension):** We know very well that we have to retire in the future and accordingly a unique plan is must for peaceful retirement life. Retirement pension plan of Indian Life Insurance Corporation is an investment portfolio which not only takes care of our retirement but also mid-life career shift. Pension plans are important today as they provide source of regular income after retirement.

(3) **Savings Plan (Endowment):** This is a plan which facilitates savings along with insurance. In these plans a lump sum amounts is paid to the policyholder either on death or on maturity at the end of the term. In these plans, bonus is declared every year which is in addition to the amount assured. However, bonus depends on the profits earned by the company in that particular year. The policy holder can select a certain term as per his convenience while obtaining the policy.

(4) **Children's Plan:** Our liabilities towards our children are unlimited. All parents want to provide them with the best but sometimes that becomes difficult to fulfill our dreams in want of funds. At the present time school education as well as higher education have become very expensive and are supposed to be getting higher with passing years. Besides, future expenditure on children's marriage is also a big burden for parents. These plans provide assured return of amount when such need arises.

(5) **Protection Plan (Term):** All the human beings are concerned about well being of their family after death. The main purpose of these plans is to provide protection to the insured instead of just an investment. Accordingly, it is quite sensible for a person to sacrifice small sums at present for the future financial security of his dependent family members in case of any unforeseen incident.

According to LIC public portal www.licindia.in, some other important features of Indian Life Insurance Corporations is as follows:

Age:

Age is the main basis of calculation of premium under life insurance policies. The following are accepted as evidence of age:

- Certified extract from Municipal or Local Body's records made at the time of birth.
- Certificate of Baptism or Certified Extract from Family Bible, if it contains age or date of birth.
- Certified Extract from School or College records, if age or date of birth is stated therein.
- Certified Extract from Service Register in the case of Government employees and employees of Quasi-Government Institutions, or,
- Passport issued by the Passport Authorities in India.

Payment of premium:

- By cash, local cheque (subject to realization of cheque), Demand Draft payable at Branch Office.

- The DD and cheques or Money Order may be sent by post.
- One can pay his premiums at any of LIC's Branches as 99 per cent of branches are networked.
- Many Banks do prepare the standing instructions to remit the premiums. So a standing instruction can be given by the banker to the policyholder to debit his account for the premium amount and to send it vide a banker's cheque to LIC, on the due dates and months mentioned in policy bond.
- Through Internet: Payment of premiums can be made through Internet through Service Providers viz. HDFC Bank, ICICI Bank, Times of Money, Bill Junction, UTI Bank, Bank of Punjab, Citibank, Corporation Bank, Federal Bank and Bill Desk.
- Premium payment can also be made through ATMs of Corporation Bank and UTI Bank.
- Premium payment can also be made through Electronic Clearing Service (ECS) which has been launched at Mumbai, Hyderabad, Chennai, Kolkata, New Delhi, Kanpur, Bangalore, Vijaywada, Patna, Jaipur, Chandigarh, Trivandrum, Ahmedabad, Pune, Goa and Nagpur, Secunderabad and Visakhapatnam. A policyholder having an account in any Bank which is a Member of the local Clearing House can opt for ECS (Electronic Clearance System) debit to pay premiums. The policyholders wishing to use this system would have to fill up a Mandate Form available at LIC's Branches/DO and get it certified by the Bank. The certified Mandate Forms are to be submitted to LIC's BO/DO.
- Citibank Kiosks at Industrial Assurance Building, Churchgate, New India Building, Santacruz, Jeevan Shikha Building, Borivali are responsible for collection of premiums through cheques.

Days of grace:

- Policyholder should pay the premiums on due dates. However, a grace period of one month but not less than 30 days will be allowed for payment of yearly/half-yearly/quarterly premiums and 15 days for monthly premiums.
- When the days of grace expire on a Sunday or a public holiday, the premium may be paid on the following working day.
- If the premium is not paid within the expiry of the days of grace, the policy lapses.

Revival of lapsed policy:

- If the policy has lapsed, it can be revived during the life time of the life assured, within a period of five years from the date of the first unpaid premium but before the date of maturity subject to certain conditions.
- The Corporation offers three convenient schemes of revival viz., Ordinary Revival, Special Revival and Installment Revival. Policies can also be revived under Loan-cum-Revival and SB-cum-Revival schemes.
- Request for revival may be made to the Branch Office servicing the policy.

Change of address and transfer of policy records:

- The policyholder should immediately intimate the change of his/her address to the Branch Office servicing the policy. The correct address facilitates better service and quicker settlement of claims.

- Policy records can also be transferred from one Branch Office to another for servicing, as requested by the policyholder.

Loss of policy document:

- The Policy Document is an evidence of the contract between the Insurer and the Insured. Hence the policyholder should preserve the Policy Bond till the contract is settled.
- Loss of the Policy Document should be immediately intimated to the Branch Office where it is serviced.

Loans:

- Loans are granted on policies to the extent of 90 per cent of Surrender Value of the policies which are in force and 85 per cent of the Surrender Value in case of policies which are paid-up, inclusive of the cash value of bonus. The rate of interest charged at present is 9 per cent p.a. payable half-yearly.
- Loans are not granted for a period shorter than six months. The conditions and privileges printed on the back of the Policy Bond states whether a particular policy is with or without the loan facility.

Relief to policyholders:

- The Corporation generally allows concessions on payment of premiums, settlement of claims, issue of duplicate policies, etc. when the policyholder is affected by natural calamities such as droughts, cyclones, floods, earthquakes, etc.

Nomination:

- Nomination is a right conferred on the holder of a policy of life assurance on his own life to appoint a person/s to receive policy money in the event of the policy becoming a claim by the assured's death. The Nominee does not get any other benefit except to receive the policy moneys on the death of the life assured. A nomination may be changed or cancelled by the life assured whenever he likes without the consent of the nominee. Ensure nomination exists in the policy for easy settlement of claims.

Assignment:

- Assignment means transfer of rights, title and interest. When an assignment is executed, all rights, title and interest in respect of the property assigned are immediately transferred to the Assignee/s and the Assignee/s becomes the owner/s of the policy subject to any lawful condition made in the assignment.
- Assignment can be either conditional or absolute. On assignment (other than to LIC), nomination automatically stands cancelled. Hence, when such a policy is reassigned, the policyholder will have to make a fresh nomination to avoid delay in settlement of claim.

Survival benefit/maturity claims:

- LIC settles survival benefit/maturity claims on or before the due date.
- Policyholders are intimated well in advance by the Branch Office which services the policy regarding the payment, and the necessary discharge voucher is also sent for execution by the assured. In case the policyholder does not get any intimation from the Branch Office concerned, he/she should contact them, quoting the Policy Number.

- Survival benefit payment up to ₹ 60,000 are settled without insisting for Policy Bond and discharge voucher.

Death claims:

- If the life assured dies during the term of the policy, death claim can be made. The death of the policyholder should be immediately intimated in writing to the Branch Office where the policy is serviced along with the following particulars:
    1. The No./s of the policy/ies.
    2. The name of the policyholder.
    3. Death Certificate issued by concerned Authority.
    4. The date of death.
    5. The cause of death, and
    6. Claimant's relationship with the deceased.
- On receipt of the intimation of death, necessary claim forms are sent by the Branch Office for completion along with instructions regarding the procedure to be followed by the claimant.
- The claims which have arisen after a period of three years are treated as non-early claims and settled within 30 days from the date of receipt of all requirements.
- The claims that have arisen within a period of two years from the date of commencement of the policy, are treated as early claims and investigation is compulsory in such cases.
- The claim is usually payable to the nominee/assignee or the legal heirs, as the case may be. However, if the deceased policyholder has not nominated/assigned the policy or if he/she has not made a suitable provision regarding the policy money by way of a Will, the claim is payable to the holder of a succession certificate or some such evidence of title from a Court of Law.
- The Corporation grants claims concessions under certain plans whereby payment of full sum assured is made, subject to the deduction of unpaid premiums with interest till the date of death and unpaid premiums falling due before the next anniversary of the policy, in the event of the death of the life assured within a period of six months or one year from the date of the first unpaid premium, provided premiums have been paid for at least three years and five years respectively.

Claim Review Committee:

The Corporation settles a large number of death claims every year. Only in case of fraudulent suppression of material information is the liability repudiated. This is to ensure that claims are not paid to fraudulent persons at the cost of honest policyholders. The number of death claims repudiated is, however, very small. Even in these cases, an opportunity is given to the claimant to make a representation for consideration by the Review Committees of the Zonal office and the Central Office. As a result of such review, depending on the merits of each case, appropriate decisions are taken. The Claims Review Committees of the Central and Zonal Offices have among their Members, a retired High Court/District Court Judge. This has helped providing transparency and confidence in operations of LIC and has resulted in greater satisfaction among claimants, policyholders and public.

Insurance Ombudsman:

The Grievance Redressal Machinery has been further expanded with the appointment of Insurance Ombudsman at different centers by the Government of India. At present there are 12 centres operating all over the country. Following type of complaints fall within the purview of the ombudsman:

(a) Any partial or total repudiation of claims by an insurer.

(b) Any dispute in regard to premiums paid if payable in terms of the policy.

(c) Any dispute on the legal construction of the policies in so far as such disputes relate to claims.

(d) Delay in settlement of claims.

(e) Non-issue of any insurance document to customers after receipt of premium.

Policyholder can approach the Insurance Ombudsman for the redressal of their complaints free of cost.

Initiatives in policy servicing areas:

- All 2048 Branches of LIC are fully computerized covering all policy servicing aspects to give prompt computerized services from new policy introduction, acceptance of renewal premium, revivals, loans, etc., to final claims settlement.
- Green Channel facility has been introduced for the speedy completion of proposals.
- Payment of premiums can be made through internet through service providers, viz., HDFC Bank, ICICI Bank, Times of money, Bill Junction, UTI Bank, Bank of Punjab, Citibank, Corporation Bank, Federal Bank and Bill-desk.

Grievance Redressal Machinery:

Machinery for redressal of policyholders grievances exist in all the offices of the Corporation. These are headed by designated Officers who are available at their respective Offices every Monday between 2.30 pm and 4.30 pm. except holidays. Policyholder can approach these officers to get their grievances redressed. The Designated Officers at the various offices of the Corporation are:

(i) At Branch Office — Sr./Branch Manager

(ii) At Divisional Office — Marketing Manager

(iii) At Zonal Office — Regional Manager (Mktg)

(iv) At Central Office — Executive Director (Mktg/IO/CRM)

Citizens' Charter:

- Citizens' Charter was presented to the Nation in November, 1997. In the Charter the benchmarks are prescribed for 30 servicing areas.

11.7 DEVELOPMENT

LIC continues to be the dominant life insurer even in the liberalised scenario of Indian insurance and is moving fast on a new growth tract surpassing its own past records. LIC has issued over one crore policies during the year 2010. It has crossed the milestone of issuing 1,01,32,955 new policies by 15th Oct, 2005, posting a healthy growth rate of 16.67 per cent over the corresponding period of the previous year.

From then to now, LIC has crossed many milestones and has set unprecedented performance records in various aspects of life insurance business. The same motives which inspired LIC's forefathers to bring insurance into existence in this country inspires LIC to take this message of protection to light the lamps of security in as many homes as possible and to help people in providing security to their families.

Some of the important milestones in the life insurance business in India are:

1818: Oriental Life Insurance Company, the first life insurance company on Indian soil started functioning.

1870: Bombay Mutual Life Assurance Society, the first Indian life insurance company started its business.

1912: The Indian Life Assurance Companies Act was enacted as the first statute to regulate the life insurance business.

1928: The Indian Insurance Companies Act enacted to enable the government to collect statistical information about both life and non-life insurance businesses.

1938: Earlier legislation consolidated and amended to by the Insurance Act with the objective of protecting the interests of the insuring public.

1956: 245 Indian and foreign insurers and provident societies were taken over by the central government and then nationalised. LIC was formed by an Act of Parliament, viz. LIC Act, 1956, with a capital contribution of ₹ 5 crore from the Government of India.

Today LIC functions with 2048 fully computerized branch offices, 109 divisional offices, 8 zonal offices, 992 satellite offices and the corporate office. LIC's Wide Area Network covers 109 divisional offices and connects all the branches through a Metro Area Network. LIC has tied up with some Banks and Service providers to offer on-line premium collection facility in selected cities. LIC's ECS and ATM premium payment facility is an addition to customer convenience. Apart from on-line Kiosks and IVRS, Info Centres have been commissioned at Mumbai, Ahmedabad, Bangalore, Chennai, Hyderabad, Kolkata, New Delhi, Pune and many other cities. With a vision of providing easy access to its policyholders, LIC has launched its SATELLITE SAMPARK offices. The satellite offices are smaller, leaner and closer to the customer. The digitalized records of the satellite offices will provide facilities service anywhere and many other conveniences in the future.

11.7.1 Advancement by application of "Information and technology"

Data pertaining to almost 10 crore policies is being held on computers in LIC. LIC has gone in for relevant and appropriate technology over the past few years.

1964 saw the introduction of computers in LIC. Unit Record Machines were introduced in late 1950's were phased out in 1980's and replaced by Microprocessor based computers in Branch and Divisional Offices for back office computerization. Standardisation of hardware and software commenced in 1990's. Standard Computer Packages were developed and implemented for ordinary and Salary Savings Scheme (SSS) policies.

(a) Front end operations: With a view to enhancing customer responsiveness and services, in July 1995, LIC started a drive of On Line Service to Policyholders and Agents through Computer. This on line service enabled policyholders to receive immediate policy status report, prompt acceptance of their premium and get revival quotation, loan quotation on demand. Incorporating change of address can be done online. Quicker completion of proposals and dispatch of policy documents have become a reality. All 2048 branches of LIC across the country has been covered under front-end operations. Thus all 100 divisional offices of LIC have achieved the distinction of 100 per cent branch computerization. New payment related Modules pertaining to both ordinary and salary saving scheme policies have been added to the Front End Package catering to Loan, Claims and Development Officers' Appraisal. All these modules help to reduce time-lag and ensure accuracy.

(b) Metro area network: A Metropolitan Area Network, connecting 74 branches in Mumbai was commissioned in November, 1997, enabling policyholders in Mumbai to pay their Premium or get their status report, surrender value quotation, loan quotation etc. from any branch in the city. The System has been working successfully. More than 10,000 transactions are carried out over this network on any given working day. Such networks have been implemented in other cities also.

(c) Wide area network: All 7 Zonal Offices and all the MAN centres are connected through a Wide Area Network (WAN). This enables a customer to view the policy data and pay premium from any branch of any MAN city. As on November 2005, LIC has 91 centers in India with more than 2035 branches networked under WAN.

(d) Interactive Voice Response Systems (IVRS): IVRS has already been made functional in 59 centers all over the country. This would enable customers to ring up LIC and receive information (e.g. next premium due, status, loan amount, maturity payment due, accumulated Bonus etc.) about their policies on the telephone from the LIC. This information could also be faxed on demand to the customer.

(e) LIC on the Internet: LIC's Internet site is an information bank. LIC has displayed information about LIC and its offices. Efforts are on to upgrade web site of LIC to make it dynamic and interactive. The addresses/e-mail Ids of LIC's zonal offices, zonal training centers, management development center, overseas branches, divisional offices and also all branch offices with a view to speed up the communication process.

(f) Payment of premium and policy status on internet: LIC has given its policyholders a unique facility to pay premiums through the internet absolutely free and also view their policy details on Internet premium payments. There are 11 service providers with whom LIC has signed the agreement to provide this service.

(g) Information kiosks: LIC has set up 150 Interactive Touch screen based Multimedia KIOSKS in prime locations in metros and some major cities for dissemination information to general public on products and services of LIC. These KIOSKS provide policy details and accept premium payments.

(h) Info centres: LIC has also set up 8 call centres, manned by skilled employees to provide us with information about products, policy services, branch addresses and other organizational information.

11.8 EVALUATION

The slogan of LIC 'Yogakshemam Vahamyaham' is derived from 'Bhagavad Gita' which interprets from Sanskrit to English as 'Your welfare is our responsibility' or 'I carry what you require'. This slogan is written in Devanagiri script below the hands holding its authorized logo. From the date of its inception, the Life Insurance Corporation of India has been a largest insurance group and investment company in India. Being state-owned, 100 per cent stock has been acquired by the Government of India. It has assets estimated of ₹ 13.25 trillion (US$ 239.83 billion) in 2010.

Its head quarter is situated in Mumbai which is the financial and commercial capital of India, the Life Insurance Corporation of India currently has 8 zonal offices and 113 divisional offices located in different parts of India, around 3500 servicing offices including 2048 branches, 54 customer zones, 25 metro area service hubs and a number of satellite offices located in different cities and towns of India and has a network of 13,37,064 individual agents, 242 corporate agents, 79 referral agents, 98 brokers and 42 banks (as on 31.3.2011) for soliciting life insurance business from the public. The following concerns are subsidiaries of Life Insurance Corporation:

- LIC Housing Finance.
- LIC Cards Services.
- LIC Nomura Mutual Fund.

Growth of Indian Life Insurance Corporation:

With the entry of private insurers in life insurance business, it is obvious that some proportion of new business will go in the hands of private life insurers. The share of private insurers and LIC in total new business has also been studied.

Table 11.1: Growth of Indian LIC

Year	*Total Premium Earned*				
	LIC		*Private Companies*		
	Total Premium (₹ in crore)	*Market Share (%)*	*Total Premium (₹ in crore)*	*Market Share (%)*	*Total (₹ in Crore)*
2001-01	34890.02	99.98	6.45	0.02	34898.47
2001-02	49821.91	99.46	272.55	0.54	50094.46
2002-03	54628.49	97.99	1119.06	2.01	55747.55
2003-04	63533.43	95.32	3120.33	4.68	66653.75
2004-05	75127.29	90.67	7727.51	9.33	82854.80
2005-06	90792.22	85.75	15083.54	14.25	105875.76
2006-07	127822.84	81.92	28218.95	18.08	156041.79
2009-10	61718.52	71.18	24980.33	28.81	86698.85
2010-11	67135.31	70.67	27864.73	29.33	95000.05

Source: Annual Report of IRDA, 2009-10.

Premium received from policyholders is a major source of income for life insurance industry. According to the above table, it reveals that the continual growth rate of LIC is 37.6 per cent during the period of study. Similarly, private life insurers have also made growth rate of 250.4 per cent during the period of study. On comparative study, it is observed that market share of LIC is gradually reducing from 99.46 per cent to 70.67 per cent during the study period.

From study of facts and figures related to LIC and other private life insurers, it reveals that growth of LIC is more consistent as compared to private life insurers. Undoubtedly, the market share of other private insurers has been increased gradually during last decades but Life Insurance Corporation of India acquiring more than 2/3rd market share is still the biggest insurance group and investment company in India. Moreover, investors have faith on LIC which creates a favorable climate of investment and growth of LIC.

11.9 SUMMARY

- The Parliament of India passed the Life Insurance Corporation Act on the 19th of June 1956, and the Life Insurance Corporation of India was created on 1st September, 1956. It was founded in 1956 with the merger of 243 insurance companies and provident societies.
- The objective of LIC is to spread life insurance much more widely and in particular to the rural areas with a view to reach all insurable persons in the country, providing them adequate financial cover at a reasonable cost.
- The basic function of LIC is (i) carry on life insurance business, whether in or outside India to the best advantage of the community; (ii) protection or realisation of any investment made by the public; (iii) carry on its business by itself and a subsidiary of any insurer and (iv) carry on other business whichever profitable to corporation.
- LIC operates different plans for insurance and investment such as — Growth Plan (ULIP), Retirement Plan (Pension), Savings Plan (Endowment), Children's Plan, Children's Plan.
- Today LIC functions with 2048 fully computerized branch offices, 109 divisional offices, 8 zonal offices, 992 satellite offices and the corporate office.
- Life Insurance Corporation of India with its estimated assets ₹ 13.25 trillion is the largest insurance group and investment company in India. It is a state-owned where Government of India has 100 per cent stake.
- The study shows that growth of LIC was more consistent as compared to private life insurers.

EXERCISES

(A) Long answer type questions:

1. Trace the history of life insurance? Elaborate the establishment of LIC.
2. What are the basic objectives of LIC? Discuss its origin.
3. Describe the functions of Life Insurance Corporation of India?
4. Describe the function of LIC with special reference to Life Insurance Act 1957.
5. Write an essay on the development of LIC and evaluate the present status of LIC.
6. Discuss the impact of privatization on LIC.

(B) Short answer type questions:

1. Write a brief history of LIC.
2. 'LIC is the largest insurance and investment group of company'. Comment.
3. What types of insurance plans are available with LIC? Please explain it.
4. Explain the functions of LIC.
5. What are the objectives of Life Insurance Corporation of India?
6. Describe the function of LIC.
7. Explain the different investment and insurance plans provided by LIC.
8. Describe the development of LIC along with important milestones of it.
9. Discuss the advancement by application of 'Information and technology' in LIC.
10. Evaluate the growth of LIC during last decade.

(C) Write a brief note on the following:

1. Vision and Mission of LIC.
2. Growth ULIP Plans of LIC.
3. Retirement (Pension) of LIC.
4. Savings Plan (Endowment) of LIC.
5. Protection Plan (Term) of LIC.
6. Children's Plan of LIC.
7. Payment of premium in LIC.
8. Revival of lapsed policy.
9. Loans on LIC policy.
10. Survival benefit/maturity claims.
11. Death claims in LIC.
12. Claim Review Committee.
13. Insurance Ombudsman.
14. Grievance Redressal Machinery.
15. Growth of LIC.

(D) Multiple type questions: (Choose any one of the given options)

Que. (1) Oriental Life Insurance Company was started by Europeans in Calcutta. It was the first life insurance company is stated in year ...

(a) 1918 (b) 1818
(c) 1828 (d) None of these.

Que. (2) Bharat Insurance Company (1896) was established in India in the year......:

(a) 1918 (b) 1818
(c) 1896 (d) None of these.

Que. (3) The sentence 'A trans-nationally competitive financial conglomerate of significance to societies and Pride of India.' is related to LIC as:

(a) Vision (b) Mission
(c) Objective (d) None of these.

Que. (4) The Parliament of India passed the Life Insurance Corporation Act 1956:

(a) 19th July 1956 (b) 19th June 1956
(c) 19th June 1965 (d) None of these.

Que. (5) On which date the Life Insurance Corporation of India was created:

(a) 1st September 1956 (b) 1st November 1956
(c) 1st July 1965 (d) None of these.

Que. (6) Which company(ies) was established in 1906:

(a) The United India in Madras (b) National Insurance
(c) Co-operative Assurance (d) All of these.

Que. (7) Which one is a subsidiary concern of LIC:

(a) LIC Housing Finance (b) LIC Cards Services
(c) LIC Nomura Mutual Fund (d) All of these.

[Answer: 1-(b), 2-(c), 3-(a), 4-(b), 5-(a), 6-(d), 7-(d)]

(F) Match the pair:

(1) LIC plan is a mixed product of insurance and investment	(a) Endowment.
(2) This is a plan which facilitates savings along with insurance	(b) ULIP
(3) Oriental Life Insurance Company was established in	(c) 1912
(4) Bombay Mutual Life Assurance Society,	(d) 1818
(5) The Indian Life Assurance Companies Act was enacted as the first statute in	(e) 1870

[Answer: 1-(b), 2-(a), 3-(d), 4-(e), 5-(c)]

References:

1. www.licindia.in
2. En.wikipedia.org

❑ ❑ ❑

CHAPTER 12

INSURANCE POLICIES IN PRACTICE

Main insurance policies in practice: Introduction; Life Insurance Policies in Practice, Salient Features of Some Important Policies of Life Insurance Corporation. General Insurance Policies in Practice and Salient Features of some Important Policies of New Insurance Corporation of India.

12.1 OBJECTIVES OF LEARNING

- *Understand the existing insurance policies are in practice.*
- *Describe the important policies of life insurances offered by Life Insurance Corporation.*
- *Discuss the various general insurance policies are offered by insurers, and*
- *Explain the features of general insurance policies in practice.*

12.2 INTRODUCTION

According to various needs of individuals, a variety of life insurance and non-life or general insurance policies are available in present time. In case of life insurance, whole life insurance policy, term policy, endowment policy, pension plan, child plan, money back policy ULIPs etc., are vital and in existing in practice. On the other hand a variety of personal, social, industrial, commercial, liability insurance policies are available under general insurance.

As it has already been stated in previous chapters that, in addition to public insurers there many private players who are operating their insurance business for life and general insurance. There are hundreds types of policies offered by these insurers and in this chapter it is not possible to include to discuss all the policy and plans in detail. Hence some important insurance policies/plans are discussed here to provide a general idea about insurance policies existing in practice. According to nature, the life and non-life insurance policies are required to be discussed separately.

12.3 LIFE INSURANCE POLICIES IN PRACTICE

(i) Term policy

Term policy provides life insurance coverage for a specified period. It is the cheapest insurance policy as the premium rates are comparatively very low than other policies. The policy does not accumulate cash value. In this policy, if the policyholder survives till the end of policy term, the risk cover lapses and no insurance benefit payment is made to him. However, a fixed sum of money is paid to the designated beneficiaries if the policyholder dies during the policy term. For instance, if an individual buys a term policy of ₹ 5 lakh for a period of 10 years, his family will get a sum of ₹ 5 lakh if he dies within that 10 year period otherwise the premiums paid are not returned back. This plan is most suitable for those who are initially not capable to pay high premium but have need of life cover for a high amount.

Some of the Life Insurance companies offering Term Insurance Plans are:

Life Insurance Companies	*Policies*
ICICI-Prudential	Protect
HDFC Life	Term Assurance Plan
LIC	Anmol Jeevan

(ii) Endowment life policy

Endowment life policy is very popular among life insurance policies as it includes risk cover with financial savings. In this policy the insurer undertakes to policyholder to pay a particular sum of money to him or his successor on his death or on the maturity of the policy, whichever is earlier. Usually, the liability of insurer ends with the maturity of policy. In such policies, the premium is paid by the policyholder till the maturity of the policy or until the death of the assured whichever is first. The premium rate for endowment policy is comparatively higher than the whole life policy as it provides double benefit to the policyholder. In case of death during the term of policy, the beneficiary gets the sum assured. In other condition, policyholder himself gets back the premiums paid by him with other benefits like bonuses.

Some of the noted companies providing Endowment Insurance Plans are:

Life Insurance Companies	*Policies*
Met Life	Met Suvidha
SBI Life	SBI Life Sudarshan
Kotak Life	Endowment Plan

(iii) Unit Linked Insurance Plans (ULIP)

Unit Linked Insurance Plans (ULIP) are well-liked by the investors now-a-days as it provides benefit of life insurance as well as mutual benefits to the policyholders. These are market-linked life insurance products and include life cover and fund accumulation options. In this plan, certain part of premium paid by the policyholder is invested in bonds, equities or debt funds for maximizing returns while the rest is used for risk coverage on life. However, if one applies for this plan then he should be ready for the risks related to stock market. In this plan, buyers have the liberty to choose the best option suitable to him from a variety of fund options depending on their risk appetite. ULIPs may be helpful for getting different long-term financial objectives such as planning for retirement, child's education, marriage etc.

The table below to know more on various ULIP plans offered by different companies:

Life Insurance companies	*Policies*
Max-New York Life Insurance	Life Maker
Bajaj-Allianz	Unit-Gain
TATA-AIG Life Insurance	Invest Assure

(iv) Pension Plans

A good pension plan is must for a respectful and independent retirement life. Pension plan is one kind of insurance policy which helps to provide better pension benefit to policyholder in return of his savings during his earning years. In such plan, the policy holder can pay either lump sum amount or premiums for definite years to get pension in later years.

Here are some of the Pension Plans:

Life Insurance Companies	*Policies*
LIC	Jeevan Nidhi
Aviva Life Insurance	Secure Pension
Kotak Life	Retirement Income Plan

(v) Money-Back Plan

Money-back plan is best for the people who look for both insurance coverage and savings. It gives periodic part payments to the policy holders during the term of policy. In other words, a portion of the assured sum is paid out at regular intervals. Policyholder gets the balance sum assured with bonus (as admissible) if he survives till the end of the term. In this policy, policyholders pay certain premiums for a fixed period and after completion of the period they are benefited with reasonable rate of returns along with the final lump sum return if insured is alive till maturity. However, a fixed lump sum is paid to the designated beneficiary in case of death of insured which occurs during the period of term.

Some of the prominent money-back plans are:

Life Insurance Companies	*Policies*
Aviva Life Insurance	Aviva Money back
LIC	Jeevan Surabhi
SBI	Sanjeevan Supreme

Common Benefits

Approximately all the above mentioned life insurance policies serve as a benefit to face the uncertainties in life courageously. Some of the general benefits of these plans are as follows.

(i) *Death Benefits:* The majority of the Life Insurance Policies provides protection to the family or the nominee in case of unfortunate death of the insured.

(ii) *Maturity Benefits:* At the time of maturity, policy holder gets the guaranteed money back plus other added benefits such as bonus or interest etc. as mentioned in the plan. In some of the plans there is also an option to take out certain money during regular interval.

(iii) *Tax Benefit:* As per Section 80C of the Income Tax Act of India, the amount policyholders pay as a premium are benefit for them in relation to their tax amount, however this is limited upto A 1,00,000 per annum. Additionally, according section 10D of the IT Act, any returns obtained as death benefits or maturity benefits is free from tax liability except the case wherein premium per annum does not exceed 20 per cent of assured sum.

(iv) *Loan Facility:* Some of the Insurance Policies let the policyholders take a loan against their insurance policy.

(v) *Riders:* Riders are some extra benefits along with the life insurance coverage. Some of the insurance policies permit the policy holders to invest part of their premium amount on market shares thereby they get a chance of selection to gain extra bonus.

12.4 IMPORTANT PRODUCT OF LIFE INSURANCE CORPORATIONS

Each individual's insurance needs and requirements are different from that of the others. LIC's Insurance Plans are policies that talk individually and give the most suitable options that can fit requirement.

(I) Bima Account Plans: (1) Bima Account-1; and (2) Bima Account-2.

(II) Endowment Plus: (1) Endowment Plus.

(III) Children Plans:

(1) Jeevan Anurag.
(2) CDA Endowment Vesting at 21.
(3) Komal Jeevan.
(4) CDA Endowment Vesting at 18.
(5) Marriage Endowment.
(6) Jeevan Kishore.
(7) Child Career Plan.
(8) Jeevan Ankur.
(9) Educational Annuity Plan.
(10) Jeevan Chaya.
(11) Child Futute Plan.

(IV) Plans for Handicapped Dependents:

(1) Jeevan Adhar, and
(2) Jeevan Vishwas.

(V) Endowment Assurance Plans:

(1) The Endowment Assurance Plans.
(2) New Janaraksha.
(3) Jeevan Anand.
(4) Jeevan Amrit.
(5) The Endowment Assurance Policy-Limited Payment.
(6) Jeevan Mitra (Triple Cover Endowment Plan).

(7) Jeevan Vaibhav (Single Premium Endowment Assurance Plan).

(8) Jeevan Mitra (Double Cover Endowment Plan).

(VI) Plans for high worth individuals:

(1) Jeevan Shree-I; and

(2) Jeevan Pramukh.

(VII) Money Back Plans:

(1) The Money Back Policy - 20 year.

(2) The Money Back Policy - 15 year.

(3) Jeevan Surabhi - 15 year.

(4) Jeevan Surabhi - 20 year.

(5) Jeevan Surabhi - 25 year.

(6) Bima Bachat.

(VIII) Special Money Back Plan for women: (1) Jeevan Bharati -I.

(IX) Whole Life Plans:

(1) The Whole Life Policy..

(2) The Whole Life Policy - Limited Payment.

(3) The Whole Life Policy - Single Payment

(4) Jeevan Tarang.

(5) Jeevan Anand.

(X) Term Assurance Plans:

(1) Two years Temporary Assurance Policy.

(2) The Convertible Term Assurance Policy.

(3) Anmol Jeevan-I.

(4) Amulya Jeevan-I.

(XI) Joint Life Plan:

(1) Jeevan Saathi.

12.5 HIGHLIGHTS OF SOME POLICIES

For getting a general idea about insurance policies, some of the insurance policies offered by the Life Insurance Corporations are briefly discussed below:

(I) Bima Account-I

LIC's Bima Account-I is a simple non-linked plan under which the insured can be covered without undergoing any medical examination subject to certain conditions. This plan offers policyholders everything they think of an insurance plan like —(1) Simplicity; (2) Liquidity; (3) Guaranteed minimum return; (4) No medical examination; (5) Transparent charges; (6) Risk cover.

Under this plan, the premiums paid by policyholders, after deduction of charges, will be credited to the Policyholder's Account maintained separately for each policyholder. The risk cover will be provided by deduction of mortality charges from the Policyholder's Account. If all due premiums are paid, the amount held in Policyholder's Account will earn an annual interest rate of 6 per cent p.a. which will be guaranteed for whole of the policy term. In addition to this guaranteed return, if all due premiums are paid, policyholder may earn an additional return depending upon the experience under this plan. Policyholder will also have an option to pay additional (Top-up) premiums without any increase in risk cover.

(II) Endowment Plus

This is a unit linked endowment plan which offers investment cum insurance cover during the term of the policy. One can choose the level of insurance cover within the limits, which will depend on the mode and level of premium he agrees to pay. He has a choice of investing his premiums in one of the four types of investment funds available. Premiums paid after deduction of allocation charge will purchase units of the fund type chosen. The Unit Fund is subject to various charges and value of units may increase or decrease, depending on the Net Asset Value (NAV).

(III) Jeevan Anurag

LIC's Jeevan ANURAG is specifically designed to take care of the educational needs of children. The plan can be taken by a parent on his or her own life. Benefits under the plan are payable at pre-specified durations irrespective of whether the Life Assured survives to the end of the policy term or dies during the term of the policy. In addition, this plan also provides for an immediate payment of Basic Sum Assured amount on death of the Life Assured during the term of the policy.

Assured Benefit: Payment of 20 per cent of the Basic Sum Assured at the start of every year during last 3 policy years before maturity. At maturity, 40 per cent of the Basic Sum Assured along with reversionary bonuses declared from time to time on full Sum Assured for the full term and the Terminal bonus, if any shall be payable. For example, if term of the policy is 20 years, 20 per cent of the Sum assured will be payable at the end of the 17th, 18th, 19th year and 40 per cent of the Sum Assured along with the reversionary bonuses and the terminal bonus, if any, at the end of the 20th year.

Death Benefit: Payment of an amount equal to Sum Assured under the basic plan immediately on the death of the life assured.

(IV) Jeevan Adhar

This plan may be offered to a person who has a handicapped dependant satisfying conditions as specified in Section 80DDA of Income Tax Act, 1961. The plan provides life insurance cover throughout the lifetime of the purchaser. The benefits under the plan are for the handicapped dependant which are partly in lump sum and partly in the form of an annuity. The premiums paid under this plan are eligible for Income Tax relief under Section 80DDA of Income Tax Act.

Premiums: Premiums are payable yearly, half-yearly, quarterly, monthly or through salary deductions, as opted by the policy holder, within the selected premium paying terms of 10, 15, 20, 25, 30 or 35 years or till the earlier death. Alternatively, the premiums may be paid in one lump sum (Single Premium).

Guaranteed Additions: The policy provides for the Guaranteed Additions at the rate of A 100 per thousand Sum Assured for each completed policy year. The Guaranteed Additions will accrue upto age 65 of the life assured or till his/her death, if earlier.

Terminal Additions: This is a with-profits plan and participates in the profits of the Corporation's life insurance business. It gets a share of the profits in the form of Terminal Additions. The policy will be entitled for Terminal Additions if at least 10 years premiums have been paid. The Terminal additions would depend on the future experience of the Corporation.

(V) The Endowment Assurance Policy

This policy not only makes provisions for the family of the life assured in the event of his early death but also assures a lump sum at a desired age. The lump sum can be reinvested to provide an annuity during the remainder of his life or in any other way considered suitable at that time. Premiums are usually payable for the selected term of years or until death if it occurs during the term period.

Disability Benefit: In case the policy holder becomes totally and permanently disabled due to an accident before reaching the age of 70 and the policy is in full force, he will not be required to pay further premiums, (the Disability Benefit is available in respect of the first ₹ 20,000 sum assured on any one life) and the policy will continue to be in force.

Accident Benefit: By paying a small extra premium of ₹ 1 per ₹ 1000 sum assured per year he or his family are entitled to the following benefits on death or permanent disability caused by accident. Even students above the age of 18 years can avail of this benefit.

Premium Stoppage: If payment of premiums ceases after atleast THREE years' premiums have been paid, a free paid-up policy for a reduced sum assured will be automatically securec provided the reduced sum assured, exclusive of any attached bonus, is not less than ₹ 250. The reduced sum assured will become payable on the event as stipulated in the policy.

Bonus: Every year the Life Insurance Corporation distributes its surplus among policyholder to 'with profits' polices in the form of bonuses. Substantial bonuses have been declared in the past after each valuation of policy liabilities.

(VI) Jeevan Shree-I (For High worth individuals)

Product summary: This is an Endowment Assurance plan offering the choice of many convenient premium paying terms. It provides financial protection against death throughout the term of plan with the payment of maturity amount on survival to the end of the policy term.

Premiums: Premiums are payable yearly, half-yearly, quarterly or through salary deductions, as opted by policy holder, throughout the premium paying term or till earlier death. Alternatively, premium may be paid in one lump sum (Single premium).

Guaranteed Additions: The policy provides for the Guaranteed Additions at the rate of A 50/- per thousand of sum assured for each completed year for first five years of the policy. The Guaranteed Additions are payable along with the Basic Sum Assured at the time of claim.

Bonuses: The policy participates in the profits of the Corporation's life insurance business from the 6th year onwards. It will get a share of the profits in the form of bonuses. Simple Reversionary Bonuses will be declared per thousand Basic Sum Assured annually at the end of each financial year. Once declared, they will form part of the guaranteed benefits of the plan.

(VII) Money Back with Profit

Unlike ordinary endowment insurance plans where the survival benefits are payable only at the end of the endowment period, this scheme provides for periodic payments of partial survival benefits as follows during the term of the policy, of course so long as the policy holder is alive. In the case of a 20-year Money-Back Policy, 20 per cent of the sum assured becomes payable each after 5, 10, 15 years, and the balance of 40 per cent plus the accrued bonus become payable at the 20th year. For a Money-Back Policy of 25 years, 15 per cent of the sum assured becomes payable each after 5, 10, 15 and 20 years, and the balance 40 per cent plus the accrued bonus become payable at the 25th year.

An important feature of this type of policy is that in the event of death at any time within the policy term, the death claim comprises full sum assured without deducting any of the survival benefit amounts, which have already been paid. Similarly, the bonus is also calculated on the full sum assured.

(VIII) Jeevan Bharathi-I

LIC's Jeevan Bharati-I - is a plan exclusively for women. It is a with profit plan having special features considering the needs of women. The plan also provides for Accident Benefit, Critical Illness Benefit and Congenital Disability Benefit as optional Riders

Encashment of Survival Benefit as and when needed: The policyholder at her option may avail the survival benefit any time on or after its due date. If opted to avail later, increased survival benefit at the rate decided by the corporation from time to time will be payable.

Flexibility to pay premiums in advance: The mode of premium payment is only yearly under this plan. However, policyholder may pay the next yearly premium in advance in installments (maximum upto 3 installments) during the year. If premiums are paid in advance a premium rebate may be allowed as may be decided by the Corporation from time to time.

Option to receive maturity proceeds in the form of an annuity: The policyholder shall have the option to receive the maturity proceeds in the form of annuity. The rate of annuity will be based on the annuity rates prevalent at the time of stipulated Date of Maturity.

Auto Cover: After two years premiums have been paid, whenever premium payment is discontinued, the life cover for full sum assured will continue for 3 years from the due date of first unpaid premium. If death occurs during the Auto Cover period, then death benefit after deducting unpaid premiums, with interest is payable alongwith the vested bonus, if any.

(IX) The Whole Life Policy

This plan is mainly devised to create an estate for the heirs of the policyholder as the plan basically provides for payment of sum assured plus bonuses on the death of the policyholder. However, considering the increased longevity of the Indian population, the Corporation has amended the above provision, thereby providing for payment of sum assured plus bonuses in the form of maturity claim on completion of age 80 years or on expiry of term of 40 years from date of commencement of the policy whichever is later.

The premiums under the policy are payable up to age of 80 years of the policyholder or for a term of 35 years whichever is later. If the payment of premium ceases after 3 years, a paid-up policy for such reduced sum assured will be automatically secured provided the reduced sum assured exclusive of any attached bonus is not less than ₹ 250. Such reduced paid-up policy is not entitled to participate in the bonus declared thereafter but the bonuses already declared on the policy will remain attached, provided the policy is converted into a paid-up policy after the premiums are paid for 5 years.

Suitable For: This policy is suitable for people of all ages who wish to protect their families from financial crises that may occur owing to the policyholder's premature death.

(X) Two Year Temporary Assurance Policy

- The Two Year Temporary Assurance policy is designed for the insuring public who require risk cover for a maximum of two years.
- Under the Two Year Temporary Assurance policy a single premium is required to be paid at the outset of the policy to cover the entire period of term.
- The proposer is required to pay the medical examination fee. The proof of age must also accompany the proposal.
- The policy issued will be only under the 'Without Profits' plan.
- The policy is not entitled to any surrender value.
- No loan will be granted against the Two Year Temporary Assurance policy.

Suitable For: The Two Year Temporary Assurance policy caters to the individuals who specifically require insurance cover against risk for a short period of two years, for instance persons who are required to go on tours for instance for a year or so.

(XI) Jeevan Saathi

This is an Endowment Assurance Plan issued on the lives of husband and wife. The plan provides financial protection against death of both the lives. It pays the maturity amount on survival of one or both the lives to the end of the policy term.

Premiums: Premiums are payable yearly, half-yearly, quarterly, monthly or through salary deductions as opted by policyholder throughout the term of the policy or till the first death of the lives covered, whichever is earlier.

Bonuses: This is a with-profit plan and participates in the profits of the Corporation's life insurance business. It gets a share of the profits in the form of bonuses. Simple Reversionary Bonuses are declared per thousand sum assured annually at the end of each financial year. Such bonuses are to be added till date of maturity or the second death of the lives covered, whichever is earlier. Final (Additional) Bonus may also be payable provided policy has run for certain minimum period.

12.6 NON-LIFE OR GENERAL INSURANCE

Complete list of existing life and non-life insurance police, as mentioned in IRDA report 2010-11, is provided separately in Appendix- 'B' at the end of the book. However, for the purpose of brief study of general insurance policies in practice, list of insurance products offered by the New Assurance Company limited (a public sector insurer) and salient features of some important insurance policies are discussed as follows:

12.6.1 Products of New India Assurance Company Ltd.:

(i) Personal Insurance:

- Pravasi Bharatiya Bima Yojana Policy.
- Mediclaim 2007 Policy.
- Family Floater Mediclaim Policy.

- Janata Mediclaim Policy.
- Senior Citizen Mediclaim Policy.
- Personal Accident Policy.
- Overseas Mediclaim Policy.
- Householder's Policy.
- Motor Policy.
- Money Insurance.
- Rasta Apatti Kavach (Road Safety Insurance).
- Suhana Safar Policy.
- TV/VCR/VCP Insurance.
- Mobile/Cellular Phone Insurance.
- Other Personal Insurance.
- Group Mediclaim Policy.

12.6.2 Salient features of general insurance policies:

Medi-claim 2007 Policy

This insurance is available to persons between the age of 18 years to 60 years. Children between the age of 3 months to 18 years can be covered provided parents are covered simultaneously. The persons beyond 60 years can continue their insurance provided they are insured under Medi-claim policy with our Company without any break. The policy covers hospitalization expenses for the treatment of illness/injury provided hospitalization is more than 24 hours. Pre-hospitalization expenses for 30 days and post hospitalization expenses for 60 days are also payable. Pre-existing conditions like Hypertension, Diabetes, and their complications are covered after two years of continuous insurance on payment of additional premium.

Exclusions

(1) Diseases contracted within 30 days of insurance.

(2) Dental treatment except arising out of accident.

(3) Debility and General Run Down Conditions.

(4) Sexually transmitted diseases and HIV (AIDS).

(5) Circumcision, Cosmetic surgery, Plastic surgery unless required to treat injury or illness.

(6) Vaccination and Inoculation.

(7) Pregnancy and child birth.

(8) War, Act of foreign enemy, ionising radiation and nuclear weapon.

(9) Treatment outside India.

(10) Naturopathy.

(11) Domiciliary Treatment.

(12) Experimental or unproven treatment.

(13) All external equipments such as contact lenses, cochlear implants etc.

(ii) Social Insurance:

- Universal Health Insurance Scheme for BPL families.
- Universal Health Insurance Scheme for APL families.
- Jan Arogya Bima Policy.
- Raj Rajeshwari Mahila Kalyan Yojana.
- Bhagyashree Child Welfare Policy.
- Janata Personal Accident Insurance.
- Student Safety Insurance.
- Ashrya Bima Yojana .
- Rural Insurance.

Ashrya Bima Yojana

Coverage of this policy is available for on-going companies only. The Company should paying statutory dues regularly. Apart from this, the company:

- Should be registered under ID Act or Factories, Shops and Establishment Act, as applicable.
- Should not have been closed for a continuous period over 30 days during last 12 months from the date of proposal.
- Should not have any immediate plan to go for re-engineering and upgradation at the time of proposing the cover.

Eligible Employees

- Employees should be contributing to EPF for at least 12 months at the time of proposing the cover.
- Employees' salary should not be more than ₹ 10000 per month; (salary for this purpose means Basic + D.A.

Claims Payment Procedure

- The sustenance allowance is payable upto 12 months or until employee secures alternate employment whichever is earlier.
- An undertaking from the affected employee and certificate by an authorized official of the employer to be obtained to secure monthly payment from the authorized banker.
- After obtaining claim form and other certificates as mentioned in the claim form and ascertaining that a valid claim is payable under the policy, a banker near to the affected unit shall be designated and authorized to pay the amounts to the affected employees before the 7th of every month.
- Insurance company countersigns the certificate issued by the insured/employer and sends it to the bank for transfer of sustenance allowance to the respective accounts of the employees.

(iii) Commercial Insurance:

- Jewellers Block Policy.
- Bankers Indemnity Policy.

- Shopkeeper's Policy.
- Marine Cargo Policy.
- Plate Glass Insurance.
- Special Contingency Policy.
- Neon Sign Insurance.
- Multi Peril Policy for L.P.G. Dealers.
- Fidelity Guarantee Insurance Policy.
- Marine Hull Policy.
- Aviation Insurance.

Marine Cargo Policy

This policy covers goods, freight and other interests against loss or damage to goods while being transported by rail, road, sea and/or air. Different policies are available depending on the type of coverage required ranging from an all risk cover to a restricted fire risk only cover. This policy is freely assignable and is basically an agreed value policy.

Scope

Transportation of goods can be broadly classified into three categories: (1) Inland Transport; (2) Import and (3) Export. The types of policies issued to cover these transits are:

For Inland Transit

1. **Specific Policy** — For covering a specific single transit.
2. **Open Policy** — For covering transit of regular consignments over the same route. The policy can be taken for an amount equivalent to three months dispatches and premium paid in advance.
3. **Special Declaration Policy** — For covering inland transit of goods wherein the value of goods transported during one year exceeds ₹ 2 crores.
4. **Multi-transit Policy** — For covering multiple transits of the same consignment including intermediate storage and processing. For e.g., covering goods from raw material supplier's warehouse to final distributor's godown of final product.

For Import/Export

1. **Specific Policy** — or covering a specific import/export consignment.
2. **Open cover** — This policy which is issued for a policy period of one year indicates the rates, terms and conditions agreed upon by the insured and insurer to cover the consignments to be imported or exported.
3. **Custom duty cover** — This policy covers loss of custom duty paid in case goods arrive in damaged condition. This policy can be taken even if the overseas transit has been covered by an insurance company abroad, but it has to be taken before the goods arrive in India.

Process of Claim

The following steps should be taken in event of a loss or damage to goods insured:

(i) Take immediate steps to minimize loss.

(ii) Inform nearest office of the insurance company or claim settling agent mentioned on the policy.

(iii) In case of damage to goods whilst on ship or port, arrange for joint ship survey or port survey.

(iv) Lodge monetary claim with carrier within stipulated time period.

(v) Submit duly assigned insurance policy/certificate alongwith the original invoice and other documents required to substantiate the claim.

Fidelity Guarantee Insurance Policy

The policy covers the employer in respect of any direct financial loss which he may suffer as a result of employee's dishonesty.

Scope

The Company agrees to indemnify the insured against a direct financial loss sustained by reason of any act of fraud/dishonesty committed:

1. On or after the date of commencement of this policy.
2. During uninterrupted service with the Insured and discovered during the continuance of this policy or within twelve calendar months of the expiration thereof.
3. In the case of death, dismissal or retirement of the employee with twelve calendar months of such death, dismissal or retirement whichever of these events shall first happen.

Conditions

1. The liability of the company shall not exceed (1) in respect of any employee the sum insured stated against his name or as declared herein; and (2) in respect of all claims under this policy, the total sum insured.
2. If this policy shall continue in force for more than one period of indemnity or if any liability shall exist on the part of the company under this policy and also under any other Policy in respect of fraud or dishonesty of the employee, the liability of the company hereunder shall not be accumulated or increased thereby but the aggregate liability of the company during any number of periods of indemnity and for any number of acts of fraud or dishonesty committed by the employee shall not exceed the sum insured hereunder or the sum insured under any other such policy as aforesaid whichever is greater.
3. The company shall not be liable to pay more than one claim in respect of the action of any one employee.

(iv) Industrial Insurance:

- Fire Policy.
- Burglary Policy.
- Machinery Breakdown Policy.
- Electronics Equipment Policy.
- Consequential Loss Policy.
- Contractors All Risk Policy.
- Marine cum Erection/Storage cum Erection Policy.
- Advanced Loss of Profit/Delay in Start-up Policy.

- Contractor Plant and Machinery Policy.
- Mega Package Policies.

Fire insurance

The Standard Fire and Special Perils Policy covers all properties on land (excluding cost of land), moveable or immoveable, at various locations against named perils. Special types of policies are designed for Stocks, Building, Plant and Machinery keeping in mind the nature of property, proposers' requirements and basis of indemnification. Policy can be extended to cover certain additional perils and expenses at additional premium. Certain perils can be deleted with discount in premium rates. Discount in premium is available for good claims experience for sum insured more than ₹ 50 crores in one location and for installation of fire extinguishing appliances. Concept of 'one risk one rate' for all properties in an Industrial or Manufacturing Complex is applied for administrative convenience of the proposer.

Scope

Building, Plant and Machineries, equipment and accessories, stocks, other miscellaneous contents such as furniture, fixtures and fittings cables, spares, tools and stores household goods etc. are covered under this policy. Besides, some other specific items such as bullion, unset precious stones, curios, work of arts, manuscripts, plans, drawings, securities, obligations or documents, stamps, coins or paper money, cheques, books of accounts, computer system records, explosives.

Perils Covered

(1) Fire, (2) Lightning, (3) Explosion, (4) Aircraft damage, (5) Riot, strike, malicious and terrorism damage, (6) Natural calamities such as Storm, thunderstorm, Flood, Inundation, Hurricane, Cyclone, Typhoon and Tornado, (7) Impact by any Rail/Road vehicle or animal (8) Subsidence/Landslide including rockslide, (9) Bursting and/or overflowing of water tanks, apparatus, (10) Leakage form Automatic Sprinkler Installation, (11) Missile testing Operation, (12) Pollution or contamination resulting from any of the above perils, (13) Any insured peril resulting from pollution and contamination; and (14) Bush Fire.

Perils not covered

(1) War and allied perils, (2) Ionizing radiations and contamination by radioactivity, (3) Pollution or Contamination,

Properties not covered

(i) Items like manuscripts etc. unless specifically declared.

(ii) Cold storage stocks due to change of temperature.

(iii) Loss/damage/destruction of any electrical and/or electronic machine, apparatus, fixture or fitting arising from over running, excessive pressure, short circuiting, arcing, self heating or leakage of electricity, from whatever cause including lightning, and

(iv) Loss/damage/destruction of Boilers, Economizers or other Vessels in which steam is generated machinery or apparatus subject to Centrifugal force, by its own explosion/implosion.

Period of Coverage

1. Fire Policy is an annual policy, generally, renewable each year.
2. Long Term policy (for a minimum period of three years) can be considered for covering 'dwellings' only with suitable discounts in premium.

(v) Liability Insurance:

- Public Liability Policy.
- Products Liability Policy.
- Professional Indemnity Policy.
- Directors and Officers Liability Policy.
- Lift (Third Party) Insurance.
- Employers' Liability Policy.
- Carrier's Liability Insurance.
- Liability Insurance Act Policy.
- Golfers Indemnity Insurance.

Public Liability Policy

This policy covers the amount which the insured becomes legally liable to pay as damages to third parties as a result of accidental death, bodily injury, loss or damage to the property belonging to a third party. One can insure more than one unit situated in different locations under a single policy. The policy offers a benefit of Retroactive period on continuous renewal of policy whereby claims reported in subsequent renewal but pertaining to earlier period after first inception of the policy, also become payable.

Scope

New Assurance Company issues three types of Public Liability Policies:

(1) **Public Liability Non-Industrial Risk:** For offices, hotels, cinema houses, hospitals, schools etc.

(2) **Public Liability Industrial Risk:** For godowns, warehouses and factories.

(3) **Public Liability Insurance Act, 1991:** This is a mandatory policy to be taken by owners, users or transporters of hazardous substance as defined under Environment (Protection) Act, 1986 in excess of the minimum quantity specified under the Act.

The Public Liability Policy can be extended to cover the following risks on payment of an additional premium.

(1) Natural calamities like flood, earthquake etc.

(2) Pollution Risk subject to NOC from Pollution Control Board.

(3) Transportation Risk.

In case of any event likely to give rise to a liability claim as described above, insurance company should be informed immediately. The event giving rise to the claim should have occurred during the period of insurance or retroactive period and the claim first made in writing against the insured during the policy period.

In case of Public Liability Insurance Act 1991 Policy, any award which exceeds assured value limit will be paid by the government through Environment Relief Fund to which the insured has to contribute an amount equivalent to the premium paid under the Public Liability Insurance Act Policy.

The policy will not pay for claims arising out of contractual liability, intentional non-compliance of any statutory provision, loss of goodwill, slander, fines, penalties, libel, false arrest, defamation, mental injury etc.

12.7 SUMMARY

- According to various needs of individuals, a variety of life insurance and non-life or general insurance policies are available in present time.
- In case of life insurance, whole life insurance policy, term policy, endowment policy, pension plan, child plan, Money back policy ULIPs etc., are vital and in existing in practice.
- Term policy provides life insurance coverage for a specified period. Term assurance plan of HDFC, iprotect of ICICI and Anmol Jeevan of LIC are examples of term policy.
- Endowment life policy is very popular among life insurance policies as it includes risk cover with financial savings. Some policies in practice are — Met Life of Met Suvidha, SBI Life Sudarshan of SBI Life, and Endowment plan of Kotak Life in India.
- Unit Linked Insurance Plans (ULIP) are market-linked life insurance products include life cover and fund accumulation options. Life make of Max-New York Life Insurance, Unit-Gain of Bajaj-Allianz; and Invest Assure of TATA-AIG Life insurance policies are in practice in present days.
- Pension Plans is one kind of insurance policy which helps to provide better pension benefit to policyholder in return of his savings while his earning years. Some of the Pension Plans are Jeevan Nidhi of LIC, Secure Pension of Aviva Life Insurance; and Retirement Income Plan of Kotak Life.
- Money-Back Plan is best for both insurance coverage and savings. It gives periodic part payments to the policy holders during the term of policy. Some of the prominent money-back plans are- Aviva Money Back of Aviva Life insurance, Jeevan Surabhi of LIC and Sanjeevan Supreme of SBI Life.
- Death Benefit; Maturity Benefits, Tax Benefits, Loan Facilities and riders are some common benefits which are attached with all most life insurance policies.
- A variety of personal, social, industrial, commercial, liability insurance policies are available under general insurance.

EXERCISES

(A) Long answer type questions:

1. What are the types of life insurance policies in practice? Explaining the types, give the names of different policies offered by various insurers.
2. Discuss the various life insurance policies designed by Life Insurance Corporation of India for different needs of the individuals.
3. Discuss the various general insurance policies designed to cater the different Socio-economic needs of the societies. Discuss with special reference to cater to products of New Assurance Company Ltd.

(B) Short answer type questions:

1. Jeevan Adhar is an insurance policy of LIC, specially designed for protection of physically handicapped. Discuss its salient features.
2. Explain the salient features of 'The Endowment Assurance Policy of LIC'.
3. Jeevan Shree-I is an insurance policy specially designed for high worth individuals. Explain its distinct features.
4. LIC's Jeevan Bharati-I is a plan exclusively for women. Comment.
5. *'Medicalim 2007 Policy'* is an insurance product for health care coverage. Discuss its important features.
6. *'Ashrya Bima Yojana'* provides insurance coverage for on-going companies only. Briefly discuss.
7. Fidelity Guarantee Insurance Policy is a commercial insurance. Highlight its features.
8. Explain the distinct features of Fire insurance offered by the New Assurance Company of India.
9. Highlight the Public Liability Policy of New Insurance Company of India.

(C) Write a brief note on the following:

(i) Term policy.
(ii) Endowment life policy.
(iii) Unit Linked Insurance Plans(ULIP).
(iv) Pension Plans.
(v) Money-Back Plan.
(vi) Common Benefits of Life insurance policies.
(vii) LIC's Bima Account - I.
(viii) Endowment Plus of LIC.
(ix) Jeevan Anurag of LIC.
(x) LIC's The Whole Life Policy.
(xi) Two Year Temporary Assurance Policy.
(xii) Jeevan Saathi.

(D) Multiple type questions: (Choose any one of the given options)

Que (1) Life insurance includes:
(a) whole life insurance policy (b) Term policy
(c) ULIPs (d) All of these.

Que (2) Unit Linked Insurance Plans (ULIP) include:
(a) Life insurance cover (b) Fund accumulation
(c) Both (a) and (b) above (d) None of these.

Que (3) Approximately, all the life insurance policies also provide:
(a) Maturity benefits (b) Tax Benefits
(c) Loan Facilities (d) All of these.

Que (4) Janata Mediclaim Policy, Motor Policy, Suhana Safar Policy, Personal Accident Policy, Rasta Apatti Kavach (Road Safety Insurance) etc. are the insurance products of New India Assurance Company Ltd. included in:
(a) Commercial Insurance (b) Industrial Insurance
(c) Personal Insurance (d) None of these.

Que (5) Which is not treated as a commercial insurance policy:

(a) Jewellers Block Policy (b) Marine Cargo Policy

(c) Aviation Insurance (d) Motor insurance policy.

[Answer: 1-(d), 2-(c), 3-(d), 4-(c), 5-(d)]

(E) Match the pair:

(1) ICICI-Prudential	(a) Term Assurance Plan
(2) HDFC Life	(b) Anmol Jeevan
(3) LIC	(c) iProtect
(4) Met Life	(d) Endowment Plan
(5) Kotak Life	(e) Suvidha
(6) Max-New York Life Insurance	(f) Unit-Gain
(7) Bajaj-Allianz	(g) Invest Assure
(8) TATA-AIG Life Insurance	(h) Life Maker
(9) LIC	(i) Jeevan Surabhi
(10) Aviva Life Insurance	(j) Retirement Income Plan
(11) Kotak Life	(k) Jeevan Nidhi
(12) LIC	(l) Sanjeevan Supreme
(13) SBI life	(m) Secure Pension

[Answer: 1-(c), 2-(a), 3-(b), 4-(e), 5-(d), 6-(h), 7-(f), 8-(g), 9-(k), 10-(m), 11-(j), 12-(i); and 13-(l)]

❐ ❐ ❐

APPENDIX-I

THE GAZETTE OF INDIA: EXTRAORDINARY [Part III — Sec. 4]

INSURANCE REGULATORY AND DEVELOPMENT AUTHORITY, NEW DELHI

NOTIFICATION

New Delhi, the 14th July, 2000

Insurance Regulatory and Development Authority (Licensing of Insurance Agents) Regulations, 2000

F.No.IRDA/Reg./7/2000. —

In exercise of the powers conferred by sub-section (6) of section 42 and clauses (k), (l), (m), (n), (o) and (p) of sub-section (2) of section 114A of the Insurance Act, 1938 (4 of 1938), the Authority, in consultation with the Insurance Advisory Committee, hereby makes the following regulations, namely:

1. Short title and commencement — (1) These regulations may be called Insurance Regulatory and Development Authority (Licensing of Insurance Agents) Regulations, 2000.

(2) They shall come into force on the date of their publication in the Official Gazette.

2. Definitions — In these regulations, unless the context otherwise requires, -

(a) *'Act'* means the Insurance Act, 1938 (4 of 1938);

(b) *'Approved Institution'* means an Institution engaged in education and/or training particularly in the area of insurance sales, service and marketing, approved and notified by the Authority;

(c) *'Authority'* means the Insurance Regulatory and Development Authority established under the provisions of Section 3 of the Insurance Regulatory and Development Authority Act, 1999 (41 of 1999);

(d) *'Composite insurance agent'* means an insurance agent who holds a licence to act as an insurance agent for a life insurer and a general insurer;

(e) *'Corporate Agent'* means a person other than an individual as specified in clause (i);

(f) *"Designated person"* means an officer normally in charge of marketing operations, as specified by an insurer, and authorised by the Authority to issue or renew licences under these regulations;

(g) *'Examination Body'* means an Institution, which conducts pre-recruitment tests for insurance agents and which is duly recognised by the Authority;

(h) *'Licence'* means a certificate of licence to act as an insurance agent issued under these regulations;

(i) *'Person'* means —

(i) an individual;

(ii) a firm; or

(iii) a company formed under the Companies Act, 1956 (1 of 1956), and includes a banking company as defined in clause (4A) of section 2 of the Act;

(j) *'Practical Training'* includes orientation, particularly in the area of insurance sales, service and marketing, through training modules as approved by the Authority;

(k) *'Proposal form'* means an application for purchase of an insurance product which shall be the basis of insurance contract;

(l) *'Prospect'* means a potential purchaser of an insurance product;

(m) *'Recognised Board or Institution'* means such board or institution as may be recognised by any State Government or the Central Government.

(2) All words and expressions used herein and not defined but defined in the Insurance Act, 1938(4 of 1938), or in the Insurance Regulatory and Development Authority Act, 1999 (41 of 1999), shall have the meanings respectively assigned to them in those Acts.

3. Issue or renewal of licence — (1) A person desiring to obtain or renew a licence (hereinafter referred to as 'the applicant') to act as an insurance agent or a composite insurance agent shall proceed as follows:

(a) the applicant shall make an application to a designated person —

(i) in Form IRDA-Agents-VA, if the applicant is an individual;

(ii) in Form IRDA-Agents-VC, if the applicant is a firm or a company:

Provided that the applicant, who desires to be a composite insurance agent, shall make two separate applications.

(b) The fees payable by the applicant to the Authority shall be as specified in Regulation 7.

(2) The designated person may, on receipt of the application alongwith the evidence of payment of fees to the Authority, and on being satisfied that the applicant, —

(i) possesses the qualifications as specified under Regulation 4;

(ii) possesses the practical training as specified under Regulation 5;

(iii) has passed the examination as specified under Regulation 6;

(iv) has furnished the application complete in all respects;

(v) has the requisite knowledge to solicit and procure insurance business; and

(vi) is capable of providing the necessary service to the policyholders;

Grant or renew, as the case may be, a licence in Form IRDA-Agents-VB, alongwith identity card in Form IRDA-Agents-VZ:

Provided that in the case of a corporate agent, the identity card shall be in Form IRDA-Agent-VY.

Provided further that such identity card from one life insurer and such identity card from one general insurer shall be provided to the applicant seeking licence to act as a composite insurance agent.

Provided further that in the case of a firm or a company, all of its partners or directors, as the case may be, shall fulfil the requirements of sub-clauses (i) to (iii).

Provided further a licence issued in accordance with this regulation shall entitle the applicant to act as insurance agent for one life insurer or one general insurer or both, as the case may be.

(3) If the designated person refuses to grant or renew a licence under this regulation, he shall give the reasons therefor to the applicant.

4. Qualifications of the applicant — The applicant shall possess the minimum qualification of a pass in 12th Standard or equivalent examination conducted by any recognised Board/Institution, where the applicant resides in a place with a population of five thousand or more as per the last census, and a pass in 10th Standard or equivalent examination from a recognised Board/ Institution if the applicant resides in any other place.

5. Practical Training — (1) The applicant shall have completed from an approved institution, at least, one hundred hours' practical training in life or general insurance business, as the case may be, which may be spread over three to four weeks, where such applicant is seeking licence for the first time to act as insurance agent.

Provided that the applicant shall have completed from an approved institution, at least, one hundred fifty hours' practical training in life and general insurance business, which may be spread over six to eight weeks, where such applicant is seeking licence for the first time to act as a composite insurance agent.

(2) Where the applicant, referred to under sub-regulation (1), is —

(a) an Associate/Fellow of the Insurance Institute of India, Mumbai;

(b) an Associate/Fellow of the Institute of Chartered Accountants of India, New Delhi;

(c) an Associate/Fellow of the Institute of Costs and Works Accountants of India, Calcutta;

(d) an Associate/Fellow of the Institute of Company Secretaries of India, New Delhi;

(e) an Associate/Fellow of the Actuarial Society of India, Mumbai;

(f) a Master of Business Administration of any Institution/University recognised by any State Government or the Central Government; or

(g) possessing any professional qualification in marketing from any Institution/University recognised by any State Government or the Central Government — he shall have completed, at least, fifty hours practical training from an approved institution.

Provided that such applicant shall have completed from an approved institution, at least, seventy hours practical training in life and general insurance business, where such applicant is seeking licence for the first time to act as a composite insurance agent.

(3) An applicant, who has been granted a licence after the commencement of these regulations, before seeking renewal of licence to act as an insurance agent, shall have completed, at least twenty-five hours practical training in life or general insurance business, as the case may be, from an approved institution.

Provided that such applicant before seeking renewal of licence to act as a composite insurance agent shall have completed from an approved institution, at least, fifty hours practical training in life and general insurance business.

6. Examination — The Applicant shall have passed the pre-recruitment examination in life or general insurance business, or both, as the case may be, conducted by the Insurance Institute of India, Mumbai, or any other examination body.

7. Fees payable — (1) The fees payable to the Authority for issue or renewal of licence to act as insurance agent or a composite insurance agent shall be rupees two hundred and fifty.

(2) The additional fees payable to the Authority, under the circumstances mentioned in sub-section (3) of section 42 of the Act, shall be rupees one hundred.

8. Code of Conduct — (1) Every person holding a licence, shall adhere to the code of conduct specified below:

(i) Every insurance agent shall —

(a) identify himself and the insurance company of whom he is an insurance agent;

(b) disclose his licence to the prospect on demand;

(c) disseminate the requisite information in respect of insurance products offered for sale by his insurer and take into account the needs of the prospect while recommending a specific insurance plan;

(d) disclose the scales of commission in respect of the insurance product offered for sale, if asked by the prospect;

(e) indicate the premium to be charged by the insurer for the insurance product offered for sale;

(f) explain to the prospect the nature of information required in the proposal form by the insurer, and also the importance of disclosure of material information in the purchase of an insurance contract;

(g) bring to the notice of the insurer any adverse habits or income inconsistency of the prospect, in the form of a report (called 'Insurance Agent's Confidential Report') alongwith every proposal submitted to the insurer, and any material fact that may adversely affect the underwriting decision of the insurer as regards acceptance of the proposal, by making all reasonable enquiries about the prospect;

(h) inform promptly the prospect about the acceptance or rejection of the proposal by the insurer;

(i) obtain the requisite documents at the time of filing the proposal form with the insurer; and other documents subsequently asked for by the insurer for completion of the proposal;

(j) render necessary assistance to the policyholders or claimants or beneficiaries in complying with the requirements for settlement of claims by the insurer;

(k) advise every individual policyholder to effect nomination or assignment or change of address or exercise of options, as the case may be, and offer necessary assistance in this behalf, wherever necessary;

(ii) No insurance agent shall —

(a) solicit or procure insurance business without holding a valid licence;

(b) induce the prospect to omit any material information in the proposal form;

(c) induce the prospect to submit wrong information in the proposal form or documents submitted to the insurer for acceptance of the proposal;

(d) behave in a discourteous manner with the prospect;

(e) interfere with any proposal introduced by any other insurance agent;

(f) offer different rates, advantages, terms and conditions other than those offered by his insurer;

(g) demand or receive a share of proceeds from the beneficiary under an insurance contract;

(h) force a policyholder to terminate the existing policy and to effect a new proposal from him within three years from the date of such termination;

(i) have, in case of a corporate agent, a portfolio of insurance business under which the premium is in excess of fifty per cent of total premium procured, in any year, from one person (who is not an individual) or one organisation or one group of organisations;

(j) apply for fresh licence to act as an insurance agent, if his licence was earlier cancelled by the designated person, and a period of five years has not elapsed from the date of such cancellation;

(k) become or remain a director of any insurance company;

(iii) Every insurance agent shall, with a view to conserve the insurance business already procured through him, make every attempt to ensure remittance of the premiums by the policyholders within the stipulated time, by giving notice to the policyholder orally and in writing;

9. Cancellation of licence — The designated person may cancel a licence of an insurance agent, if the insurance agent suffers, at any time during the currency of the licence, from any of the disqualifications mentioned in sub-section (4) of section 42 of the Act, and recover from him the licence and the identity card issued earlier.

10. Issue of duplicate licence — The Authority may issue a duplicate licence replace a licence lost, destroyed, or mutilated on payment a fee of rupees fifty.

11. Non-application to existing insurance agents — Nothing contained in Regulations 4 to 6 of these Regulations shall apply to the existing agents before the commencement of these Regulations

❒ ❒ ❒

APPENDIX-II

According to annual report of IRDA 2010-11, life insurance products of various public and private insurers cleared during the financial year 2010-12 are appended below:

Sl. No.	*Name of the Insurer*	*Name of the Product*	*UIN**
1.	Aegon Religare	Aegon Religare Health Plan	138N021V01
		Aegon Religare Money Back Plus Plan	138N022V01
		Aegon Religare Pension plan	138N029V01
		Aegon Religare Endowment Plan	138N031V01
		Aegon Religare Endowment Advantage Plan	138N032V01
		Aegon Religare Future Protect Plan	138L023V01
		Aegon Religare Future Protect Plus Plan	138L024V01
		Aegon Religare Assure Plan	138L025V01
		Aegon Religare Rising Star Plan	138L026V01
		Aegon Religare Future Protect Premier Plan	138L027V01
		Aegon Religare Assure Plus Plan	138L028V01
		Aegon Religare iMaximise Plan	138L030V01
		Aegon Religare Group Gratuity Plan	138L033V01
2.	Aviva	Aviva Group Life Protect	122N080V01
		Aviva Life Shield Advantage	122N081V01
		Aviva Sampoorna Suraksha Bima Yojana	122N084V01
		Aviva Dhana Varsha	122N088V01
		Aviva Life Shield Platinum	122N089V01
		Aviva Young Scholar Secure	122N092V01
		Aviva I Life	122N093V01
		Aviva Pension Builder	122N094V01
		Aviva Lifesaver Advantage	122L082V01
		Aviva Freedom Life Advantage	122L083V01
		Aviva Young Scholar Advantage	122L085V01
		Aviva Life Bond Advantage	122L086V01
		Aviva Life Sachin Extra Cover Advantage	122L087V01
		Aviva Group Gratuity Advantage	122L090V01
		Aviva New Group Leave Encashment Plan	122L091V01
		Aviva Child Education Rider	122B015V01
		Aviva Health Guard Rider	122B016V01
		Aviva Term Plus Rider	122B017V01

* UIN: Unique Identification Number.

3.	Bajaj Allianz	Bajaj Allianz Group Credit Protection Plus	116N094V01
		Bajaj Allianz Super Cash Gain Insurance Plan	116N102V01
		Bajaj Allianz Cash Rich Insurance Plan	116N103V01
		Bajaj Allianz Wealth Insurance Plan	116L095V01
		Bajaj Allianz Max Advantage Insurance Plan	116L096V01
		Bajaj Allianz Shield Insurance Plan	116L097V01
		Bajaj Allianz Assured Protection Insurance Plan	116L098V01
		Bajaj Allianz Life iGain III	116L099V01
		Bajaj Allianz Smart Insurance Plan III	116L100V01
		Bajaj Allianz Money Secure Insurance Plan	116L101V01
		Bajaj Allianz Group Employee Benefit Plan	116L104V01
		Bajaj Allianz Group Wealth Insurance Plan	116L105V01
		Bajaj Allianz Group Terminal Illness Rider	116B025V01
4.	Bharti AXA	Bharti AXA Life Group Term Cover	130N034V01
		Bharti AXA Life Life Protect Plus	130N037V01
		Bharti AXA Life Family Income Secure	130N038V01
		Bharti AXA Life Aajeevan Anand	130N039V01
		Bharti AXA Life Jan Suraksha	130N040V01
		Bharti AXA Life Premier Home Shield	130N042V01
		Bharti AXA Future Champs	130N043V01
		Bharti AXA Wonder Years Retirement Plan	130N044V01
		Bharti AXA Life Bright Star Edge	130L035V01
		Bharti AXA Life True Wealth	130L036V01
		Bharti AXA Life Wealth One	130L041V01
		Bharti AXA Life Premium Waiver Rider	130C005V01
		Bharti AXA Group Accidental Death Benefit Rider	130B006V01
5	Birla Sun Life	BSLI Bachat (Endowment) Plan	109N056V01
		BSLI Bachat (Money Back) Plan	109N057V01
		BSLI Bachat (Child) Plan	109N058V01
		BSLI Hospital Cash Plan	109N059V01
		BSLI Rainbow Plan	109N063V01
		BSLI Vision	109N068V01
		BSLI Group Capital Assured Traditional Plan	109N070V01
		BSLI Dream Endowment Plan	109L060V01
		BSLI Classic Endowment Plan	109L061V01
		BSLI Platinum Advantage Plan	109L062V01
		BSLI Dream Life Plan	109L064V01
		BSLI Dream Child Plan	109L065V01
		BSLI Classic Child Plan	109L066V01
		BSLI Classic Life Plan	109L067V01
		BSLI Foresight Plan	109L069V01
		BSLI Surgical Care Rider	109C015V01
		BSLI Hospital Care Rider	109C016V01
		BSLI Waiver of Premium Rider	109C017V01

		BSLI Accident Death and Disability Rider	109C018V01
		BSLI Critical Illness Rider	109C019V01
		BSLI Group Critical Illness Premier Rider	109B020V01
		BSLI Group Accelerated Critical Illness Premier Rider	109B021V01
		BSLI Group Accelerated Terminal Illness Rider	109B022V01
		BSLI Accidental Death Benefit Rider	109B014V01
6.	Canara HSBC OBC	Canara HSBC OBC Life Group Traditional Plan	136N014V01
		Canara HSBC OBC Life Insurance Secure Smart Plan	136N017V01
		Canara HSBC OBC Life Insurance Dream Smart Plan	136L015V01
		Canara HSBC OBC Life Insurance Grow Smart Plan	136L016V01
		Canara HSBC OBC Future Smart Plan	136L018V01
		Canara HSBC OBC Insure Smart Plan	136L019V01
7.	DLF Pramerica	DLF Pramerica Dhan Suraksha	140N020V01
		DLF Pramerica Assure Money +	140N021V01
		DLF Pramerica Tatkal Suraksha Gold	140N024V01
		DLF Pramerica Roz Bima	140N026V01
		DLF Pramerica Future Idols Gold	140N027V01
		DLF Pramerica Rakshak	140N028V01
		DLF Pramerica Wealth + Premier	140L022V01
		DLF Pramerica Ezee Wealth+	140L023V01
		DLF Pramerica Wealth+ Ace	140L025V01
8.	Future Generali	Future Generali Dream Guarantee Plan	133N029V01
		Future Generali Care Plus	133N030V01
		Future Generali Smart Life	133N031V01
		Future Generali NAV Insure Plan	133L032V01
		Future Generali Select Insurance Plan	133L033V01
		Future Generali Nivesh Preferred Plan	133L034V01
		Future Generali Pramukh Nivesh	133L035V01
		Future Generali Wealth Protect Plan	133L036V01
		Future Generali Unit Linked Life Guardian Rider	133A018V02
		Future Generali Saral Term Benefit Rider	133B020V01
9.	HDFC Standard	HDFC SL Group Savings Plan	101N062V01
		HDFC SL New Money Back Plan	101N063V01
		HDFC SL Sarvgrameen Bachat Yojana	101N069V01
		HDFC SL Group Conventional Plan	101N070V01
		HDFC SL Endowment Gain	101N071V01
		HDFC SL Group Traditional Plan	101N075V01
		HDFC SL Classic Assure Insurance Plan	101N076V01
		HDFC Life Classic Pension Insurance Plan	101N077V01
		HDFC Life Sampoorn Samridhi Insurance Plan	101N078V01
		HDFC SL Crest	101L064V01
		HDFC SL Youngstar Super II	101L065V01
		HDFC SL ProGrowth Super II	101L066V01

		HDFC SL ProGrowth Maximiser	101L067V01
		HDFC SL Young Star Super Premium	101L068V01
		HDFC SL ProGrowth Flexi	101L072V01
		HDFC SL Group Unit Linked Option I	101L073V01
		HDFC SL Pension Maximus	101L074V01
10.	ICICI Prudential	ICICI Pru Hospital Care II	105N108V01
		ICICI Pru iProtect	105N110V01
		ICICI Pru Guaranteed Savings Insurance Plan	105N114V01
		ICICI pru Whole Life	105N116V01
		ICICI Pru Future Secure	105N117V01
		ICICI Pru Group Term Plan	105N119V01
		ICICI Pru LifeLink Wealth SP	105L111V01
		ICICI Pru Life Time Premier	105L112V01
		ICICI Life Link Pension SP	105L113V01
		ICICI Pinnacle II	105L115V01
		ICICI Pru Life Stage Wealth II	105L118V01
		ICICI Pru Smart Kid Premier	105L120V01
		ICICI Pru Pinnacle Super	105L121V01
		ICICI Pru Waiver of Premium on Critical Illness Rider	105C024V01
11.	IDBI Federal	IDBI Federal Loansurance Group Life Plan	135N013V01
		IDBI Federal Termsurance Group Life Plan	135N015V01
		IDBI Federal Bondsurance Advantage Insurance Plan	135N016V01
		IDBI Federal Retiresurance Guaranteed Pension Plan	135N017V01
		IDBI Federal Term Assurance Premier Insurance Plan	135N019V01
		IDBI Federal Termsurance Seniors Insurance Plan	135N021V01
		IDBI Federal Wealthsurance Milestone Plan	135L014V01
		IDBI Federal Wealthsurance Premier Insurance Plan	135L018V01
		IDBI Federal Retiresurance Milestone Pension Plan	135L020V01
12.	IndiaFirst	India First Life Plan	143N007V01
		India First Simple Life Plan	143N008V01
		India First Anytime Plan	143N009V01
		India First Secure Save Plan	143N012V01
		India First Smart Save Plan	143L010V01
		India First Young India Plan	143L011V01
		India First Employee Benefit Plan	143L013V01
		India First Term Rider	143B001V01
13.	ING Vysya	ING Immediate Annuity with return of purchase price	114N050V01
		ING Aashirvad	114N051V01
		ING Aashirvad	114N051V02
		ING Creating Star Guaranteed Future	114N052V01
		ING Ace Life	114N058V01
		ING Ace Pension	114N059V01
		ING Uttam Jeevan - SP	114L053V01

		ING Uttam Jeevan	114L054V01
		ING Prospering Life	114L055V01
		ING Market Shield	114L056V01
		ING Prospering Life SP	114L057V01
14.	Kotak Mahindra	OM Kotak e-Preferred Term Plan	107N060V01
		Kotak e-Term	107N061V01
		Kotak Fixed Return plan	107N068V01
		Kotak Assured Income	107N069V01
		Kotak Saral Suraksha	107N070V01
		Kotak Secure Invest Insurance	107L062V01
		Kotak Wealth Insurance Plan	107L063V01
		Kotak Ace Investment Plan	107L064V01
		Kotak Single Invest Advantage	107L065V01
		Kotak Headstart Child Assure	107L066V01
		Kotak Platinum	107L067V01
15.	LIC LIC's Group	Flexible Income Plan	512N262V01
		LIC's Bima Account -I	512N263V01
		LIC's Bima Account -II	512N264V01
		LIC's Pension Plus	512L260V01
		LIC's Endowment Plus	512L261V01
		LIC's Samridhi Plus	512L265V01
16.	Max New York	Max New York Life Platinum Protect	104N060V01
		Max New York Life Smart Bond	104N063V01
		Max New York Life College Plan	104N065V01
		Max New York Shubh Invest	104L061V01
		Max New York Shiksha Plus II	104L062V01
		Max New York Life Flexi Fortune	104L064V01
17.	Met Life	Met Grameen Ashray	117N063V01
		Met Monthly Income Plan - 7 pay	117N064V01
		Met Protect	117N065V01
		Met Group Savings Plan	117N067V01
		Met Smart Platinum	117L066V01
		Met Smart One	117L068V01
		Met Easy Super	117L069V01
18.	Reliance	Reliance Life Care for You Plan	121N078V01
		Reliance Money Multiplier Plan	121N079V01
		Reliance Life Classic Plan	121L076V01
		Reliance Life Highest NAV Advantage Plan	121L077V01
		Reliance Life Insurance Classic Plan – Limited Premium	121L080V01
		Reliance Life Insurance Group Gratuity Plus Plan	121L081V01
		Reliance Life Insurance Five Pay Plan	121L082V01

19.	Sahara	Sahara Shikhar Jeevan Bima	127L021V01
		Sahara Utkarsh Jeevan Bima	127L022V01
		Sahara Sugam Jeevan Bima	127L023V01
		Sahara Sanchit Jeevan Bima	127L024V01
20.	SBI Life	SBI Life Hospital Cash	111N065V01
		SBI Life - Saral Shield	111N066V01
		SBI Life - Smart Shield	111N067V01
		SBI Life - Saral Life	111N071V01
		SBI Life - Gaurav Jeevan	111N076V01
		SBI Life - RiNn Raksha	111N078V01
		SBI Life - Smart Performer	111L068V01
		SBI Life - Unit Plus Super	111L069V01
		SBI Life - Saral maha Anand	111L070V01
		SBI Life - Smart Elite	111L072V01
		SBI Life - Smart Scholar	111L073V01
		SBI Life - Smart Horizon	111L074V01
		SBI Life - Smart Pension	111L075V01
		SBI Life - Smart Wealth Assure	111L077V01
21.	Shriram Life	Shriram Credit Guard	128N033V01
		Shriram Ujjwal Life	128L034V01
		Shriram Ujjwal Life (SP)	128L035V01
		Shriram Life Wealth Plus	128L036V01
		Shriram Group Gratuity Protector	128L037V01
		Shriram Extra Cover Rider	128B009V01
		Shriram Critical Illness Cover Rider	128C010V01
22.	Star Union Dai-ichi	SUD Life Defined Benefit Endowment Plan	142N023V01
		SUD Life Defined Growth Endowment Insurance Plan	142N027V01
		SUD Life Dhan Suraksha 3	142L024V01
		SUD Life Dhan Suraksha Premium 3	142L025V01
		SUD Life Prabhat Tara 3	142L026V01
		SUD Life Dhan Suraksha Express	142L028V01
23.	TATA AIG	Tata AIG Life Group Total Suraksha	110N088V01
		Tata AIG Maha Life Guarantee	110N089V01
		Tata AIG Life Maha Guarantee Flexi	110N093V01
		Tata AIG Life Invest Assure Flexi Supreme	110L090V01
		Tata AIG Life Lakshya Supreme	110L091V01
		Tata AIG Life Invest Assure Plus Supreme	110L092V01
		Tata AIG Life United Ujwal Bhavishya Supreme	110L094V01
		Tata AIG Life Invest Apex Supreme	110L095V01
		Tata AIG Life Insurance Swarna Pratigya	110L096V01
		Tata AIG Life Invest Assure Gold Supreme	110L097V01
		Tata AIG Life Group Disability Rider	110B022V01

According to annual report of IRDA 2010-11, general insurance products of various public and private insurers cleared during the financial year 2010-12 are as follows:

Sl. No.	*Name of the Insurer*	*Name of the Product*
1.	Agriculture Insurance Company	Cardamom plant & yield insurance
2.	Apollo Munich Health	Maxima Insurance Optima Plus Easy Health Insurance Easy Health Group Insurance
3.	Bajaj Allianz	Commercial Package SIB Health Assist Mausam Hifazat
4.	Cholamandalam	Weather Insurance (Index) Chola MS Individual Healthline Insurance Domestic Travel Insurance Chola MS Critical Healthline Insurance
5.	Future Generali	Future Event Insurance Future Cine Suraksha Health Suraksha — Revision Travel Suraksha — Standard Plan — Additional Benefits
6.	HDFC Ergo	Card Sure Package Policy Weather Insurance Event Cancellation Policy Crop Insurance Policy Information Communication Technology Errors & Ommission (Revised International wordings) Janata Personal Accident (JPA) Gramin Arogya Nidhi Marine Cargo Open Policy (Revision of Marine Institute of Cargo Clauses)
7.	ICICI Lombard	Crop Insurance Crop Insurance Policy (Revision/add-on covers)
8.	IFFCO Tokio	Janta Bima Yojana Policy (MI Product) Fasal Bima Yojna
9.	L&T General	Industrial All Risks Policy Advance Loss of Profits Insurance Policy Machinery Loss of Profits insurance policy My:asset Two Wheeler Insurance My:asset Private Motor Insurance My:asset Commercial & Miscellaneous Vehicle Insurance

		Motor Liability Only Policy Burglary and Housebreaking Insurance My Jeevika Standard Fire & Special Perils Policy Contractors All Risk Policy Erections All Risk Policy Contractors Plant & Machinery Policy Machinery Breakdown Policy Electronic Equipments Insurance Policy Workmens' Compensation Insurance Public Liability (Act) Insurance Fire Loss of Profits Insurance Policy All Risks Insurance Neon Sign Insurance Money Insurance Baggage Insurance Plate Glass Insurance Money Insurance Commercial General Liability Insurance Combined Public & Product Liability Insurance My:Jeevika Personal Accident Micro Insurance Marine Cargo Insurance
10.	Max Bupa Health	International Medical Emergency PoLICy Swasthya Pratham Micro Insurance Product HeartBeat Employee First Health Insurance Plan
11.	National Insurance	Package Insurance (Private Cars & Two Wheelers)
12.	New India Assurance	Jan Suraksha Laghu Bima
13.	Raheja QBE	Multimedia Professional Indemnity Professional Indemnity (Medical Malpractice) Transporters Liability Policy D&O Liability Insurance Excess Policy D&O and Company Reimbursement Insurance
14.	Royal Sundaram	Motor Add-ons for Commercial Vehicles Health Shield - Gold Health Shield - Normal Health Shield - Premier Family Health Protector Top up insurance - Health XS and Super Health XS Insurance Critical Illness Lumpsum Insurance Family Good Health Family Health Floater

15.	SBI General	Long Term Insurance (Fire) Burglary Insurance Motor Add-ons (PC/TW/CV) Plate Glass Insurance Policy Business Package Motor Add-ons (2) Re-filed Advance Loss of Profits Insurance Policy Money Insurance (revised) Machinery Breakdown Policy Contractors Plant & Machinery Policy Boiler & Pressure Plant Policy Erection All Risks Policy Machinery Loss of Profits Policy Aviation Hull Package Industrial All Risks Policy Money Insurance Policy Loss of Profit Group Health Insurance Marine Cargo Insurance
16.	Star Health and Allied	Star Shri Individual Care Insurance Star Shri Family Care Insurance Star Unique Health Insurance Star Wedding Gift Insurance Senior Citizen Red Carpet Insurance Health All Care Insurance Policy
17.	Shriram General	Industrial All Risk Policy Neon sign/Glow sign/Hoardings Insurance Policy Agriculture Pumpset Insurance Policy Plate Glass Insurance Policy Burglary Insurance (Revision) Baggage Insurance All Risk Insurance Jewellers Block Insurance Policy Business Protector Commercial General Liability Insurance Janata Personal Accident (Group) Sales Turnover Policy
18.	TATA AIG General	Pashu Suraksha Bima Add-ons for Two Wheeler Package Policy Rashtriya Swasthya Bima Yojana Wellsurance Marine Cargo Insurance

19.	United India	Nil Depreciation (Add-on) Workmen Medicare Policy Individual Health Insurance — Senior Citizen Individual Health Insurance — Platinum Individual Health Insurance — Gold IOB Health Care Plus
20.	Universal Sompo	Motor Add-ons (8) Advance Loss of Profits Policy Fine Arts Insurance Policy Individual Health Insurance — Sampoorna Swasthya Kavach

❑ ❑ ❑

APPENDIX-III

GLOSSARY OF INSURANCE

Accidental Death Benefit – In a life insurance policy, benefit in addition to the death benefit paid to the beneficiary, should death occur due to an accident. There can be certain exclusions as well as time and age limits.

Actual Cash Value – Cost of replacing damaged or destroyed property with comparable new property, minus depreciation and obsolescence. For example, a 10-year-old sofa will not be replaced at current full value because of a decade of depreciation.

Actuary – A specialist in the mathematics of insurance who calculates rates, reserves, dividends and other statistics. (Americanism: In most other countries the individual is known as 'mathematician.')

Adjuster – A representative of the insurer who seeks to determine the extent of the insurer's liability for loss when a claim is submitted.

Admitted Assets – Assets permitted by state law to be included in an insurance company's annual statement. These assets are an important factor when regulators measure insurance company solvency. They include mortgages, stocks, bonds and real estate.

Agent – A licensed person or organization authorized to sell insurance by or on behalf of an insurance company.

Aggregate Limit – Usually refers to liability insurance and indicates the amount of coverage that the insured has under the contract for a specific period of time, usually the contract period, no matter how many separate accidents might occur.

Annuity – An agreement by an insurer to make periodic payments that continue during the survival of the annuitant(s) or for a specified period.

Assets – Assets refer to 'all the available properties of every kind or possession of an insurance company that might be used to pay its debts'. There are three classifications of assets: invested assets, all other assets, and total admitted assets. Invested assets refer to things such as bonds, stocks, cash and income-producing real estate. All other assets refer to non income producing possessions such as the building the company occupies, office furniture, and debts owed, usually in the form of deferred and unpaid premiums. Total admitted assets refer to everything a company owns. All other plus invested assets equals total admitted assets. By law, some states don't permit insurance companies to claim certain goods and possessions, such as deferred and unpaid premiums, in the all other assets category, declaring them 'non admissible'.

At and From Clause – The subject matter is covered under this clause while it is lying at the port of departure and until it reaches the port of destination. If the policy comprises of the word 'from' only instead of 'at and from', the risk is covered only from the time of departure of the ship. It is used in voyage policies.

Attained Age – Insured's age at a particular time. For example, many term life insurance policies allow an insured to convert to permanent insurance without a physical examination at the insured's then attained age. Upon conversion, the premium usually rises substantially to reflect the insured's age and diminished life expectancy.

Automobile Liability Insurance – Coverage if an insured is legally liable for bodily injury or property damage caused by an automobile.

Barratry Clause – Losses suffered by the ship owner or the cargo owner due to willful conduct of the master or crew of the ship is covered under this clause.

Benefit Period – In health insurance, the number of days for which benefits are paid to the named insured and his or her dependents. For example, the number of days that benefits are calculated for a calendar year consist of the days beginning on Jan. 1 and ending on Dec. 31 of each year.

Broker – Insurance salesperson that searches the marketplace in the interest of clients, not insurance companies.

Broker-Agent – Independent insurance salesperson who represents particular insurers but also might function as a broker by searching the entire insurance market to place an applicant's coverage to maximize protection and minimize cost. This person is licensed as an agent and a broker.

Burglary Insurance – Coverage against loss as a result of forced entry into premises.

Capital – Equity of shareholders of a stock insurance company. The company's capital and surplus are measured by the difference between its assets minus its liabilities. This value protects the interests of the company's policyowners in the event it develops financial problems; the policyowners' benefits are thus protected by the insurance company's capital. Shareholders' interest is second to that of policyowners.

Captive Agent – Representative of a single insurer or fleet of insurers who is obliged to submit business only to that company, or at the very minimum, give that company first refusal rights on a sale. In exchange, that insurer usually provides its captive agents with an allowance for office expenses as well as an extensive list of employee benefits such as pensions, life insurance, health insurance, and credit unions.

Career Agent – Represents only one company and sells only its policies. This agent is paid on a commission basis in much the same manner as the independent agent.

Casualty Insurance – That type of insurance that is primarily concerned with losses caused by injuries to persons and legal liability imposed upon the insured for such injury or for damage to property of others. It also includes such diverse forms as plate glass, insurance against crime, such as robbery, burglary and forgery, boiler and machinery insurance and Aviation insurance. Many casualty companies also write surety business.

Casualty – Liability or loss resulting from an accident.

Claim – Notice to an insurer that under the terms of a policy, a loss maybe covered.

Claim – A demand made by the insured, or the insured's beneficiary, for payment of the benefits as provided by the policy.

Coinsurance – In property insurance, requires the policyholder to carry insurance equal to a specified percentage of the value of property to receive full payment on a loss. For health insurance, it is a percentage of each claim above the deductible paid by the policyholder. For a 20 per cent health insurance coinsurance clause, the policyholder pays for the deductible plus 20 per cent of his covered losses. After paying 80 per cent of losses up to a specified ceiling, the insurer starts paying 100 per cent of losses.

Collision – When the ship collides with another ship or with other objects, causing damage.

Collision Insurance – Covers physical damage to the insured's automobile (other than that covered under comprehensive insurance) resulting from contact with another inanimate object.

Commission – Fee paid to an agent or insurance salesperson as a percentage of the policy premium. The percentage varies widely depending on coverage, the insurer and the marketing methods.

Comprehensive Insurance – Auto insurance coverage providing protection in the event of physical damage (other than collision) or theft of the insured car. For example, fire damage or a cracked windshield would be covered under the comprehensive section.

Concurrent Periods – In hospital income protection, when a patient is confined to a hospital due to more than one injury and/or illness at the same time, benefits are paid as if the total disability resulted from only one cause.

Continuation Clause – This clause authorizes the vessel to continue and complete her voyage even if the time of the policy has expired. This clause is used in a time policy. The insured has to give prior notice for this and deposits a monthly prorate premium.

Contract of Marine Insurance – means a contract of marine insurance as defined by section3 of Marine Act.

Convertible – Term life insurance coverage that can be converted into permanent insurance regardless of an insured's physical condition and without a medical examination. The individual cannot be denied coverage or charged an additional premium for any health problems.

Coverage Area – The geographic region covered by travel insurance.

Coverage – The scope of protection provided under an insurance policy. In property insurance, coverage lists perils insured against, properties covered, locations covered, individuals insured, and the limits of indemnification. In life insurance, living and death benefits are listed.

Death Benefit – The limit of insurance or the amount of benefit that will be paid in the event of the death of a covered person.

Deductible – Amount of loss that the insured pays before the insurance kicks in.

Direct Premiums Written – The aggregate amount of recorded originated premiums, other than reinsurance, written during the year, whether collected or not, at the close of the year, plus retrospective audit premium collections, after deducting all return premiums.

Direct Writer – An insurer whose distribution mechanism is either the direct selling system or the exclusive agency system.

Dividend – The return of part of the policy's premium for a policy issued on a participating basis by either a mutual or stock insurer. A portion of the surplus paid to the stockholders of a corporation.

Employers Liability Insurance – Coverage against common law liability of an employer for accidents to employees, as distinguished from liability imposed by a workers' compensation law.

Encumbrance – A claim on property, such as a mortgage, a lien for work and materials, or a right of dower. The interest of the property owner is reduced by the amount of the encumbrance.

Exclusions – Items or conditions that are not covered by the general insurance contract.

F.A.A. Clause – F.A.A.(Free of All Average) relieves the insurer from liability arising from both particular average and general average.

F.P.A. Clause – The F.P.A. (Free of Particular Average) clause relieves the insurer from particular average liability.

F.S.R. and C.C. Clause – Implies that if any loss is occurred due to strike, riots or civil commotion the insurer would not be responsible for compensate the losses.

First Premium Receipt – Receipt given to the assured after the risk has been accepted by the insurer.

Floater – A separate policy available to cover the value of goods beyond the coverage of a standard renters insurance policy including movable property such as jewelry or sports equipment.

Free of Capture and Seizure Clause – This clause relieves the insurer from the liability of making compensation for the capture and seizure of the vessel by enemy countries. The insured can insure such abnormal risks by taking an extra 'war risks' policy.

Freight – Includes the profit derivable by a ship-owner from the employment of his ship to carry his own goods or other movables, as well as freight payable by a third party, but does not include passage money.

Future Purchase Option – Life and health insurance provisions that guarantee the insured the right to buy additional coverage without proving insurability. Also known as 'guaranteed insurability option'.

General Liability Insurance – Insurance designed to protect business owners and operators from a wide variety of liability exposures. Exposures could include liability arising from accidents resulting from the insured's premises or operations, products sold by the insured, operations completed by the insured, and contractual liability.

Grace Period – The length of time (usually 31 days) after a premium is due and unpaid during which the policy, including all riders, remains in force. If a premium is paid during the grace period, the premium is considered to have been paid on time. In Universal Life policies, it typically provides for coverage to remain in force for 60 days following the date cash value becomes insufficient to support the payment of monthly insurance costs.

Impaired Insurer – An insurer which is in financial difficulty to the point where its ability to meet financial obligations or regulatory requirements is in question.

Inchmaree Clause – This clause covers the loss or damage caused to the ship or machinery by the negligence of the master of the ship as well as by explosives or latent defect in the machinery or the hull.

Income Taxes – Incurred income taxes (including income taxes on capital gains) reported in each annual statement for that year.

Indemnity – Restoration to the victim of a loss by payment, repair or replacement.

Independent Agent – represents at least two insurance companies and (at least in theory) services clients by searching the market for the most advantageous price for the most coverage. The agent's commission is a percentage of each premium paid and includes a fee for servicing the insured's policy.

Insurable Interest – Interest in property such that loss or destruction of the property could cause a financial loss.

Insurable Property – Means any ship, goods or other movables which are exposed to maritime perils.

Investment Income – The return received by insurers from their investment portfolios including interest, dividends and realized capital gains on stocks. It doesn't include the value of any stocks or bonds that the company currently owns.

Jettison – This is throwing of cargo overboard due to either a deliberate act or at the wake of grave danger.

Jettison Clause – Jettison means throwing overboard a part of the ship's cargo so as to reduce her weight or to save other goods. This clause covers the loss arising out of such throwing of goods. The owner of jettisoned goods is compensated by all interested parties.

Liability Insurance – Insurance that pays and renders service on behalf of an insured for loss arising out of his responsibility, due to negligence, to others imposed by law or assumed by contract.

Liability – Broadly, any legally enforceable obligation. The term is most commonly used in a pecuniary sense.

Licensed for Reinsurance Only – Indicates the company is a licensed (admitted) insurer to write reinsurance on risks in this state.

Liquidity – Liquidity is the ability of an individual or business to quickly convert assets into cash without incurring a considerable loss. There are two kinds of liquidity: quick and current. Quick liquidity refers to funds — cash, short-term investments, and government bonds — and possessions which can immediately be converted into cash in the case of an emergency. Current liquidity refers to current liquidity plus possessions such as real estate which cannot be immediately liquidated, but eventually can be sold and converted into cash. Quick liquidity is a subset of current liquidity. This reflects the financial stability of a company and thus their rating.

Living Benefits – This feature allows you, under certain circumstances, to receive the proceeds of your life insurance policy before you die. Such circumstances include terminal or catastrophic illness, the need for long-term care, or confinement to a nursing home. Also known as 'accelerated death benefits'.

Lost or Not Lost Clause – Under this clause, the insurer is liable even if the ship insured is found not to be lost prior to the contact of insurance, provided the insurer had no knowledge of such loss and does not commit any fraud. This clause covers the risks between the issue of the policy and the shipment of the goods.

Maritime Perils – means the perils consequent on, or incidental to, the navigation of the sea, that is to say, perils, of the seas, fire, war perils pirates, rovers, thieves, captures, seizures, restraints and detainments of princes and peoples, jettisons, barratry and any other perils which are either of the like kind or may be designed by the policy

Maturity Date – Date at which insurance policy expires.

Memorandum Clause – This phrase is used for perishable goods.

Mortality and Expense Risk Fees – A charge that covers such annuity contract guarantees as death benefits.

Mortgage Insurance Policy – In life and health insurance, a policy covering a mortgagor with benefits intended to pay off the balance due on a mortgage upon the insured's death, or to meet the payments due on a mortgage in case of the insured's death or disability.

Movables – Means any movable tangible property, other than the ship, and includes money, valuable securities and other documents.

Mutual Insurance Companies – Companies with no capital stock, and owned by policyholders. The earnings of the company — over and above the payments of the losses, operating expenses and reserves — are the property of the policyholders. There are two types of mutual insurance companies. A nonassessable mutual charges a fixed premium and the policyholders cannot be assessed further. Legal reserves and surplus are maintained to provide payment of all claims. Assessable mutuals are companies that charge an initial fixed premium and, if that isn't sufficient, might assess policyholders to meet losses in excess of the premiums that have been charged.

Named Perils – Perils specifically covered on insured property.

Net Premium – The amount of premium minus the agent's commission. Also, the premium necessary to cover only anticipated losses, before loading to cover other expenses.

Net Premiums Earned – The adjustment of net premiums written for the increase or decrease of the company's liability for unearned premiums during the year. When an insurance company's business increases from year to year, the earned premiums will usually be less than the written premiums. With the increased volume, the premiums are considered fully paid at the inception of the policy so that, at the end of a calendar period, the company must set up premiums representing the unexpired terms of the policies. On a decreasing volume, the reverse is true.

Occurrence – An event that results in an insured loss. In some lines of business, such as liability, an occurrence is distinguished from accident in that the loss doesn't have to be sudden and fortuitous and can result from continuous or repeated exposure which results in bodily injury or property damage neither expected not intended by the insured.

Out-of-Pocket Limit – A predetermined amount of money that an individual must pay before insurance will pay 100 per cent for an individual's health-care expenses.

Peril – The cause of a possible loss.

Piracy – It is forcible robbery at sea, whether committed by thieves or by mariners or passengers within it.

Policy – The written contract effecting insurance, or the certificate thereof, by whatever name called, and including all clause, riders, endorsements, and papers attached thereto and made a part thereof.

Premium – The price of insurance protection for a specified risk for a specified period of time.

Profit – A measure of the competence and ability of management to provide viable insurance products at competitive prices and maintain a financially strong company for both policyholders and stockholders.

Reinsurance Ceded – The unit of insurance transferred to a reinsurer by a ceding company.

Reinsurance – In effect, insurance that an insurance company buys for its own protection. The risk of loss is spread so a disproportionately large loss under a single policy doesn't fall on one company. Reinsurance enables an insurance company to expand its capacity; stabilize its underwriting results; finance its expanding volume; secure catastrophe protection against shock losses; withdraw from a line of business or a geographical area within a specified time period.

Renewal – The automatic re-establishment of in-force status effected by the payment of another premium.

Risk – Uncertainty as to the outcome of an event when two or more possibilities exist.

Risk Class – Risk class, in insurance underwriting, is a grouping of insureds with a similar level of risk. Typical underwriting classifications are preferred, standard and substandard, smoking and nonsmoking, male and female.

Running down Clause – This clause covers the risk arising out of collision between two ships. The insurer is liable to pay compensation to the owner of the damaged ship. This clause is used in hull insurance.

Ship – includes every description of vessel used in navigation.

Solvency – Having sufficient assets — capital, surplus, reserves and being able to satisfy financial requirements — investments, annual reports, examinations — to be eligible to transact insurance business and meet liabilities.

Standard Auto – Auto insurance for average drivers with relatively few accidents during lifetime.

Subrogation – The right of an insurer who has taken over another's loss also to take over the other person's right to pursue remedies against a third party.

Sue and Labour Clause – This clause authorizes the insured to take all possible steps to avert or minimize the loss or to protect the subject matter insured in case of danger. The insurer is liable to pay the expenses, if any, incurred by the insured for this purpose.

Suit – includes counter-claim and set-off.

Sum Assured – Sum Payable by insurance company to the assured/his beneficiary.

Surrender Charge – Fee charged to a policyholder when a life insurance policy or annuity is surrendered for its cash value. This fee reflects expenses the insurance company incurs by placing the policy on its books, and subsequent administrative expenses.

Surrender Period – A set amount of time during which you have to keep the majority of your money in an annuity contract. Most surrender periods last from five to 10 years. Most contracts will allow you to take out at least 10 per cent a year of the accumulated value of the account, even during the surrender period. If you take out more than that 10 per cent, you will have to pay a surrender charge on the amount that you have withdrawn above that 10 per cent.

Term Life Insurance – Life insurance that provides protection for a specified period of time. Common policy periods are one year, five years, 10 years or until the insured reaches age 65 or 70. The policy doesn't build up any of the nonforfeiture values associated with whole life policies.

Third Party – In insurance, it is an arrangement of covering damage or injury suffered by a person other than an insured.

Touch and Stay Clause – This clause requires the ship to touch and stay at such ports and in such order as specified in the policy. Any departure from the route mentioned in the policy or the ordinary trade route followed will be considered as deviation unless such departure is essential to save the ship or the lives on board in an emergency.

Touch and Stay – this phrase implies that the ship will travel via prescribed harbors (staying at these specific harbors). The insurance liability is ceased if the journey of ship is performed from other than prescribed route. Therefore the ship should not deviate from prescribed route.

Umbrella Policy – Coverage for losses above the limit of an underlying policy or policies such as homeowners and auto insurance. While it applies to losses over the dollar amount in the underlying policies, terms of coverage are sometimes broader than those of underlying policies.

Underwriter – The individual trained in evaluating risks and determining rates and coverages for them. Also, an insurer.

Underwriting – The process of selecting risks for insurance and classifying them according to their degrees of insurability so that the appropriate rates may be assigned. The process also includes rejection of those risks that do not qualify.

Valuation – A calculation of the policy reserve in life insurance. Also, a mathematical analysis of the financial condition of a pension plan.

Waiver of Premium – A provision in some insurance contracts which enables an insurance company to waive the collection of premiums while keeping the policy in force if the policyholder becomes unable to work because of an accident or injury. The waiver of premium for disability remains in effect as long as the ensured is disabled.

Warehouse to Warehouse Clause – This clause is inserted to cover the risks to goods from the time they are dispatched from the consignor's warehouse until their delivery at the consignee's warehouse at the port of destination.

Whole Life Insurance – Life insurance which might be kept in force for a person's whole life and which pays a benefit upon the person's death, whenever that might be.